D1131017

THE
VIRGIN

THE
VIRGIN

GEOFFREY ASHE

ROUTLEDGE & KEGAN PAUL
LONDON AND HENLEY

First published in 1976
by Routledge & Kegan Paul Ltd
39 Store Street,
London WC1E 7DD, Broadway House, Newtown Road,
Henley-on-Thames, RG9 1EN
Set in 12 pt. Monotype Perpetua
and printed in Great Britain by
Ebenezer Baylis & Son Limited
The Trinity Press, Worcester, and London

ISBN 0 7100 8342 4

Contents

v

Illustrations

vi

PROLOGUE

The angel Gabriel was sent from God to a city of Galilee named Nazareth, to a virgin betrothed to a man whose name was Joseph, of the house of David; and the virgin's name was Mary. And he came to her and said, 'Hail, O favoured one, the Lord is with you!' But she was greatly troubled at the saying, and considered in her mind what sort of greeting this might be. And the angel said to her, 'Do not be afraid, Mary, for you have found favour with God. And behold, you will conceive in your womb and bear a son, and you shall call his name Jesus. . . .'

And Mary said to the angel, 'How shall this be?' (Luke 1:26–31, 34).

How indeed? Her first recorded state of mind is bewilderment, and her first recorded speech is a question. Jesus Christ, according to the faith of his Church, was born through a miracle. But a birth, however miraculous, requires a mother. God's alarming favour sets Mary strangely apart, both inside and outside the divine counsels, with a mystery she herself is aware of.

Catholic Christianity has hailed her over the centuries as the Blessed Virgin, Mother of God, Queen of Heaven; as Our Lady of Lourdes, Walsingham, Guadalupe, Czestochowa; as Flower of Carmel, House of Gold, Ark of the Covenant. She is the Madonna, patroness of countless churches, prayed to in countless guises and garbs. She is the spiritual mother of all the faithful. She is Co-Redeemer with her Son, the only human being besides him who is the theme of an article of faith. Twice over, indeed. Two doctrines concern Mary alone, distinct from

1

Christ. She herself (it is taught) was conceived immaculate: that is, as the chosen vessel, she was uniquely exempted from the least fault – even the original stain of all Adam's children – and never sinned. After death (it is further taught) she never suffered mortal corruption but was taken up from earth, body and soul, into a holier realm where she now lives glorified.

These two millennially old beliefs, the 'Immaculate Conception' and the 'Assumption', have hardened in the largest Christian communion to the status of dogma. Yet so long as that communion holds to its Gospel, with the story of the angel's visit, its almost deified Virgin can never lose another quite different quality, unknown among goddesses; a quality out of key with a would-be progressive Christianity, yet still able to disturb. In Bernanos's novel, *The Diary of a Country Priest*, the Curé de Torcy struggles to find words for it:

> She is Our Mother – the mother of all flesh, a new Eve. But she is also our daughter. The ancient world of sorrow, the world before the access of grace, cradled her to its heavy heart for many centuries, dimly awaiting a *virgo genetrix*. For centuries and centuries those ancient hands, so full of sin, cherished the wondrous girl-child whose name even was unknown. A little girl, the queen of the Angels. And she's *still* a little girl, remember! . . .
>
> The Virgin was Innocence. Think what we must seem to her, we humans. Of course she hates sin, but after all she has never known it. . . . The eyes of Our Lady are the only real child-eyes that have ever been raised to our shame and sorrow. . . . They are eyes of gentle pity, wondering sadness, and with something more in them, never yet known or expressed, something which makes her younger than sin, younger than the race from which she sprang, and though a mother, by grace, Mother of all grace, our little youngest sister.

If, today, Rome discourages Marian excesses, it has not ceased to draw lessons for the faithful from the same source. On 22 March 1974 Pope Paul VI extolled the mother of Jesus as 'the ideal of the New Woman': Mary of Nazareth, devoted to God's will, yet neither timidly submissive nor repellently pious.

2

Why should it be held so important, in a religion she did not found, to keep her at the forefront? How did it all start? In venturing to explore the origins of her cult I am aware of the difficulties. One might well ask whether it is a topic for history at all. Can it be fruitfully discussed, except in terms of commitment for or against? This is not simply a question of 'religion'. With large parts of the Bible, and its ecclesiastical sequels, the historian can maintain balance. The facts make it possible. Faced, for example, with books portraying the Israelites as the Lord's Chosen People, he can say: 'Israel's leaders reflected on such-and-such events, reacted to such-and-such influences, political, economic and so forth. As a result they formed certain ideas about Israel's place among the nations, and interpreted their traditions in that spirit.' With care such statements can be worded so that believers and unbelievers can both accept them. The believer need only add: 'Yes, that is how the Israelites thought – and they were right.'

But with Mary the problem is subtler and more daunting. As an earthly person, she almost defeats the technologies of research. We have no data except, scantily, in the Christian writings themselves. There is no way of checking from outside them. Archaeology is irrelevant to her. She has no certain ancestry or background. If Christ himself existed, Christ's mother did; but a sceptic who questioned whether we know any more would have a case.

When we turn from Mary on earth to Mary glorified, history is in danger of complete incoherence. Near-silence during the first Christian centuries gives way to an apotheosis which seems to have no real cause, no proportion to the facts at the point of origin, no development behind it to span the gap. Yet it happens. It is a phenomenon of history, to be handled and accounted for. And when we follow the Virgin's cult further still, into the minds and hearts of her devotees, we strike yet another obstacle. The phenomenon has a life, a strength, a passion, which defy cool analysis. It has something of the quality of being in love. The cool analyst is supposed to stay outside the experience, but if he does, he is outside the understanding of it. He may call it fantasy, he may rationalize it, he may explain it away with words like 'myth' and 'complex'. Those who have been within can simply retort:

'Sorry, but we know it first-hand, and it isn't like that. It is more valid than any argument you can bring against it.'

Apparently the right mode of approach might be to steep one-self in the language of Marian devotion: in the Litany and the Rosary, the *Salve Regina*, the prayer in the last canto of the *Divine Comedy*. Apparently; not actually. These things are far along in the story, and only the beginning belongs at the beginning. The cult takes shape through a series of facts in time. Yet the devotional path is not a false trail, to ignore utterly. There is a non-historic dimension in this, and a need to remain conscious of it. The final key to the historian's problem, to the mystery of the cult and its strange unfolding, may lie on a level of human nature which is still mysterious itself.

Two who have tried to chart that level are C. G. Jung and Robert Graves, Jung by way of psychology, Graves by way of poetic imagination. We need not believe unreservedly in the Collective Unconscious, or the White Goddess, to value the kinds of thinking which led to them. As a reverent inquirer into the Mary cult I have supplemented the usual techniques of history. But I have tried not to break its rules, or depart from its standards, or relax from a proper scepticism. After all, Mary herself is a sceptic for as long as anybody in the New Testament. She first opens her mouth with an incredulous query; she is still perplexed about her Son more than twelve years later; she shows unease in the full tide of his Galilean triumph; and we cannot be quite certain where she stands even at our last glimpse of her, middle-aged, in the Acts of the Apostles.

Pursued thus, the inquiry suggests conclusions which may seem subversive. In a sense, I believe, Catholic teaching has been true; indeed it has not gone far enough. Rome has been right to stress Mary as a tangible figure, with much more to be said about her than appears on the surface. Rome has been right, also, to give her a high place in its scheme of things. Far from treating Mary-worship in Protestant style as a disease of Christianity, we should confess that in at least one crisis it actually saved Christianity, which would have dwindled to nullity for the lack of what it supplied. But while there is a voice that has said to me, 'Rome is right', there is another that has whispered, 'Yes, but not in the way Rome would like to think. You are missing something.'

4

Naturally I enter my claim to have found out what the 'something' is. If valid, it implies a startling extension of the meaning of Christianity. I cannot help that. It furnishes ammunition for one school of thought in the present radical-feminist movement. I cannot help that. It also hints that if the churches are to renew their vocation, and to have (humanly speaking) any future, the ecumenical trendiness of their current stance is not merely inadequate but partly mistaken. I cannot help that, either.

Chapter 1

EWIG-WEIBLICHE

I

In 1963 a group of Anglicans published a book of essays. It was entitled *The Blessed Virgin Mary*, and it surveyed her cult from various angles, notably in its bearing on inter-church relationships. Times were already changing: most of these heirs of the Reformation approved Mariolatry within decent limits, and none was wholly hostile. John de Satgé, however, an evangelical canon, summed up what he considered to be the case against it under four headings. The last was by far the most important, and here, in their entirety, are his remarks under it. I do not think anyone in the Church of England has added much to them since (or, indeed, to the book's message in general).

> The evangelical has a strong suspicion that the deepest roots of the Marian cultus are not to be found in the Christian tradition at all. The religious history of mankind shows a recurring tendency to worship a mother-goddess. Three factors in particular suggest that the cult of Mary may be an intrusion into Christianity from the dark realms of natural religion. First, it seems that historically the earliest traces of Marian devotion seem to come from Christian circles to some extent at least tainted with syncretizing Gnosticism. The second is the ease with which the devotion becomes associated with local holy places so that the faithful make their prayers to our Lady of a particular shrine. May it not be the case, the evangelical wonders, that what we have here is in reality an older religion, a paganism which has

been too lightly baptized into Christ and whose ancient features persist under a thin Christian veil? The third factor is an apparent correlation between Marian devotion and an elevation of chastity to a point of esteem where marriage and sexual intercourse are depreciated if not reprehended. Is the increasing emphasis on a female object of devotion in some way a form of psychological compensation?

A few pages farther on, Canon de Satgé tries to show how such facts might be accepted without precluding a cautious veneration. We need not follow him into his second passage. It is even briefer, and tentative in the last degree. The immediate point is that he is the only contributor who ventures into this region at all. His fellow essayists dissect Mary's cult eruditely without leaving the safety of Christian ground. They never once risk a glance at the paganism behind her. Nor do they mention – de Satgé himself does not – that the earliest documented worship of her is not as Christ's mother (a human creature, however holy) but as a divinity in her own right.

All Christians exploring Marian country confront the issue by implication. Having done so, nearly all remain silent. These Anglicans confront it as directly as any, and remain as silent as any. Yet the problem begins to loom as soon as the major doctrines are scrutinized. Here is the first sentence of another contributor, Dr H. S. Box: 'The Immaculate Conception cannot be regarded by Anglicans as an article of the faith, because it is not read in Holy Scripture, "nor may be proved thereby".' When he comes to the Assumption he says it again.

> For Roman Catholics it has been defined as a divinely revealed dogma that 'Mary, when the course of her earthly life was run, was assumed to heavenly glory in body and soul'. Anglicans cannot regard it as an article of the faith, because it does not satisfy the criterion of being capable of being proved by Holy Scripture, which 'containeth all things necessary to salvation'.[1]

Quite so. Whatever the genesis of the Marian dogmas, neither is rooted in any fact or tradition which the Bible attests. Roman theologians concede as much. Scripturally, the most anyone can claim for these doctrines is that a few passages yield a richer meaning if read with them in mind. Thus the 'flawlessness' of the Beloved in the Song of Songs (4:7; 6:9) may be taken, if one cares for such exercises, as an inspired hint at the stainless Virgin. But there is no text which clearly states either doctrine; there is no text from which an unbiased person would infer either; there is no hint of them even in the prophecies, canonical and otherwise, which helped to prepare a way for Christ. Medieval attempts to reason them out, legends supplying fanciful details, are only afterthoughts about beliefs planted already by obscurer causes. How early they were planted, no document exactly shows. Certainly too far back to allow a facile explaining-away as popish imposture.

The same mystery overhangs other aspects of Mary's cult. She faces us in fact with a paradox at the outset, and the first questions to ask, however adroitly Christians may dodge them, are the ones which it poses. Christianity justifies its teachings by the appeal to a sacred book. Nevertheless, right in the mainstream and not so immensely far from the source, we find convictions clustering round the mother of Christ which the book does not prove or even clearly support. Texts are quoted, but they are not really thought of as proofs, rather as hints confirming what is already 'given' for prior reasons. Belief persists for centuries with increasing fervour and little protest. Several Christian bodies do at last challenge some of the Marian ideas, but the largest maintains them, and, after a long delay, defines the aforementioned two as articles of faith – the Immaculate Conception in 1854, the Assumption in 1950.

To urge that this process does not make sense is to invite the retort that Christianity doesn't. The point, however, is that the process appears to make no sense even within Christianity's own logic. Failing the vital scriptural warrant, what produced these beliefs in the first place? Where did they find a footing? Why were they so compulsive, what gap did they fill in a system supposedly perfect and complete? The case of Christ himself highlights the difficulty with a vivid contrast. Prophecies in the Bible, or deriving from it, had prepared and authorized Jews to believe wondrous things about the Messiah. By those who saw Jesus as the fulfilment, such things were believed. Not a single prophecy had aroused any expectations about the Messiah's mother; yet such things were believed of her too. The Gospels, when added to the Old Testament, assured that she would be held in honour but did not enjoin any steps beyond.

Canon de Satgé seems to be at least partly right. The victorious dayspring of the cult cannot be explained solely from inside Christianity. We must look first to factors outside, in what he pleases to call 'the dark realms of natural religion'. Mary's history begins long before she is born. And afterwards we must bear in mind that however loftily she was enthroned in the Church, she preserved something pre-Christian which explained much, which was part of her, and without which she would have been viewed very differently.

2

Over a large part of the world, before the rise of any verified gods, human beings did indeed worship goddesses. More precisely they worshipped The Goddess: in Goethe's phrase, the Ewig-Weibliche or Eternal-Womanly.

Early Stone Age art gives us no proven images of male deity. But it does give us female ones – figurines with gross breasts and bellies, exaggerated tokens of motherhood. These were carved in Siberia and Europe before 10,000 BC as cult-objects of hunting tribes. Presently we find the motif spreading to agricultural peoples in the Indus Valley and Middle East, where the figurines are made of ivory, terracotta or clay, with more realism, and in a context of more advanced art.

The primitive sculptors leave no message, and the precise meaning of their work is open to challenge. But as the theme undergoes its long-drawn transitions, it flowers without dispute into the imagery of a Goddess-centred religion. When we pass from prehistory to the oldest recoverable rituals and myths, the divine features come ever more clearly into view. However fragmented she may be before, the Eternal-Womanly is One at her apogee – not always through conscious intercommunion of cults, but psychologically One, under many names and aspects.[2]

Few surviving myths portray her wholly alone. Nearly always

she enters our field of vision in the company of other divine beings. But she is senior to them. Her protean nature comes through at different stages in theogony, some far more primitive than others. We meet her in myth at the Dawn of All, and we meet her under various masks among the older and younger gods. Sometimes she is a world-matriarch of immeasurable age, sometimes she is a wife or mistress, sometimes she is a maiden. She takes on animal forms as well as human. Occasionally one aspect of her encounters another.

In Sumeria four or five thousand years ago she was Nin-Khursag or Nintu the life-giver, 'mother of all', 'queen of the gods'. She was also the alluring Inanna. In Babylon she had a dark and monstrous shadow-aspect before creation, and a refulgent one in the city pantheon as Ishtar. For Canaanites she was the all-mother Asherah. Asherah's variant, Ashtoreth or Astarte, was worshipped in Syria. Canaan itself knew a more sophisticated version called Anath, voluptuous, beautiful and martial. Such Goddess-forms of Middle Eastern religion were not sharply distinguished. They could not be. All were sovereign bestowers of life and fertility. Inanna and Ishtar were acknowledged to be the same. Ishtar and Asherah were both known as 'the Goddess' pure and simple. Asherah, Ashtoreth and Anath, despite a growth of myth that gave them conflicting personalities, tended in practice to overlap and fuse.[3]

In Egypt the Goddess was primarily Neith, secondarily Isis, an anomalous form with a special destiny, one of several that attracted the title Queen of Heaven. In central Asia Minor she was Cybele, the Mighty Mother, ruler over wild nature. In its western zone she was Artemis, whom the Romans called Diana and saluted as Lady of the Moon. On the Greek mainland she was Earth, mother of all beings, including the Titans who were the eldest of deities. But she was also the chief Titaness Rhea, and sovereign of many shrines under other names.

Multi-faceted, multi-visaged, yet mysteriously constant, she had something of the sea about her. As Aphrodite (afterwards Venus) she rose out of the foam and took possession of Cyprus, then glided over the waves to Greece; the Greeks identified Aphrodite with Astarte the Syrian. In the sea empire of Minoan Crete the Goddess was chief divinity without rival, a gracious

Mistress of Animals like Cybele, in an island at peace. Westward over the Mediterranean she was the deity of the seafaring megalith-builders, worshipped in their ponderous Maltese temples, confronted by Odysseus in the charming guise of Calypso. Her cult flourished wherever the great stone structures arose – in other Mediterranean islands, in the Iberian peninsula, and out on the Atlantic fringe in Brittany and the British Isles.[4]

The Goddess's high summer belongs to the later Stone Age and the early and middle Bronze. It fades in the second millennium BC. Attempts have been made to link it with a state of society: a quiet and fairly stable state, where the round of life was un-altered from year to year and nothing radical ever happened. Agriculture, a female pursuit, was paramount; male talents, such as prowess in war and hunting, had only marginal value. There was even (it has been argued) a matriarchy. Everywhere the Goddess reigned in the person of an arch-priestess, and kings were not overlords but sacred functionaries, ritually married to the priestess, and put to death at regular intervals.

To speak of matriarchy may be extreme. But women may well have been powerful then through a monopoly of the arts of magic, and the Eternal-Womanly powerful with them.[5] There are hints at an honoured status for women in traces of matrilinear custom – that is, inheritance through the mother and not the father. The reason for the custom was not what we should now regard as the practical one, that a child's mother is known whereas the father's identity may be doubtful. It went deeper, and the nature of the Goddess was bound up with it. Ancient peoples were hazy on procreation itself. In the presence of birth, they were doubtful not merely about the father's identity but about his existence. Sex-relations often occurred without pregnancy; why should not pregnancy occur without sex-relations? Woman alone was the visible life-bestower. The Goddess as Mother Earth, woman's cosmic counterpart, obviously produced life in a medley of ways, and often for no known cause at all.

This is the background of many legends of impregnation by strange means, such as swallowing a blade of grass or standing against the wind. In the more civilized tales of this type, the agency, whatever it is, tends to be interpreted as the mask of a male god: thus Danaë becomes pregnant by a shower of gold which is really Zeus in disguise. But farther back the external male is absent. And in that primal phase the Goddess, correspondingly, exists and gives life without him and embodies all functions.

In some of her forms she can generate other deities unaided. Neith gives birth to the Sun-God Ra by her own power. At a slightly later, transitional stage we have myths where a male element within the Goddess splits off and is turned into a partner for her. That is how Cybele, whose original cosmic femininity contains maleness itself, acquires a consort named Attis. A Greek myth portrays 'Earth' conceiving the Titans through fecundation by 'Heaven' or 'the Sky', Uranus. But in the beginning, as myths from other nations make clear, Earth and Heaven are not distinct. They are a single being, the matrix of life, and the male sky-figure Uranus results from fission.[6]

Being prior to the male, the Goddess in her earliest forms was, after a fashion, Virgin as well as Mother. She might – as in her Neith identity – have no spouse at all. She might project an Attis-type companion out of herself. As Anath (in the civilized coastal part of Canaan), she had a blatant sex life but somehow retained her maidenhead: Anath was the Mother of Nations, but she was also the Virgin, and these titles were habitually paired together. Even in a later world where the male had conquered, ambiguity still clung to at least one residual version of the Goddess, the Artemis or Diana of classical myth. She was coolly virginal, a 'Queen and Huntress chaste and fair' . . . yet in her temple at Ephesus she presided, still, as a many-breasted image of cosmic motherhood. The ancient concept persisted as a matter of attitude rather than physical integrity. Artemis gave herself to no male in particular, and none was necessary to her or had any claim on her. Without inconsistency she was the patroness of childbirth and the helper of women in labour.[7]

Male projections from the Goddess included not only Attis but all those Young Gods resembling him, made familiar by *The Golden Bough*. The Young God was Tammuz, Adonis, Osiris, her mystically dual sexual companion. In his origins he was clearly her junior, a dependent figure, even a son. Later he was more like an equal, but he did not break free into a totally unrelated status. As Anath's consort Baal, and as Isis's consort Osiris, he was a brother – in the case of Isis, a twin. Incest taboos were for humans only. It is possible that Anath's virginity, despite a sex life and motherhood, means that as her brother was in a sense one with herself, intercourse with him did not count. Always the companion-god was the Goddess's doomed and tragic lover, who died annually with the green life of nature and was reborn in spring.

His, however, was not the only shape masculinity assumed in its budding-off from her. It could also be overtly phallic. Sometimes we find her accompanied by a serpent, or several serpents. In Crete she holds them up in her hands. In Sumeria she sits with a human-faced consort beside a tree or staff with snakes coiling up it. Her serpents are mysterious, 'chthonic', associated with caves and the underworld. They are also divine like her, and charged with numinous energy.[8]

It must be repeated that very few myths, in their extant form, take us back as Neith's does to the Goddess reigning by herself. But many – however re-edited, diluted, distorted – take us back to an age when she was still ascendant, if not so toweringly. In classical myth this is the age of the gods-before-the-gods, when Zeus was still unborn, and the Titans and Titanesses were supreme over mankind; their head, Cronus or Saturn, being the Goddess's son (in her capacity as Earth) and also her brother-husband (in her capacity as Rhea).[9] That age's atmosphere comes through to us with a disquieting ambivalence. It is 'other', it is weird. Notorious monsters such as the Gorgons are survivors from it. Yet it is also, nostalgically, the Golden Age. Greeks such as Hesiod look back on it as a time when men lived without toil and were just and carefree. The Golden People, they say, had no fear of death, and indeed are still alive as invisible benign spirits.

That last point is a clue to the nostalgia, and essential to bear in mind. It agrees with facts which can be inferred about the Goddess's world on firmer grounds. She was (let it be stressed again) the universal life-bestower: not only in human birth, but in the fertility of crops, in the magic that ensured this, and, on another level, in the inspiration of seers and bards – whence her role as Muse. Therefore, having life in her hand, she could renew it as well as give it. One of her oldest names, the Sumerian

Nin-Khursag, means 'she who gives life to the dead'. Her
serpents symbolized not only sex but rebirth, through the shed-
ding of the old skin and growth of a new one. Her megalithic
sepulchres were also wombs, where her dead were laid to rest
with grave-goods, for use in the afterlife she was expected to
bring them into. When she was at her zenith, or not too far
declined from it, belief in that future rebirth was strong. Hesiod
transmits authentic tradition when he says that death did not
terrify. But the Goddess was superseded, and in most places the
comforting faith waned with her.[10]

3

During the second millennium BC, male deities took command:
partly through the ever-strengthening institution of kingship,
partly through changes in relations between the sexes, partly
through war and conquest. There was a rough correlation with
progress in astronomy and the precision of time-reckoning. The
Female was lunar, the Male solar. The moon's natural connection with women, through monthly periodicity, had fitted
well into a social milieu where it governed the calendar – as, at
first, it did. In remoter Middle Eastern antiquity it was preferred
to the sun. It was a cool and kindly orb, lighting the traveller by
night, not burning him up by day. It was easier to watch, and its
phases marked the passage of time. Over most, perhaps all, of
the Goddess's ancient territory the original calendar was
fittingly lunar. Observation of the sun, however, led to greater
accuracy, and the new calendars corresponded to the advance of
the Male.

Zeus, the Roman Jupiter, was the sky-god of Hellenic
invaders from the north who overran Greece and transformed its
religious system. The Olympians sung by Homer are buccaneer-
ing chiefs with inferior female partners. Olympian myth made
Zeus into a son of Cronus who had ousted his father and the other
Titans. The Goddess was demoted and split up into sharply
distinct goddesses, all far less than her original self. Zeus's many
amours are myths about his takeover of shrines where the
Goddess had been worshipped in various guises. Some of her
other guises, such as Aphrodite and Artemis, were re-interpreted

as his daughters. Her attributes were shared out. Athene (afterwards, to Romans, Minerva) acquired her snakes. Artemis had the wild creatures. Aphrodite kept the lover Adonis. All were cut down, nearer to the human level. This was especially true of Aphrodite, whom the trend of art reduced to a nubile young woman, a mere exciter of male desire, endowed in such figures as the Medici Venus with human modesty.

The predominance of male gods corresponded to new outlooks and new notions of world order. It brought with it a blackening of their predecessors. In Greek lands the Goddess's lingering presence was so great and elusive that it prevented direct calumny. But femininity was attacked through the myth of Pandora's jar or box, which unleashed every woe upon mankind. Also the Goddess's Titan brood were made out to have been anarchic and brutish. Ugly stories, probably borrowed from the Hittites, were told of their leader Cronus – despite the fact that the era when he ruled mankind was confessed to have been the Golden Age.[11]

In Semitic nations this revision of values had already gone further. At each New Year festival, Babylonian priests chanted a Creation Epic telling how the god Marduk had created the world by destroying a she-monster of chaos, Tiamat, and re-arranging her fragments. The Goddess's serpents, formerly wise and benign, were now portrayed as malicious. In the Babylonian Epic of Gilgamesh the snake is not an emblem of man's ascendancy over decay and death but an enemy who filches it from him. Most familiar, yet strangest because we see only its end product, is the Female's change of status among the Israelites. She is embodied in the person of Eve, 'Life', the mother of all living (Genesis 3:20). As such she is introduced to us in a paradisal state, a Hebrew Golden Age. She walks naked through the garden of Eden, beside the tree of life (2:9) and the stream that divides into four great rivers, sources of fertility for the whole earth. But the story as we now have it shows her already cut down and traduced, with more severity than the Greeks ever ventured. She has dwindled to being merely the first woman, a trouble-maker, created from a rib of the senior and dominant first man.

The reason for this lies in the character of Yahweh, the male Lord God of Israel, with his fierce ethical demands and his intolerance towards idols. He led the Israelites out of Egypt into Canaan, their Promised Land. Israel's faith took shape partly through a violent rejection, at (so to speak) policy-making levels, of the cults of the native Canaanites. In the up-country areas settled by Israel their most conspicuous version of the Goddess was Asherah. Their dying-and-rising god of the seasonal cycle was, in various forms, Baal. The Israelite settlers were constantly tempted to placate these powers of the land, planting trees for Asherah, and paying their respects to the local Baals with a vague mental excuse that they were aspects or deputies of Yahweh.

Yahweh's spokesmen, the priests and prophets, laboured to stamp such practices out. For them the Female meant the abomination of Canaan, and in that east Mediterranean zone some of the forms of Goddess-worship and Baal-worship really were rather abominable. Therefore the official religion grew more rigidly male than most, and Hebrew myths and traditions were rewritten accordingly, though Canaanite literary influence lay heavy on them.[12]

Whatever the Life-Goddess Eve was originally like, she appears in Genesis as a Hebrew Pandora, the villainess in a story about the origin of human misfortunes. A serpent appears too, twining round a tree like his Sumerian forebears who accompanied the Goddess. But now he is Eve's tempter. Succumbing to his guile, she eats forbidden fruit and persuades her husband Adam to do the same. Thus the Female and her reptile companion are both presented as wicked. The fact that Eve must on no account be viewed as a goddess herself is underlined by her delusion that the fruit will make her one (3:4–5); and the final slide into a purely human condition is marked – we may recall the humanized Venus of art – by sexual self-consciousness and bodily shame. Through the first couple's fall, mankind is tainted with sin and alienated from Yahweh. The brief Golden Age ends, and its ending, as elsewhere, brings death into the world as a terror hitherto unknown (2:17; 3:19). To prevent man from ever vanquishing it, his Creator bars him out from the garden where the tree of life is (3:22–3).

As Hesiod shows, the new and bitter finality of death was not confined to Yahweh's Israel. Even though paternity was now understood, male deities could never bestow life of their own nature as the Mother had done. Zeus and his colleagues were immortal, but they did not transmit that quality to their human subjects; in fact it was their chief point of distinction. Through most civilized and semi-civilized lands west of Persia, death ceased to be a passage to future life. In Babylonia (as we know from the Epic of Gilgamesh) and in Greece (as we know from Homer) the dead were no longer pictured as significantly existing. They were reduced to feeble, bloodless shades in a gloomy underworld. For the Greeks this was 'Hades'. The odd exception might occur through special divine favour. A few heroes had been translated alive to Elysium, a kind of Eden in the far west. Heracles had been promoted to godhead. But there was no hope for the vast majority. In Babylonia there was none for anybody. With the fading of the Eternal-Womanly, with her cutting-down or anathematization, death had become the end with no prospect of rebirth.

Israel's shift of ideas was similar. Grave-goods attest belief in an afterlife among the pioneer settlers of Canaan. But the triumph of Yahweh-worship ended this, as the worship of the Male did in other contexts. Except in a few late texts showing foreign influence, the Old Testament has no doctrine of survival or return. As in Babylonia, as in Greece, the dead become shades. They go down to an underworld called Sheol, The Grave. Ecclesiastes is quite explicit. Make the most of life while you can, says this book which the Christian Bible retains as inspired, 'for there is no work or thought or knowledge or wisdom in Sheol, to which you are going' (9:10). The dead are still dimly present in their descendants, but their own lives are finished. The sole Israelite immortality is collective. It belongs to Israel itself, God's chosen community, the nation through which he reveals his will on earth.[13]

4

In most of the Middle East, therefore, and in most of the Graeco-Roman region, the last centuries BC were haunted by a sense of a far-off loss: of a 'fall' which might or might not be conceived morally but, whatever its nature, had brought death into the world or at least made it terrible. Hence there was a deep, unconsciously perceptive nostalgia for the life-giving divine Female and all she had implied. The male gods' state-endowed priests had almost effaced memory of her in her true majesty. Yet the sense of loss gave a haunting magic to the rituals which had once centred on her and still, disjointedly, persisted.

Nor was her eclipse ever absolute. She survived; not – for most – in her pristine integrity, but fragmentarily, through myths and special aspects and local cults. She never, for example, lost her old status as mistress of inspiration. Apollo had staked his claim as god of poetry, but the actual Muses, nine facets of the Goddess, remained feminine. A resurgent worship of Cybele, as Great Mother of the Gods, spread from Asia Minor to Italy and won a popular following (she was credited with ending the invasion by Hannibal). In Egypt male deity had rooted itself early through the pharaohs' divine kingship. But Isis retained her dignity as sister-wife of the prototype divine ruler Osiris; and the Greek conquest of Egypt under Alexander brought a partial reconstitution of the Goddess. Greeks learned to see their own reduced goddesses as aspects of a senior figure, even though, in her origins, she was not really one of the primordial Mothers. Demeter became Isis-as-provider-of-corn; Aphrodite was Isis-as-goddess-of-love; Hera, Zeus's consort, was Isis-as-wife-of-the-chief-god; Hecate, mistress of magic, was Isis-as-goddess-of-the-magical-arts; and so on.[14] The reigning Ptolemies imitated the sacred Osiris-Isis coupling by marrying their sisters. Hereditary chance in that dynasty gave the country a most bewitching queen, in whom female deity was briefly reborn on earth. Shakespeare's insight is sound when he describes Cleopatra wearing 'the habiliments of the goddess Isis', and gives her a final scene of transfiguration with an echo of Christ.

> Give me my robe, put on my crown; I have
> Immortal longings in me; now no more
> The juice of Egypt's grape shall moist this lip.

Truly, I say to you, I shall not drink again of the fruit of the vine until that day when I drink it new in the kingdom of God.

(Mark 14:25 – the Last Supper)

More significant perhaps was the Goddess's return in the Mysteries. These were cults for initiates, not the masses, but a high proportion of the initiates were people of wealth and standing, whose effect on the spirit of the times was out of proportion to their numbers. Without any sudden or spectacular upsurge, the Mysteries survived for hundreds of years. Their chief gift was that precious one which the Goddess had offered long ago and her male supplanters, generally speaking, did not – the overcoming of death. At Eleusis she presided as Demeter or Ceres, the Earth-Mother, paired with the maiden Kore, in other words her own younger, virginal aspect. When her initiates passed to the next world it was not for them as it was for the multitude. To quote Sophocles: 'Thrice blessed are those among men who, after beholding these rites, go down to Hades. Only for them is there life, all the rest will suffer an evil lot.' In other Mysteries the saviour who conferred a new birth was not so much the Goddess directly as the Young God, her spouse and in a sense her son, whose own annual rebirth was spring itself, perpetuating the theme in a male figure projected from her. Attis and Adonis found a new, select company of adorers.[15]

With their Egyptian colleague Osiris the Mysteries were double. The Goddess, as his wife Isis, was personally present too. In the refashioning of their cult as a religion of individual salvation, she was the more important. Their divine partnership held a special allure for immortality-seekers because, in Egypt, belief in an afterlife had been more durable than elsewhere, without the same decline from an early prevalence. The Roman author Apuleius, in his serio-comic fantasy, *The Golden Ass*, reveals all that he feels free to disclose about his own initiation into Isis-worship. His account of a moonlight vision beside the sea-shore is the finest and fullest homage any classical writer devotes to her. It shows how an educated man of his period – the second century AD – could draw the scattered Goddess-figures together again, regard contemporaries as children of one Eternal-Womanly even in ignorance, and thus evoke the pre-Olympian aeon.[16]

I [Lucius, the narrator] offered this soundless prayer to the supreme Goddess:

'Blessed Queen of Heaven, whether you are pleased to be
known as Ceres, the original harvest mother who in joy at
the finding of your lost daughter Proserpine abolished the
rude acorn diet of our forefathers and gave them bread
raised from the fertile soil of Eleusis; or whether as celestial
Venus, now adored at sea-girt Paphos, who at the time of
the first Creation coupled the sexes in mutual love and so
contrived that man should continue to propagate his kind
for ever; or whether as Artemis, the physician sister of
Phoebus Apollo, reliever of the birth pangs of women, and
now adored in the ancient shrine of Ephesus; or whether as
dread Proserpine to whom the owl cries at night, whose
triple face is potent against the malice of ghosts, keeping
them imprisoned below earth; you who wander through
many sacred groves and are propitiated with many different
rites – you whose womanly light illumines the walls of every
city, whose misty radiance nurses the happy seeds under the
soil, you who control the wandering course of the sun and
the very power of his rays – I beseech you, by whatever
name, in whatever aspect, with whatever ceremonies you
deign to be invoked, have mercy on me in my extreme
distress. . . .'

The apparition of a woman began to rise from the middle
of the sea with so lovely a face that the gods themselves
would have fallen down in adoration of it. First the head,
then the whole shining body gradually emerged and stood
before me poised on the surface of the waves. . . .

Her long hair fell in tapering ringlets on her lovely neck,
and was crowned with an intricate chaplet in which was
woven every kind of flower. Just above her brow shone a
round disc, like a mirror, or like the bright face of the
moon, which told me who she was. Vipers rising from the
left-hand and right-hand partings of her hair supported this
disc, with ears of corn bristling beside them. Her many-
coloured robe was of finest linen; part was glistening white,
part crocus-yellow, part glowing red, and along the entire
hem a woven bordure of flowers and fruit clung swaying in
the breeze. But what caught and held my eye more than
anything else was the deep black lustre of her mantle. She

wore it slung across her body from the right hip to the left shoulder, where it was caught in a knot resembling the boss of a shield; but part of it hung in innumerable folds, the tasselled fringe quivering. It was embroidered with glittering stars on the hem and everywhere else, and in the middle beamed a full and fiery moon. . . .

All the perfumes of Arabia floated into my nostrils as the Goddess deigned to address me: 'You see me here, Lucius, in answer to your prayer. I am Nature, the universal Mother, mistress of all the elements, primordial child of time, sovereign of all things spiritual, queen of the dead, queen also of the immortals, the single manifestation of all gods and goddesses that are. . . . Though I am worshipped in many aspects, known by countless names, and propitiated with all manner of different rites, yet the whole round earth venerates me. The primeval Phrygians call me Pessinuntica, Mother of the gods; the Athenians, sprung from their own soil, call me Cecropian Artemis; for the islanders of Cyprus I am Paphian Aphrodite; for the archers of Crete I am Dictynna; for the trilingual Sicilians, Stygian Proserpine; and for the Eleusinians their ancient Mother of the Corn. . . .

'But both races of Aethiopians, whose lands the morning sun first shines upon, and the Egyptians who excel in ancient learning and worship me with ceremonies proper to my godhead, call me by my true name, namely, Queen Isis. I have come in pity of your plight, I have come to favour and aid you. Weep no more, lament no longer; the hour of deliverance, shone over by my watchful light, is at hand.'

A being conceived thus, even by a coterie only, was not dead. At the very least she was a Goddess-shaped yearning which no emptily thundering Jove could appease. 'I and I alone,' she says in the same scene, 'have power to prolong your life beyond the limits appointed by destiny.' Later, in response to a further visit from her, Lucius goes on to be initiated into the rites of Osiris also. But this is rather perfunctory. It is Isis that he cares about.

5

In cults such as these, branching out from Asia and Egypt during the early years of the *Pax Romana*, a sprinkling of pagans groped their way back towards female deity through a sense of absence and loss. The Jews, heirs of ancient Israel, had already struggled with the same problems – mortality, futility, things closing in on them. But their own male God seemed too tremendous to allow a maternal answer. He had spoken through the Torah or teaching communicated by Moses, and from that there could be no dissent, no appeal. What the Jews did instead was to add new doctrines brought from Persia, and begin hoping (some of them, though not the Sadducees) for a bodily resurrection of the dead and a paradisal World to Come.

They also envisaged a saviour of their own, though not one like Attis or Adonis. Male, of course, he was pictured in various ways, but always as in the future. He would be a king, a royal descendant of King David, who would deliver Israel as a nation rather than individually. Or he would be a divine agent from celestial regions, the Son of Man. These and kindred ideas tended to converge, and the Old Testament motif of a monarch's 'anointing' caused the images to coalesce in a single figure, the Messiah, God's earthly Anointed or in Greek the Christ, who would usher in a world-transformation. At the beginning of the Christian era this coalescence was still incomplete. There was no Messianic orthodoxy. But David's anointed heir was always conceived as an earthly leader, who, whatever else he did, would free the Jews from Roman subjection and set up an earthly kingdom, drawing even the Gentiles into the Lord's service. Those who believed in a resurrection tended to equate this kingdom with the glorious World to Come, and prophesy that the righteous dead would return to life to enjoy it.

Can it be said, then, that Judaism found a path of its own and kept the Eternal-Womanly out? Not quite. Alongside the apocalyptic excitements, she did creep back. She had quietly found a footing in holy writ – several footings – and therefore, though subordinate, she could not be altogether suppressed, or deprived of her power to work on imaginations.

In the first place, while the only clear immortality was the perennial life of Israel, some of the prophets had represented Israel itself as a human figure; and in many such passages the symbol of Yahweh's elect community was a woman. Israel was his 'betrothed' (Hosea 2:19). Israel, centred on the holy city Jerusalem, was the 'daughter of Zion' or 'of Judah'. That image occurred with variations in the oldest of the prophetic books, Amos (5:2); in the most important, Isaiah (1:8; 10:32, and elsewhere); and in five others. Sometimes the prophets pictured Sometimes she was tormented or disgraced, sometimes triumphant.[17]

Thus we read in Jeremiah (4:31; 18:13, 15):

> I heard a cry as of a woman in travail . . .
> the cry of the daughter of Zion gasping for breath,
> stretching out her hands.

> The virgin Israel
> has done a very horrible thing . . .
> My people have forgotten me,
> they burn incense to false gods.

And in Lamentations (1:15; 2:13):

> The Lord has trodden as in a wine press
> the virgin daughter of Judah.

> What can I say for you, to what compare you,
> O daughter of Jerusalem?
> What can I liken to you, that I may comfort you,
> O virgin daughter of Zion?
> For vast as the sea is your ruin;
> who can restore you?

Her downfall and sufferings were not in vain. They came to be seen as birth-pangs of a new hope, the hope of deliverance, and, some day, the Messiah.

> Writhe and groan, O daughter of Zion,
> like a woman in travail;

for now you shall go forth from the city
   and dwell in open country;
   you shall go to Babylon.
There you shall be rescued,
   there the Lord will redeem you
   from the hand of your enemies.

(Micah 4:10)

Thus says the Lord . . .
Again I will build you, and you shall be built,
   O virgin Israel!
Again you shall adorn yourself with timbrels,
   and shall go forth in the dance of the merrymakers. . . .

Return, O virgin Israel,
   return to these your cities.
How long will you waver,
   O faithless daughter?

(Jeremiah 31:2, 4, 21–2)

Behold, the Lord has proclaimed
   to the end of the earth:
Say to the daughter of Zion,
   'Behold, your salvation comes;
Behold, his reward is with him,
   and his recompense before him.'

(Isaiah 62:11)

Sing aloud, O daughter of Zion;
   shout, O Israel!
Rejoice and exult with all your heart,
   O daughter of Jerusalem! . . .
The King of Israel, the Lord, is in your midst;
   you shall fear evil no more.

(Zephaniah 3:14–15)

Sing and rejoice, O daughter of Zion; for lo, I come and I will
dwell in the midst of you, says the Lord.

(Zechariah 2:10)

Rejoice greatly, O daughter of Zion!
Shout aloud, O daughter of Jerusalem!
Lo, your king comes to you.

(Zechariah 9:9)

It was this personification that enabled the rabbis to come to terms with the Song of Songs. Faced with that ecstatic drama of profane love, embedded in the sacred writings, they tamed it as allegory. The Beloved, they declared, was Israel, and the book was about God's love for her. But its language went so far beyond what was needed for such a message that the image of a living person – not indeed a divine one, but a woman-immortal combining unique beauty with high and holy meaning – was inexorably evoked.

The other bridgehead of the Female in Jewish scripture was, and still is, more mysterious. She entered as a demi-goddess called Wisdom, in Hebrew Chokmah, with *ch* as in 'loch'. We meet this lady in Proverbs, a book that was compiled late (between 300 and 250 BC), despite its biblical placing. Proverbs reflects alien influences, busy in such places as Alexandria where Jews lived alongside Gentiles. Its eighth chapter opens with Wisdom making a speech, and for some time we might suppose her to be only an allegory. But in verse 22 she starts making astounding claims. She existed before the world and even helped Yahweh in bringing order out of chaos.

'The Lord created me at the beginning of his work,
   the first of his acts of old.
Ages ago I was set up,
   at the first, before the beginning of the earth. . . .
When he established the heavens, I was there,
   when he drew a circle on the face of the deep . . .
When he marked out the foundations of the earth,
   then I was beside him, like a master workman;
And I was daily his delight,
   rejoicing before him always,
rejoicing in his inhabited world
   and delighting in the sons of men.'

Here the allegorical view becomes hard to sustain. If Wisdom is just a personified quality of wise people, how did she exist before there were any wise people? Yet if she is an actual being, why does the Genesis account of creation not mention her? Something very odd has slipped into Judaism at this point.[18]

In Proverbs Wisdom is personal without being unequivocally a person. With an effort we might still construe her as merely a symbol of the wisdom of God, his thinking, creative aspect. But in the Apocrypha she appears at greater length and as a person beyond dispute, a very splendid one. She takes up the entire twenty-fourth chapter of the book of Ben-Sira or Sirach, usually called Ecclesiasticus, composed during the second century BC by a Jewish subject of the Ptolemies.

> Wisdom will praise herself, and will glory in the midst of
>   her people.
> In the assembly of the Most High she will open her mouth,
>   and in the presence of his host she will glory:
> 'I came forth from the mouth of the Most High,
>   and covered the earth like a mist.
> I dwelt in high places,
>   and my throne was in a pillar of cloud.
> Alone I have made the circuit of the vault of heaven
>   and have walked in the depths of the abyss.
> In the waves of the sea, in the whole earth,
>   and in every people and nation I have gotten a possession.
> Among all these I sought a resting place;
>   I sought in whose territory I might lodge.
> Then the Creator of all things gave me a commandment,
>   and the one who created me assigned a place for my tent.
> And he said, "Make your dwelling in Jacob,
>   and in Israel receive your inheritance."
> From eternity, in the beginning, he created me,
>   and for eternity I shall not cease to exist.
> In the holy tabernacle I ministered before him,
>   and so I was established in Zion.
> In the beloved city likewise he gave me a resting place,
>   and in Jerusalem was my dominion.
> So I took root in an honoured people,
>   in the portion of the Lord, who is their inheritance.

I grew tall like a cedar in Lebanon,
  and like a cypress on the heights of Hermon.
I grew tall like a palm tree in En-gedi,
  and like rose plants in Jericho;
like a beautiful olive tree in the field,
  and like a plane tree I grew tall.
Like cassia and camel's thorn I gave forth the aroma of spices,
  and like choice myrrh I spread a pleasant odour,
like galbanum, onycha, and stacte,
  and like the fragrance of frankincense in the tabernacle.
Like a terebinth I spread out my branches,
  and my branches are glorious and graceful.
Like a vine I caused loveliness to bud,
  and my blossoms became glorious and abundant fruits.
I am the mother of beautiful love, of fear, of knowledge,
  and of holy hope;
  being eternal, I therefore am given to all my children,
    to those who are named by him.
Come to me, you who desire me,
  and eat your fill of my produce.
For the remembrance of me is sweeter than honey,
  and my inheritance sweeter than the honeycomb.
Those who eat me will hunger for more,
  and those who drink me will thirst for more.
Whoever obeys me will not be put to shame,
  and those who work with my help will not sin.'

Nobody knows how this demi-goddess found a place in the sacred writings. Like Solomon's Beloved, she is too vivid and complex to be 'nothing but' an allegory. Still, we can at least understand the impulse behind these texts. It was the same dissatisfaction with male deity that was bringing back aspects of the Goddess, with her satellite-myths, in other places. The emphasis was a little different, the basic thought was akin.

Israel's God had become too remote in his heaven beyond the sky. Jews felt that their long misfortunes had made him incomprehensible. He called them his Chosen, he made exacting demands on them, yet he did not reliably reward them when they obeyed . . . nor did he reliably punish sinners. That is the complaint in the book of Job, written a century or two before Proverbs. Job's lament is that he does not understand; he has been righteous, and still he suffers; man is of few days and full of trouble, even the life he has makes no sense, and he cannot confront God to demand an explanation. 'Where shall wisdom be found,' asks Job bitterly, 'and where is the place of understanding?' The personal Wisdom of the later books is in part an answer to Job's question.

She is a mediator between God and his world, enthroned in Zion. If the faithful and thoughtful Jew will attend to her, life will make sense in spite of all. She knows the divine secrets and inspires the holy words of the Torah. Indeed, just after the rhapsody quoted, Ben-Sira – or a pious interpolator – tries to preserve orthodoxy by an escape clause allowing the supposition that she is no more than a symbol of the Torah, 'the book of the covenant, the law which Moses commanded us'. This notion recurs in another apocryphal Wisdom text, Baruch 3:9–4:1. In Baruch it may just work, in Ecclesiasticus it does not. A later apocryphal book, the Wisdom of Solomon, which tries to relate Wisdom to Greek ideas, tells in its tenth chapter how she befriended various biblical characters who lived before the Torah was written. Elsewhere it tells how she guides her devotees towards immortality in the World to Come. Even within Judaism, that renewed hope is here connected with the Female. It hovers strangely alongside the more approved comfort of Messianic promise.[19]

(In later ages, aware of the problem Wisdom poses, some Christians continued the attempt to make her 'mean' something tractable. But except for a school of Russians, few theologians have ventured to face her squarely. Few artists have, either. One of them however is Michelangelo. In his Sistine Chapel painting of the Creation of Adam, Wisdom is present, young but adult and competent-looking, loosely embraced in God's left arm.[20])

As to why Wisdom in Jewish scripture is female, Ben-Sira's imagery suggests that several forms of the Eternal-Womanly have combined to mould her. The easy point to make is that she is like the Greek wisdom-goddess Athene, the virgin who sprang from the head of Zeus. But Athene is less important to Wisdom's making than her antecedents in the lands facing Cyprus.

Canaanite-Phoenician literature, at least as far back as the
seventh century BC, has a good deal to say on the theme of
'wisdom' which the passage in Proverbs appears to echo; and
when Wisdom takes the stage as a person in Ecclesiasticus, her
descent to earth and to the 'abyss' below resembles a descent to
the underworld made by the goddess Anath, Canaan's mighty
Virgin. Further details may have come from another deity of the
same region. In the opinion of Canon Wilfred Knox:

> The personified Wisdom is a female figure definitely on the
> divine side of the gulf which separates God from man. . . .
> There can be little doubt as to the original of this highly
> coloured portrait. The lady who dwells in the city of
> Jerusalem and in its Temple, who is also to be compared to
> all the forest trees of Hermon and the luxuriant verdure of
> the Jordan valley, is the great Syrian goddess Astarte, at
> once the goddess of great cities and the mother manifested
> in the fertility of nature. [21]

We must accept the fact, while acknowledging the riddle.
Somehow, in some Jewish minds, monotheism cracked so as to
let this being in. Untraceable in the Temple's official religion,
the crack may have opened because of a long-standing flirtation
with female deity by heretics. Before 600 BC Jerusalem did
harbour a cult of Astarte as Queen of Heaven, and the prophet
Jeremiah found Jews in Egypt worshipping a divinity with the
same title. They burned incense to her and made her offerings of
food – little cakes with her image stamped on them. (Jeremiah
7:18; 44:15–19.)

These apostates in Egypt may also have been adoring Astarte.
If they were, it is still hard to see any link with the emergence of
an Astarte-like Wisdom four hundred years later. But there is
another possibility. It may be that the Queen worshipped by the
Egyptian Jews was not Astarte but Anath, her often barely
distinguishable relation. Both had their votaries in Egypt apart
from the Jews, and a stele of Anath's cult under Rameses II hails
her as 'Queen of Heaven and mistress of all the gods'. At a later
time than Jeremiah's her status with Jews in Egypt is attested in
writing. Papyri dating from the fifth century BC show that
Jewish mercenaries stationed at Elephantiné near Aswan had a

small temple dedicated not only to 'Yaho' (as they called Yahweh, the God of Israel) but also to Anath. These troops and their families, probably descendants of Jeremiah's apostates, had attached Anath to the Lord as a female companion.

Elephantiné brings us much nearer in time to the Wisdom books. The last clue belongs to the Hellenistic age after Alexander's conquests, the period of the Wisdom books themselves. An inscription in Cyprus by Greek-speaking Phoenicians begins 'To Anath strength of life', and goes on to equate her with Athene: partly, it appears, because both are warrior-virgins, partly because their names are so nearly anagrams of each other (even more nearly so if the spelling 'Athena' is used).[22]

It can be proved, then, that there were Jews in Egypt who reverenced the Virgin Anath as in some sense attached to Yahweh. It can also be proved that Anath came to be merged with Athene, the Greeks' wisdom-goddess who emanated from their Sky-Father Zeus. Under the Greek Ptolemaic dynasty, which reigned over Egypt and, for a while, Palestine, it would have been easy for speculative Jews to conjure up the life-giving Lady Wisdom, Anath-Athene, at Yahweh's side; the makings of her were ready to hand; 'wisdom' as a literary motif *was* Canaanite as Anath was; and once conjured up, she would have attracted related Goddess-imagery such as Astarte's. The story as a whole is conjectural. The background presence of female deity in Judaism, towards the beginning of the Christian era, is rather more than conjectural.[23] While one set of texts evoked the Virgin Daughter of Zion, another evoked the Virgin Wisdom dwelling in Zion, trailing phantasms of a pagan past behind her. Further convergence, further coalescence, were not ruled out.

Jesus appeared in an atmosphere of expectancy which was still male in its bias. There was an obvious role for him to fill. Most Jews were waiting for their Messiah, David's royal descendant, the deliverer. Vaguer hopes of the same type had spread among Gentiles. These had inspired, for instance, Virgil's Fourth Eclogue, a prophecy of a divine child which was afterwards claimed as a pagan foreshadowing of Christ. The world-wide peace of Augustus had made such hopes less exciting and urgent, but they lingered on and could be reactivated.[24]

What is less familiar but now evident is that there was a role

31

for a woman to fill also. There was a resurgent daydream for a woman to realize. It was more complex, less definable. It did not point so positively to a real person. The Curé de Torcy's phrase about 'awaiting a *virgo genetrix*' (p. 2) over-simplifies it. Nevertheless the Curé is more right than wrong. It did exist, with limitless reserves of power from an older world. The throne of the Queen of Heaven could admit a visible occupant, a woman embodying the vision. And if any single qualification could be named, it was that she should come as a life-bestower: perhaps – like the Goddess in several of her renascent forms – through giving humanity a saviour, a rescuer from bondage to death.

Chapter 2

FROM THE SON TO THE MOTHER

I

In spite of all the preludes and predispositions, Mary's cult does not simply 'evolve'. She enters the historical scene by way of Christianity, and the trap of treating that religion as a mere growth out of older ones, a mere patchwork of pieces from them, must be sternly avoided. Though it had clear likenesses to the Mysteries, it was not derived from them. Though it began as a Jewish sect, it was not simply a new edition of Judaism – not even of Dead-Sea-Scroll Judaism, much less the speculative kind that enthroned the Lady Wisdom. When we turn to Mary and inquire who and what she was, such things give little direct help. Our prime concern is with the religion she appears in. The process that shaped the Christ of its faith is the necessary prologue to his mother's status among the faithful, and to whatever popular return of the Goddess took place through her.

In the reconstruction of Christian origins, it is an error, however often committed, to start from the New Testament as a set of documents. The basic datum of history is the early Church, a society of people who behaved in a special manner, proclaimed 'good news', told an extraordinary tale. We can infer a number of things about them from non-Christian sources, chiefly Roman, without drawing on their own statements at all. These sources tell us that they recognized a Jew named Jesus as the promised Messiah, the Christ. Since he had been executed in Judaea by Pontius Pilate, without setting up a kingdom, we can be certain that the Christians gave a new meaning to Messiahship which

33

transcended the Jewish expectation or even broke with it. We learn in fact that some at least of them worshipped Christ as divine – in Jewish eyes, a blasphemy – and that in general they proclaimed him with a fanatical fervour which got them cordially detested, but won converts in Rome and nerved many to endure martyrdom under Nero.[1]

With that picture in mind, we can turn to the New Testament itself and read it for what it is: the collective voice of the community that acted so wildly. It should be seen as *the Church's account of its own origins and status*. To insist on such careful phrasing is not to split hairs. The first object to contemplate is not the body of writings and doctrines, but the body of human beings prior to both, responsible for both, attested by outside witnesses.

Its original leaders were disciples of Jesus. They were not primarily preachers of theories or a moral code; Hebrew prophets and Greek philosophers had been doing as much for centuries. They were men who had undergone a soul-shaking experience. They had attached themselves to another man so unlike anyone else, so much more than anyone else, that he seemed to speak with the voice of God. They had been exalted, mystified, then plunged into despair by his crucifixion. After which he had raised them to a fresh, unimagined peak of faith by coming to life again.

The point here is not to ask whether he really did, or even why his followers thought so, but to realize that their experience transformed them, and was the cause of all that ensued. Paul, the first great convert, was won over not by preaching but by a vision which conveyed to him, in a flash, the essential impact of the experience. Christianity was an attempt to cope with it: to come to terms with the fact of Jesus Christ, to work out the meaning of his career, to express that meaning in a message. The Christianity of the mainstream never lost that character. Rival Christian systems appeared alongside, loosely called 'Gnostic'. But these stamped themselves as heretical by working the other way round. Their teachers invented theories of the universe, and then fitted Christ into them, re-writing his life freely to suit their needs. Orthodox Christians *started from* Christ – a living human being once encountered by other human beings, at times and

34

places more or less known – and built up their ideas by trying to interpret him.[2] The account of him given by his disciples (chiefly the apostles, who had been closest to him) determined their thinking. Of course the facts were improved upon, as in the Fourth Gospel. But Christians cannot be convicted, as the heretics can, of treating the facts as merely irrelevant, and concocting new stories in defiance of them to support notions of Christ imposed from outside. The tradition remained central.

Christianity was about a person. Therefore it was also about people connected with him: his mother, for instance. The roles assigned to such people in the Christian scheme would depend mainly on what was concluded about the Founder himself.

2

Christian doctrine was born in a traumatic crisis. Jesus had used the language of Jewish prophecy and apocalypse, speaking of an imminent Kingdom of God. His disciples assumed that he was preparing the Messianic uprising which Jews awaited. Hence, his arrest and execution seemed totally fatal to his claims, and caused most of them to desert. The Resurrection (however it came to be believed in) restored faith, yet left the riddle unanswered. On the one hand Jesus was plainly God's Anointed, as the stupendous miracle proved; he could be trusted to return some day in glory, and set up the promised kingdom. On the other hand there was no evading the fact that he had been put to death, horribly, disgracefully, and, worst of all, unexpectedly. His own followers had seen him alive afterwards, but nobody else had. Until he did return, his Messiahship was still an apparent fiasco. How to resolve the paradox?

The apostles turned to scripture and started picking out texts which could be read as prophecies of a dying and resurrected Messiah. Peter's address after Pentecost in Acts 2:14–36 includes such a text, quoted from Psalm 16. More impressive than the Psalm was a cryptic and haunting prophecy in Isaiah 52–53, about a 'Servant of the Lord' who was to suffer and die, yet live.

> Behold, my servant shall prosper,
>   he shall be exalted and lifted up,
>   and shall be very high.

As many were astonished at him –
   his appearance was so marred, beyond human semblance,
   and his form beyond that of the sons of men –
So shall he startle many nations;
   kings shall shut their mouths because of him. . . .
He was despised and rejected by men;
   a man of sorrows, and acquainted with grief;
   and as one from whom men hide their faces
   he was despised, and we esteemed him not.
Surely he has borne our griefs
   and carried our sorrows;
   yet we esteemed him stricken,
   smitten by God, and afflicted.
But he was wounded for our transgressions,
   he was bruised for our iniquities;
   upon him was the chastisement that made us whole,
   and with his stripes we are healed.
All we like sheep have gone astray;
   we have turned every one to his own way;
   and the Lord has laid on him
   the iniquity of us all.
He was oppressed, and he was afflicted,
   yet he opened not his mouth;
   like a lamb that is led to the slaughter,
   and like a sheep that before its shearers is dumb,
   so he opened not his mouth.
By oppression and judgment he was taken away;
   and as for his generation, who considered
   that he was cut out of the land of the living,
   stricken for the transgression of my people?
And they made his grave with the wicked,
   and with a rich man in his death,
   although he had done no violence,
   and there was no deceit in his mouth.
Yet it was the will of the Lord to bruise him. . . .
   He shall see his offspring, he shall prolong his days;
   the will of the Lord shall prosper in his hand;
   he shall see the fruit of the travail of his soul and be satisfied.

Jewish commentators had never been sure how to take this. Could the Servant be Israel? But Israel, as we have seen, tended to be personified as a woman, whereas the Servant was male. Those who accepted Jesus as Messiah could apply the passage to him, and they did (Acts 8:30–5). They took it as implying that he died a martyr for a backsliding people, suffering for the sins of others. Recalling his moral teachings, and his warning that the Kingdom of God was 'within', they inferred that their task was to prepare for his Second Coming by a vast work of purification. Whatever the Kingdom meant, his people must be made worthy of it, and only those who became so would share in it.[3]

There they might have halted. Probably many of the first generation did. It is impossible to tell how many of Jesus's own disciples ever regarded him as divine. For Jews it was a fearful leap to take. Paul, however, claiming a private revelation, not only took it but went much further. He said Jesus was the Son of God, and had become man and died on the cross, himself sinless, as a mystical expiation for the sins of the world. (In his extant writings Paul never discusses the Isaiah passage, but, on his showing, it has depths beyond depths.) Moreover the Resurrection was not simply a proof of Christ's mission but a victory over death, opening the gates of eternal life for all who believed in him.

Paul found himself in conflict with other Christians. His ideas gave the Messiahship an individual and spiritual bias which was alien to Jewish thought. It could be argued too that they paganized it. Christ became a Saviour with a perceptible likeness to the dying-and-rising gods of the Mysteries, Osiris, Adonis and the rest. Paul was thereby able to break out of Judaic exclusiveness and convert Gentiles, but at the cost of estranging Jews, most of whom rejected such a complication of deity, and such a seeming relapse into the iniquities of the Canaanites.

In the upshot it was Paul who gained ground. The main bulwark of Jewish Christianity, the Church in Jerusalem, was ruined in the uprising against Rome which led in AD 70 to the city's destruction. After this, Christianity became largely Gentile and non-political. Its figure of Christ, incorporating all that was agreed about him, was more Pauline than Judaic. His

Jewishness remained, but it was revalued. The three Synoptic Gospels – Matthew, Mark, Luke – portrayed him as Messiah and wonder-worker and teacher. The supplementary Fourth, ascribed to John the 'beloved disciple', theologized him further as the creative Logos or Word of God. That term was borrowed from the philosopher Philo, who was an Alexandrian Jew, but an intellectual spiritually apart from the main body.[4]

So the Christ whom the Church proclaimed as its Lord and Founder interwove several strands of prior belief. He filled several pre-ordained roles. Besides being the Messiah foretold by Jews, he was the Saviour anticipatorily worshipped in the Mysteries, and also the divine co-creator imagined by pre-Christian philosophers like Philo. Yet it is wrong to suppose that he was 'nothing but' these, a composite deity put together from older materials. With each role that he filled, he went beyond it. He was a profounder Messiah than the Jews had expected, and not what most of them had hoped for. He was far more his own master than the doomed victim-god of the Mysteries, slain and restored in an endlessly repeated cycle. He was higher in the divine scheme than Philo's Logos.

Christianity in fact centred on an idea which outsoared all the rest: the Incarnation. Jesus Christ was in some sense God (not merely *a* god). He had united the human and divine natures. He had voluntarily shared our condition, suffered with us and for us, submitted himself to death and conquered it. That happened in history, not in a mythological 'dream time', and it happened once for all. Myths and hopes, prophecies and speculations, converged on Jesus and he fulfilled them. But he also transcended them. They reappeared in him transfigured.

This is not a modern afterthought in the light of comparative religion. It is a way of looking at Jesus which began in the early Church and is attested by its writings. Matthew, for instance, quotes Old Testament texts which can be construed as prophetic hints at him. The hints, however, are less than the reality. Most of them are not clear-cut predictions which would have led a reader to expect a certain event. They make complete sense only in the light of their fulfilment by Jesus, which adds new dimensions, unforeseeably, sometimes poignantly.[5] Again, a story already cited from Acts (8: 30–5) brings the same point out with precision. The Ethiopian eunuch who is reading Isaiah 53 admits that he cannot understand it without guidance. Philip expounds it, showing how the prophecy is fulfilled in Jesus – but only now that he has actually come. No one before his coming predicted him from it, or would have been likely to. So also with the metaphysical preface to John. Others had spoken of a being called the Word of God, but there was no precedent for the doctrine of the Incarnation as stated here, 'the Word became flesh and dwelt among us' (John 1:14).

Among the characters in the early Christian scene, the motif of fulfilment was confined to Christ himself . . . almost. The Church never suggested that Peter or Paul fitted a pattern foreshadowed before their Master appeared. Dark prophecies of an Enemy, an Antichrist, were supposed for a time to have been realized by Nero, but the belief never became a doctrine and it was not held to be certain that Christ did imply a personal Antichrist. For Gentiles, however, he tended to imply someone else. In his role as dying-and-rising Saviour he could not be readily conceived as standing alone. Such gods had never normally done so. They were rooted in the world of the Goddess, and in some form she accompanied them. You could not have Osiris without Isis, or Attis without Cybele. The death-conquering Christ of the Pauline missions cast a shadow behind him, whether or not Paul was ever aware of it. He evoked a role for another to fill – a woman. The world's nostalgic desire would prepare a place for her. Doubtless, like Christ, she would transcend myth as well as fulfilling it. And the original relationship of the Young God to the Goddess made Christ's mother the best candidate.

3

With the scene thus set, we can surely move forward. The steps are obvious: first, to distil from the Gospels what little there is about Mary to be distilled; then, to trace the growth of legend about her, showing how it turned an obscure Jewish wife into the Virgin Mother of God and Queen of Heaven.

These are the obvious steps, but they are illusory. The problem of Mary is part of a larger problem posed by Christian beginnings in general. We have seen, in outline, what happened.

It is not so clear how it happened, or how we should take the documents that embody it. The normal modern view is that a purely human 'historical Jesus' had a purely human career. Then, after his death, legends and interpretations were gradually added, resulting in the New Testament. If this view were viable, our first step in inquiry would be to survey the Gospels, prune away the supernatural growths, and accept what remained as the nucleus of truth, with an unmiraculous Jesus, and an unmiraculous Mary giving birth to him.

But a huge obstacle blocks the path. It cannot be done with Jesus, and his mother's story is so intricately involved in his that it cannot be done with her either. Analysis of this type does not yield a history which accounts for the facts: for the shattering experience which Christianity was an attempt to spell out; or for the forms which the attempt took. If a quest for the historical Jesus is pursued in that spirit (as it has been, times without number), the awe-inspiring and transfiguring Christ always vanishes, and the so-called legends themselves become incomprehensible. In approaching the Gospel record we must adjust, however reluctantly, to something very strange indeed.

The 'gradual growth of legend' around Jesus was not like the growth around (for example) Buddha. It did not drift on and on for hundreds of years. The New Testament was finished, or nearly so, within a single long lifetime of the Crucifixion. That period covers virtually the entire growth. Almost everything afterwards is either doctrinal expansion of the New Testament, or mere decline into feeble apocrypha which the Church never incorporated into its account of itself. In the Gospels the canonical Christ is presented through a unique composite masterpiece, which cannot be shown evolving from earlier narratives.[6] This began to take shape with Mark about AD 65, and was complete when old people who remembered the central character were probably still living. To speak of a masterpiece is not to raise questions of literary taste. The Gospels may or may not be good writing. They may or may not be as rife as critics allege with inconsistencies, obscurities and absurdities. Their colossal impact is a datum of history. Pagan and apocryphal imitations never had anything like that impact, and to read and compare them is to see why not.

Given these four related books, can we or can we not arrive at truth by pruning away non-history? We have to decide, because Mary is embedded in them and not significantly to be found elsewhere. Clearly, to quote Ernest Renan, they are full of miracles and the supernatural. But if we draw his conclusion that they are largely fictitious, and govern the pruning process by that axiom, we are in trouble.

To begin with, where should we draw the line? Is 'pruning' perhaps too mild a word? Are the Gospels *essentially* fictitious, in the sense that the main story itself is false, a kind of novel? To take an extreme view which, though outmoded, still finds the odd supporter – did Jesus never exist? Was the Christian experience a group-fantasy? If so, it is no use looking for Jesus's mother.

But even on literary grounds the theory is suspect; and it might never have been launched at all if biblical critics had known enough about literature. It is really too much to assert the concoction of such an amazing fiction, by four geniuses suddenly sprouting together, in an age when fiction as we know it had scarcely begun to be written anywhere. The inventors would be as extraordinary as the invention, and since banishing Christ banishes Matthew, Mark, Luke and John with him, we have not the faintest clue to their identity. Who were they and why is nothing known about them? There is no point in replacing a mystery which we may at least hope to unravel with a mystery which is total.

Furthermore, if Jesus had not been a real person, somebody would have said so. In particular the Church's enemies would have said so, during Nero's persecution for instance, or later ones. What could be more damning than to retort – if there was the least ground for it – 'Your so-called Saviour never existed'? Non-Christians such as Tacitus, however hostile, accept that he did.

This last point has a wider application, and helps us, I think, to define the right attitude to the Gospels and to what they tell us of Mary. It might seem that while they cannot be essentially fiction, the true story is overlaid with miracles and religious fables, and the way to recover it is by (as said before) a process of pruning. Yet the same difficulty persists. The chief Christian statements, in and out of the Gospels, were being made publicly well within the lifetime of eye-witnesses, and in a milieu of enmity, even of persecution. If those statements were false, it is hard to see why no authority, Jewish or Roman, ever rebutted them. Why not produce witnesses to discredit the tales of miracles? Why not disprove the Resurrection by opening the tomb and showing a decayed corpse? Matthew 28:11–15 suggests that the latter refutation may well have been thought of, perhaps tried, but could not be effected because, for whatever reason, the corpse was missing.[7]

It does not follow that the orthodox version must be true after all. But criticism of it is closely and puzzlingly restricted. There is little room for a gradual growth of legend, and any dissection of the Gospels on that assumption leads to an impasse. The 'legends' which the early Christians proclaimed, orally and in writing, must have had a toughness forbidding airy dismissal. For an impartial inquirer the correct adjective takes shape: the Christian story must be read, not necessarily as 'true', but as somehow 'irrefutable'. Few of course believed it, but there was no major fact that subverted it. No Roman official produced a glaringly discrepant record of Jesus's trial. No identical twin came forward who confessed to having faked his Resurrection appearances. There was no such record and no such twin.[8]

Let me offer a parallel, showing why, for personal reasons alone, I cannot believe in a wholesale falsification of Christ's career. I live in a house formerly owned by Dion Fortune, a well-known psychologist and writer on fringe topics such as occultism. She died in 1946. The house was a rendezvous for a society which she founded. Members of it have visited me and described the house as it was then, and what went on in it. Now suppose I were to launch a cult based on grossly false claims about her. Knowing her books and milieu, I could contrive a Dion Fortune 'Gospel' having a certain plausibility, and perhaps get away with a few invented incidents. But I could not get away with a story which entirely altered her life, portraying her as (say) a famous healer by acupuncture when she was not, and describing public confrontations with Churchill and George VI which never took place. Apart from anything else, survivors of her own loyal circle would rise up to explode my falsehoods. Some gullible souls might still believe me, but the denials and disproofs would be too many to suppress. They would become overwhelming if my cult got in trouble with the law; and if it did, very few would remain convinced to the point of dying for it.

With Christian origins, irrefutability has a positive as well as a negative side. Even people with strong motives for destroying the Christians' claims, even people with strong motives for giving a rival non-miraculous story, failed (for whatever reason) to do so. There is not, until far too late to be of serious interest, any hostile 'truth about Jesus Christ' challenging the Church's account.

And nobody has produced it since: not with all the resources of modern scholarship. That is the final and crucial issue in deciding how to read the Gospels. The Christian traditionalist can still fairly ask: 'If the Church's account of its own origins is false, then what is the truth, how did it originate?' No would-be rational historian has yet answered. Or rather, too many have; Strauss tried in 1835, Renan in 1863, and a host of others afterwards. Most of their stories have owed more to the intellectual fashions of the moment of writing than to accurate logic, and they have all cancelled each other. To say so is not polemic but fact, attested by two classic works of scholarship, Albert Schweitzer's *Quest of the Historical Jesus* and Joseph Klausner's *Jesus of Nazareth*. Both are amply confirmed in this respect by all that has happened since they were published.

Every such attempt to strip away the supposed accretions, and refute the Church by isolating the 'historical Jesus' or 'Christ-myth', gives a different Jesus or a different myth. He is made out to have been a moralist, or an exorcist, or a healer, or a prophet of doomsday, or a socialist, or a pacifist, or a lunatic, or a Jewish nationalist, or an Essene Teacher of Righteousness. He is made out to have been a sun-myth or a vegetation-myth . . . or a sacred mushroom. The only plain deduction from this critical chaos is that the reality was richer than the critics care to admit. Incantatory repetition of words like 'myth' is not historical scholarship. It is an abdication of scholarship. One school of thought, Bultmann's, says 'Jesus existed but we can't know anything about him, and the message is all that matters.' I do not see how a historian can acquiesce in such a surrender, unless he wants to evade the issue; and I am thinking of some who profess Christianity as well as some who reject it.

Reason is supposed to be an objective method of arriving at truth. Here it seems to arrive at dozens of 'truths', which are not only incompatible but far more completely so than the divided Christian sects.[9] It is time, not to reject reason, but to ask whether what is here assumed to be rational inquiry actually is so. *Omnia abeunt in mysterium* indeed. Either the thing happened more or less as the Church concluded – a view which need not entail naive churchmanship today – or something else happened which remains unfathomed. But the principle of irrefutability survives. The pruning, negative approach to the Gospels will not work. It shipwrecks on the absence of ancient refutations and the hopeless confusion of modern ones.

To approach a major Gospel question, such as the truth about Mary, we must use a different method. Critical analysis is of course an aid, and may be a potent aid. But we cannot safely discard 'myths' or 'legends' which in other contexts we would discard. We are not bound to take them literally; we are bound to take them seriously, and ask what realities they express, what points they make. Obviously the Gospels pose immense problems of authorship and authority. They confront us with language, imagery, descriptive conventions and ways of putting things, which are not ours and must be treated with intelligent ruthlessness. Yet the sole hope of a useful outcome is to study the record as a whole, and do our best to make sense of it as a whole.

It might be urged that this applies only to Christ himself and not to those around him. The historical Jesus may defeat the pruning technique, but we can cut away miracles and get at a historical Peter or Paul. Perhaps. Christ's mother, however, turns out differently. She shares in the quality of her Son. Much less is said of her than of Peter or Paul, yet she resists being cut down to a historical Mary. The account given of her raises queries over her status in the authors' eyes. Texts take on various meanings according to what we judge that status to have been. We must approach them with the same breadth of outlook required for the Gospels as a whole. A basic, no-nonsense, rational reading is hard to fix upon.

By following the wiser path we can arrive at a picture of her which is much more than the brief scriptural notices. We can also disclose a group of facts involving her more closely in the making of Christianity than the New Testament ever does. Her cult is rooted in events which the Church belatedly came to terms with, but obscured in the process.

Chapter 3

THE STRENGTH OF
THE ABSURD

I

Mary figures chiefly in two groups of stories of Jesus's birth and infancy (Matthew, the first two chapters, and Luke 1:26–56 and 2:1–40). Luke adds a further story about a family pilgrimage to Jerusalem when the boy is twelve (2:41–52). Jesus works his first miracle at his mother's prompting, the changing of water into wine at Cana, and then takes her to Capernaum for a few days (John 2:1–12). During his public ministry she appears with relatives outside a house where he is staying, and sends in a message, to which his response reads like a snub (Matthew 12:46–50; Mark 3:31–5; Luke 8:19–21). Here, as in Luke 11:27–8 where he deflects a compliment that involves her, he seems to be keeping her at a certain distance. When he revisits his home town, Mary's neighbours resent all the excitement over the son of a woman whom they have known for years (Matthew 13:53–8; Mark 6:1–6). She is present at the Crucifixion. Before dying, he entrusts her to the care of John, the beloved disciple (John 19:25–7). We have a last glimpse of her in Acts 1:14 joining the apostles in prayer.

That is all. Surely such a meagre record cannot be so very hard to sort out? Indeed, surely it cannot be so very informative? All we need do is sum up the little that is said, conclude that the Mother of Christ is hardly more than a name, and go straight on to her mythification.

Yet – to look no further – even a name is something. Even if we did have no more, it could still be a clue, a sign of myth-

making potentialities which were there from the start.[1] 'Mary'
is Jewish, the same as 'Miriam'. The earliest known woman to be
so called is a sister of Moses and Aaron. She first appears by name
in Exodus 15:20, though she is commonly assumed to have been
the same sister who, long before that point in the story, kept
watch over Moses as a baby in his basket of rushes. At her entry
by name she is described as a prophetess. Beating a timbrel, she
leads the women in a song after the Israelites have passed through
the sea and Pharaoh's pursuing troops are drowned. Scholars
have maintained that the verse put in her mouth –

> Sing to the Lord, for he has triumphed gloriously;
> the horse and his rider he has thrown into the sea –

is the oldest in the whole Bible, and authentic. We have here a
kind of spiritual, made up by the singer at the time.[2] Just as
Israel's entire faith grew round this miracle of deliverance, opening the road to the Promised Land, so Israel's entire Bible (in
Christian terms, the Old Testament) grew round Miriam's song
proclaiming it. She is a curiously important person.

At this juncture Moses, Aaron and Miriam herself are united
as a prophetic family leading the people. They are so remembered
long afterwards (Micah 6:4). During the tribal wanderings,
however, Miriam rebels with Aaron's support (Numbers 12).
She objects to Moses marrying a foreign wife, and to his claim to
a monopoly of revelation: 'Has the Lord indeed spoken only
through Moses? Has he not spoken through us also?' The Lord
retorts with a crushing rebuke, telling her that he speaks directly
to Moses alone, and inflicting one of his terrifying penances.
After this we hear no more of her but her death. Nothing,
however, cancels her dignity as an inspired woman closely
concerned in her brothers' work. Jewish tradition calls her the
saviour of Israel and makes her an ancestress of David.

It is by no means certain how she pronounced her name. The
old Hebrew alphabet lacked vowels. 'Miriam' is a late form with
vowels conjecturally filled in. The Greek Old Testament, translated from the Hebrew in the third century BC, gives 'Mariam'.
This may well be correct. 'Maria', in English 'Mary', is a
variant of it.

By Christ's time, at any rate, the name was in common use

among Jews. Six women have it in the New Testament. Six more are mentioned by the historian Josephus, who was born in AD 37. The New Testament gives it twenty-five times as 'Mariam' and twenty-eight as 'Maria'. Applied to the Mother of Christ, it is 'Mariam' twelve times and 'Maria' seven. Her neighbours call her 'Mariam'.

Its derivation is doubtful. It is often said to mean 'bitterness'. The same Hebrew letters can be read *marim*, 'bitter', and the Talmud says fancifully that Miriam was born when the Egyptians 'embittered' the life of the Hebrews. Much the same thought appears in Ruth 1:20. Later, for a reason which will emerge in a moment, mystics associate 'Mary' with the bitterness of sea-water. However, the name has been construed also as meaning 'lady', 'prophetess', 'the proud', even 'the fat' – since Asians admired a full figure. Another suggested source is an Egyptian prefix *meri*, 'beloved' (feminine *merit*, but the *t* was silent). This could be combined with a god's name to make a human one: Meri-Ra was 'Beloved of Ra'. Likewise Meri-Yām, using an early form of the name of the God of Israel, might have meant 'Beloved of Yahweh'. If Moses's sister was indeed the same elder one who looked after him in infancy, she could not have been called Meri-Yām originally, because the Lord's name was not revealed till later (Exodus 3:14); but possibly she was given a new one herself, as the first woman in his service. However derived, the name 'Mariam' recalled that mighty rescue which the prophetess celebrated, the miracle which Jews saw at the root of their destiny as God's Chosen. Any woman so called would have been ripe for the play of symbolic imagination, the moment she was linked with a Messianic belief.

In the Roman Empire, with Latin as a world-wide language, the name had possibilities for Gentiles as well. In Latin the word for 'sea' was *mare*, and its plural was *maria*. Mary, therefore, could readily be connected with the sea, the vast numinous water from which, in some of her aspects, the Goddess had long ago arisen. A way was open for imagery unknown to Hebraic minds to gather about her. Christ's mother was presently to become 'Myrrh of the Sea' and 'Drop of the Sea', *Stilla Maris* – whence a more endearing title, *Stella Maris*, Star of the Sea. Was it so far-fetched? Even in Hebrew *marah* meant 'brine'. Moses's sister, the prototype-Mary so to speak, had herself passed through the sea that swallowed Pharaoh's army and saved Israel; she had hymned the victory which the sea won as Yahweh's instrument; her song saluted it.[3]

When the Gospels were written, most of these potentialities were unrealized. The author who introduces Mary as we read through them (we may call him Matthew) shows no signs of having Latin in mind. But he may well have regarded Mary as aptly named to be the agent of an even greater salvation than the sea-miracle. The moment she appears in his text she is a special person, drawn into the scheme of scriptural prophecies proving Jesus to be the Christ. His first quotation is from Isaiah 7:14: 'Behold, a virgin shall conceive and bear a son, and his name shall be called Emmanuel (which means, God with us).' The word translated 'virgin' is ambiguous in Hebrew and need not mean that. But Matthew interprets it in the light of an already-current belief that although Jesus was legally the son of Mary's husband Joseph, a carpenter, he was not begotten by Joseph or by any man. He was born to Mary without sexual intercourse through a miracle of the Holy Spirit.

2

So this crucial mystery, the Virgin Birth, faces us at once. It is the heart of the Christian view of Christ's mother. Our best hope of giving her any sort of biography does not lie in dismissing it as a legend but in meeting it head-on, trying to decide what it is all about, and working outwards from it. The case for such a procedure in general has already been stated. The objection to it in this instance is the absence of proof that the miracle was affirmed early: which suggests that the first Christians may not have believed in it. If they did not – or rather, if they believed something else – then it is not a datum for Mary's life but for her mythification afterwards, and we must look elsewhere for the facts.

This objection seems powerful, even self-evident. Yet it fails. Let us consider the Christian writings and see what they tell us.

The account of the Virgin Birth in Matthew is given from Joseph's point of view, the one in Luke from Mary's. Both these

Gospels date, in their present form, from the years between 70 and 90 AD. The immediate question is whether we can find traces of Christians farther back who had no knowledge of the miracle, or, failing that, of a conservative protest or rival version when it came to be asserted.

There are silences. Silence alone, however, is a fragile argument. Paul's Epistles, which are earlier than the Gospels, never mention the Virgin Birth. But John, written after Matthew and Luke when the belief was well established, never mentions it either. Nor does Paul ever refer to Joseph, or hint at a more commonplace birth-story.

Mark also antedates the other Gospels, and preserves more of the primitive tradition, sometimes with impressive touches of honesty – such as the fact, prudently suppressed later, that some friends of Jesus tried to lock him up as insane (3:21). It gives no birth-story at all. Its chief allusion to Jesus's family (6:1–3) is surprising. The passage is paralleled in Matthew 13:53–5, and Matthew is worth looking at first.

> Coming to his own country he taught them in their synagogue, so that they were astonished, and said, 'Where did this man get this wisdom and these mighty works? Is not this the carpenter's son? Is not his mother called Mary?'

If we now go back to Mark, ten or twenty years closer to the events, the corresponding text has a glaring difference.

> He went away from there and came to his own country . . . and many who heard him were astonished, saying, 'Where did this man get all this? What is the wisdom given to him? . . . Is not this the carpenter, the son of Mary?'

Here Jesus himself is the carpenter, with nothing about inheriting a family trade, and no father. In this earlier Gospel we do not get back to normal paternity, only to absolute non-paternity: a blank. It may of course be assumed that Joseph was dead, but Jews tended to call a man the son of his father – not his mother – long after the father's demise, and in Luke 4:22, for example, Jesus is so described. The Marcan phrase 'son of Mary' is very odd, and almost hints at a doubt or absence.[4]

By using the Bible we cannot get away from the marvel, or

behind it. Mary is given a male partner, but only by the very
authors who assert the supernatural birth. Except as spouse of
the Virgin Mother, Joseph the carpenter has no documentary
existence. The Fourth Gospel mentions his name, but may be
only echoing Matthew or Luke. To discuss Joseph as if we knew
anything about him, apart from the miracle that involves him, is
not rational but fanciful. If we cut out the supernatural birth-
stories as accretions, we are not left (as we are, say, in the case of
Buddha) with a normal couple normally producing a child. We
are left with no birth at all, and an alleged, scantily mentioned
husband for Mary, of whom the oldest Gospel has no trace
whatever.

On the face of it, then, the only way to make anything positive
of her motherhood is to use writings which assume it to be
miraculous. The Bible gives us no direct glimpse of any first-
generation Christians who can be proved to have told a different
tale. Can we find them by searching elsewhere? Negatively there
is some hope of this. Paul's Epistles, and the Acts, do prove that
the Virgin Birth was not a vital part of the earliest preaching.[5]
The Church started from Christ's adult career; his birth from a
virgin was at least not publicized officially till forty or fifty years
later. Is the New Testament's silence an active suppression –
suppression of the fact that Paul's Christian contemporaries
believed Jesus to have been born normally, and did not talk much
about his birth because they did not think of it as special? Are
there signs outside the Bible that this was so?

The question turns mainly on another one, the nature of the
'Ebionite' sect. Early in the second century, little groups of
Christians known by that name were scattered through Palestine
and neighbouring countries. If we can trust hostile reports, they
anathematized Paul and held to a purely Judaic faith. Jesus was
the Messiah of Israel's prophetic hope. He would return in glory
to be the world's overlord. He was God's Chosen, through
whom miracles were worked. But he was not in any sense God,
nor, according to the stricter Ebionites, was his birth one of the
miracles. Joseph had been his father as truly as Mary was his
mother.

Was this sect merely a reaction against the religion taught by
Paul, in other words an innovation itself; or was it a remnant of

a fully defined primal Christianity that held the field unchallenged before the Pauline remodelling? On one theory the second view is correct. The parent Jewish Church in Jerusalem was under the influence of Jesus's family and regarded him in a more or less 'Ebionite' manner. It was crushed, as we saw, when the Romans destroyed Jerusalem in 70; after which (this is the nub of the theory) the dwindling Ebionite outposts were the last relics of the Jewish Christianity which it stood for. The diehards took their name from *ebionim*, 'the poor', in the spirit of Luke 6:20. But Paul's Gentile converts changed Christianity and ousted the Ebionites as heretics.

This reconstruction may be right, but it cannot be proved, and nothing can be inferred as to the opinion held of Christ's birth in the Jerusalem Church. Even its Ebionite heirs, if that is what they were, had no written alternative birth-story. As a Gospel for their own use they had a censored text of Matthew in Hebrew, a fact suggesting a breakaway group rather than a remnant of the pre-Matthew faithful.[6]

The Ebionite protest against the Virgin Birth is a dead end. It comes too late and from outside the Church. So does that of Cerinthus, a heretic who opposes the doctrine at about the same time. Within Christianity, the only other hope of getting behind orthodoxy is to show that the Gospels have been tampered with, that the Virgin Birth is an interpolation. This claim rests on two frail pieces of evidence. In 1892 a Syriac manuscript of Matthew came to light in which verse 1:16 differed from the received text. In the standard Bible we read: 'Jacob begat Joseph the husband of Mary, of whom was born Jesus, who is called Christ.' The Syriac version said: 'Jacob begat Joseph; Joseph, to whom was betrothed Mary, the Virgin, begat Jesus, who is called Christ.' A quotation of the same verse in another ancient work says: 'Jacob begat Joseph, the husband of Mary, from whom was born Jesus who is called Christ, and Joseph begat Jesus who is called Christ.'

Since these versions disagree, it is not much use trying to argue that they give us a suppressed original text. In any case they both look like clumsy re-writings of the text which we know. In the first, why call Mary 'the Virgin' if she was not? In the second, why not say simply 'Jacob begat Joseph, and Joseph

begat Jesus who is called Christ'? Furthermore neither con-
clusively proves the writer's belief that Joseph, physically, did
beget Jesus. The word used need imply no more than official
parenthood. In another Syriac work, which embroiders the
Gospel and expressly extols Mary's virginity, the angel's message
to Joseph in Matthew 1:21 nevertheless becomes 'She shall bear
to thee a son.' It is surprising what could be said with no sense of
incongruity.[7]

Among Christians, then, the Virgin Birth is the only birth.
Granted, they might have revised their own books so thoroughly
as to leave no trace of any alternative story. But they could
hardly have given the same treatment to the books of Jews or
pagans; and these do not offer an alternative either. The Jews
had strong motives and unbroken traditions handed down from
rabbi to rabbi, yet they made no attempt to publish the 'truth
about Jesus' till the fourth century. Even then the result was a
mere farrago of fantasy called the Toledoth Jeshua, History of
Jesus, which sheds no more light on his origin than it does on
anything else.

The Jewish story of the birth was simply a kind of joke based
on the Gospels themselves. Jesus was alleged – predictably – to
have been fathered by someone other than Joseph, who seduced,
or ravished, Mary. Some such scandal was current in the second
century and is mentioned by the great Christian writer Origen.
But Jesus is never given a credible father. Instead we get a
number of contradictory versions in which the common factor is
a man with the bizarre name 'Pandera' or 'Pantere', who is
sometimes the begetter, always closely involved in the affair; and
there is nothing in this but a corruption of the Christian statement that Jesus was the son of a parthenos – virgin.[8]

So we have, it seems, an instance of the irrefutability principle.
To prepare the ground for whatever Life of Mary can be compiled, the first task is an essay in detection based on taking the
Virgin Birth seriously: not as literal truth, nor yet as a fancy to
discard, but as an event (or supposed event) which was in keeping
with all that Mary's contemporaries knew, was consistent with
all traditions that went into the Gospels, and was not disproved
by any manifest fact. When Matthew and Luke were written,
Mary was presumably dead, but many people still living had met

her. I would suggest that the authors of these Gospels wrote nothing starkly at variance with anything her friends remembered her saying.

3

Both the birth-stories start with Mary 'betrothed' to Joseph. The word translated 'betrothed' is imprecise. In Luke 2:5 it clearly means 'married', and in Matthew 1:19 Joseph is her 'husband'. The truth is that under Jewish law the distinction was little more than nominal. Betrothal was tantamount to marriage. The marriage was completed not by a ceremony or celebration, though these might be held, but simply by the couple living together – normally, by the man taking the woman to his own home.[9] It is this step which is meant when Joseph is told to 'take' his wife in Matthew 1:20. At the time when Mary conceives her child he has not yet done so. They are not under the same roof, and no consummation has occurred.

Hence, when he finds she is pregnant, he knows it cannot be by him. Rather than disgrace her in public, says Matthew, he plans to remain apart and divorce her quietly. However, an angel appears to him in a dream (this Gospel has a whole series of dreams taken as guidance) and tells him she is innocent. She has conceived through the Holy Spirit, and her son is to be called Jesus – the same as Joshua, meaning 'God is salvation' – because he will save his people from their sins. Joseph abandons the idea of divorce and they live together, but he has no sexual relations with her. We are not told where these events happen. The next chapter locates the birth in Bethlehem, as allegedly prophesied of the Christ in Micah 5:2.

Luke 1:26–38 gives Mary's side and is much more interesting. We find her living at Nazareth in Galilee. Joseph does not seem to be within call; he may be away working in some other town. The passage quoted on p. 1 mentions her virginity and describes the visit of Gabriel. The angel promises that she will conceive a child. She must name him Jesus, and he shall be called the Son of the Most High, and God will set him on the throne of David for ever – a plain Messianic pledge.

Mary's natural reaction would surely be to apply this message to her marriage, as foretelling that when Joseph is with her she will bear the child to him. But, somehow, she knows at once that he is excluded and Gabriel has another meaning. 'How shall this be,' she asks, 'since I have no husband?' (or 'no knowledge of man'; her point is the same however translated). Doubtless we have to understand some such word as 'today' in the angel's promise of conception. He replies that the event will take place, not through a sexual act, but through the Holy Spirit and the power of the Most High. He adds that her kinswoman Elizabeth has become pregnant herself in old age after a lifetime of barrenness. God has worked a wonder for Elizabeth, and is working a greater one for Mary. 'Behold,' Mary answers, 'I am the handmaid of the Lord; let it be to me according to your word.' Gabriel departs. She goes to visit Elizabeth, who lives near Jerusalem, and stays with her for about three months. The birth is at Bethlehem as in Matthew, but since Mary and Joseph are both said to live in Nazareth (2:4), a reason is given for their going there: Bethlehem is where Joseph must report for a census.

Both versions are restrained. Angels appear, in keeping with the traditions of Hebrew religious narrative, but the actual conception is merely indicated. There are no cheap marvels or anatomical details. The authors are concerned with the Virgin Birth as a simple if unique fact. But in an age of comparative religion, most people who consider this 'fact' at all would say it is anything but unique. Pagan myth, it is assumed, abounded in virgin births through divine agency. Christians merely adopted a Gentile fancy to glorify their Founder. Perhaps, too, they regarded sex as sinful, and decided that Christ had to be born without it if he was to be untainted himself. Clearly the first question to ask is how the Virgin Birth relates to older mythology. Was it indeed a bridge by which pagan themes passed over into Christianity?

On the claim that the Gentile world offers a mass of precedents, a modern investigator's comment is final. 'It is difficult to find a statement in all the literature of historical criticism which is more misleading.'[10]

Pre-Christian myth, heroic legend and dynastic flattery did speak of women bearing children through strange means. We have glanced at a few such tales already. The oldest, or at any rate the most primitive, are those that reflect a stage of society where the male role was not properly understood, and pregnancy was ascribed to a medley of causes. The wind is an agency often favoured. So are certain foods, and vaguely-imagined ghosts or spectral beings. Sunlight may be enough. Particular stories name particular magical objects, such as a blade of grass or a pebble. These are sometimes swallowed. Fo-hi, the legendary founder of China, is conceived by a girl who finds a flower clinging to her garment while bathing, and eats it. One proof of the ignorance or fantasy in such folk-tales is that conception may occur in all sorts of places – via the fingers, the navel, the ear, the crown of the head. Even when a man is involved, he can make the woman pregnant without relevant contact, by looking at her, for instance.

In a more advanced society procreation is understood, and then the birth-with-no-human-father is apt to be ascribed to a god. Early Christian authors are quite aware of such 'parallels' in the world before Christ. Justin Martyr mentions the well-known case of Danaë, who loses her maidenhead to Zeus when he comes to her as a shower of gold, the result being Perseus. It is easy to add other myths of the same type, told to account for the origin of a demigod or distinguished mortal. Zeus visits Alcmena disguised as her own husband and begets Heracles. In the shape of a swan he is the father of Helen by Leda. Apollo begets Asclepius, Mars begets Romulus.

Even in historical times such legends attached themselves to famous men. Alexander was said to have been conceived by Olympias, Philip of Macedon's wife, when Zeus coupled with her in the form of a snake. Pythagoras and Plato were said to be sons of Apollo. And so on. Outside the classical world, India was rich in these tales. A much-loved legend of Buddha tells how he took up his abode in the womb of Maya, his chosen mother, in the shape of a white elephant. Older accounts of Buddha give him a normal origin, and the elephant legend is probably too late to have any bearing on the Gospels. Still it can fairly be cited to show the universality of the idea.

But the idea, however universal, is neither a source nor a true parallel. None of these pre-Christian stories are 'virgin birth' stories. They are 'unusual impregnation' stories. The women are often married, and even when they are virgins this is seldom, perhaps never, the point of the story. Very few would have asked Mary's question 'How shall this be, since I have no husband?' In the legends about historical figures, such as Alexander, none are in a position to ask it. Moreover, male sexuality is always present when the mythology is at a level where its function is known, and in some of Zeus's amours it is paraded. With Alcmena he makes the night three times its ordinary length. Whatever these tales are, they have nothing to do with virginity and they are not prudish.

By contrast the Virgin Birth of Christ is without sex, without physical agency. Unlike all the rest, this is not a story of 'conception through an unusual impregnation', but a story of 'conception by divine fiat without impregnation', in a society that understood impregnation perfectly well. The embryo appears in the womb by a direct decree of God, a divinely ordained exception to the order of nature, making the event wholly unique. Luke has a slight concession to sexual imagery – 'the Holy Spirit will come upon you' – but the fact that God comes as Spirit precludes the idea of intercourse. Apocryphal legends were indeed to invent physical means, rather in the style of Fo-hi, but the Church firmly banished these from its own account.

It might still be urged that although the Virgin Birth is unique, its uniqueness is trivial, because it is no more than a fancy evoked by Christian prudery. This, however, is not as easy to maintain as it looks. Under careful scrutiny the belief turns out to have had a logic independent of such taboos. It was rooted in the conviction that Jesus was the Son of God. That title had its eternal meaning in heaven, where the Son was one with the Father, but it had an earthly meaning as well. Since, metaphorically, all men were sons of God, Jesus could only be distinguished as *the* Son by a special mode of entering earthly life. No human father could be allowed to have begotten him. Instead, there had to be a special divine act corresponding to procreation. The God of Israel, however, was not Zeus. To give him any bodily function would have been a blasphemous anthropomorphism. Jesus's mother had to be in some sense the bride of the Lord, therefore untouched by man; but she could not be 'touched', in the crude

57

pagan sense, by the Lord either; no other state than virginity was open to her, and her conception of his Son could only be an inscrutable divine action.

With Mary as with Christ, there is fulfilment and transcendence. But the pagan fantasies about earlier women are so much more than merely 'fulfilled' that the birth is shifted to another realm of ideas. Alexander and the rest have only marginal interest. Does the mystical virginity grow in any way from the tradition of Israel itself? We can detect a nostalgia for the far-off innocence of Eden. Presently, as we shall see, Christians begin to bracket Mary's virginity with the presumed virginity of unfallen Eve. But this is vague. Did Jewish tradition supply any specific role which Mary could fill, any specific pattern which the birth fitted?

The Old Testament has several characters in whose birth God plays a special part. Abraham, for instance, thinks he and his wife Sarah are too old to produce a child, but the Lord promises that they will, and in due course, to Abraham's surprise, they do. Jewish legend enlarged on such cases, giving marvel-attended origins to Noah, to Abraham himself, to Moses and Samuel and Samson. The Luke account of the birth of John the Baptist echoes the Abraham-Sarah story. His mother is the Elizabeth whom Gabriel mentions to Mary. Her husband, the priest Zechariah, is told by the same angel that she will bear him a son; he objects that he is too old and Elizabeth is barren, but the son is conceived, and grows up to be Christ's forerunner. It has been claimed that the Virgin Birth is an attempt to outdo the Jewish stories – to 'go one better' – and, in particular, to surpass the half-miracle of John with a complete miracle for Jesus, thus putting them in their proper relation to each other.

Perhaps. Yet, for a mind conditioned by Judaism, the leap from any of these tales to a Virgin Birth would have been a huge one – qualitative, not quantitative – and unlikely to be taken in a spirit of pure fancy, without a deeper reason. The theory might be plausible if the thing had happened somewhere else: if, for example, some emperor's flatterers had tried to exalt him above the heroes of legend by giving *him* a birth more wonderful still. It never did happen. Christians may have hit on it all the same, but if they did, they were alone in doing so.

Jewish imagination in other fields is, on the face of it, no more helpful. The philosopher Philo speaks of God-begotten children and even of virgin mothers, but only metaphorically. As for the idea that the whole notion arose from a tendentious reading of Isaiah 7:14, where the 'virgin' who is to conceive a son may be merely a 'young woman', it is true that Matthew cites this verse. It is also true, as a matter of fact, that the Hebrew word *'almah* does mean 'virgin' more often than not, and that Isaiah's prophecy may echo Canaanite and other hopes of a new era dawning through an extraordinary birth.[11] But whatever he intended, there is no sign that anybody applied his text in this way before. So far as we know, it came into Christianity as an afterthought recorded by Matthew, a prop from scripture for a belief already held.

We may dismiss the Hebrew women made fruitful by Yahweh as well as the pagan ones embraced by Olympian lovers. Precedents for Mary only appear (so far as they do) when we leave humanity behind. The Goddess herself was Virgin and Mother, and it is she, in one or two of her senior forms, that the Mother of Christ recalls. The motherhood which Mary incarnates and perpetuates is divine rather than human.

Its locale at the relevant time is Egypt. When Egypt is mentioned in this connection, the image of female deity usually cited is Isis, who is portrayed in a Madonna-like pose with her divine child, Horus. But in relation to Mary, Isis is far less interesting than Anath and Neith. Anath, in her native Canaan, was – as we have seen – 'the Virgin' and also 'Mother of Nations'. She entered Egypt early and was saluted there as Queen of Heaven. The Jewish apostates denounced by Jeremiah may have been worshipping her, and the Jewish soldiers at Elephantiné undoubtedly did. They attached her to Yahweh; whether as handmaid or as consort, the papyri do not disclose. Identified in due course with the virgin Athene, Anath may have survived, transfigured, as the Lady Wisdom of Jewish sacred writing. Some sort of mythic continuity is at least arguable, from the Canaanite Anath all the way through to the apotheosized Mary, Queen of Heaven; and the latter's virgin-motherhood during her earthly sojourn is an essential link. No mere Danaë or Alcmena could have taken her place.

There is more. The Anath-worshipping Jews at Elephantiné were doubtless familiar with a cult of Neith in the same town. Neith, or Net, is another whom we have encountered already. Migrants from Libya, her original home, brought her to Egypt during the fourth millennium BC and planted her at Saïs in the Nile delta. Under the Twenty-Sixth Dynasty, the last in Egypt before its conquest by Persia, she expanded. Her principal city Saïs became the capital, her priests became the custodians of Egyptian tradition. It was during their ascendancy that the main body of Jewish immigrants entered Egypt from Palestine. Neith was then widely regarded as the Great Goddess and mother of the gods, and at Elephantiné she was paired with a god called Khnum in an aspect of creative power.

Neith is one of the few goddesses whose myths, in their surviving form, take us back in plain terms to the primordial cosmic motherhood. She existed in the waters before the world, and gave birth to the Sun-God Ra, the pharaohs' chief deity, by her virgin power and secret knowledge. A priest told the Persian king Cambyses that 'it was Net, the mighty mother, who had given birth to Ra, that she was the first to give birth to anything, and that she had done so when nothing else had been born, and that she had never herself been born.' Yet by a bizarre twist of theology she was also declared to be Ra's daughter. This dual nature is the solitary pagan anticipation of the Christian paradox summed up in a line of Dante: 'Virgin mother, daughter of thy Son'. Mary is a child of God as all human beings are, yet she is also God's mother when he becomes incarnate. Neith likewise, and long before her, is daughter of Ra and mother of Ra, through some time-transcending mystery which leaves her sovereign in herself, unimpregnated.[12]

It does not appear that Neith and Anath were ever plainly affirmed to be the same. They were linked, however, through an intermediary. As Anath was identified with Athene, so also was Neith. Herodotus in the fifth century BC takes their equivalence for granted, even saying that Athene's costume in Greece is of Libyan origin. Hence, while we never have the equation Neith = Anath, we do have the equation Neith = Athene = Anath. Which is peculiarly interesting, in view of the likelihood of Athene being a point of contact between female theology and

Judaism. Ben-Sira's Lady Wisdom is affiliated, through her, not merely to one of the Virgin Mothers but to both. And Mary herself, in turn, has some kind of mystical connection with Wisdom. When we pass from the prelude to the sequel, we find the liturgy of her cult making use of the Wisdom texts, and Christian thought in the east drawing them together. This is a topic to revert to in its place.

If any hint from the constellation of senior deities crept into Christian minds, it was probably subconscious and its nature is quite uncertain. But they are relevant to Mary as the divinely fertilized women are not, even though their own motherhood is outside history and humanity. The Virgin Birth does not bring Mary close to Olympias or the mother of Fo-hi. It does bring her close to Anath and Neith, and more especially to Neith. It places her on a supramundane level, with a sense of standing at the Beginning, of a fresh creation.[13]

4

We must turn next to the biographical issue. Apart from an act of faith, can these assertions yield information for Mary's life? Certainly it is no use discarding the Virgin Birth and then trying to restore Christ's mother without it. Without it, she is virtually not there. She can only be approached *through* her legend . . . or whatever it is. But can she be profitably approached even thus? Can we infer anything from the belief, and the stories embodying it, which is sound enough to build on?

If the miracle stood alone, the answer would be 'no'. Christians would be free to take it on faith, but they could not expect anybody else to accept it as history, because, when the miraculous enters, normal rules of evidence no longer apply. Historical exceptions to the order of nature cannot be disproved, but they cannot be proved either, and they must always be unlikely. The case for probing these stories further rests on the fact that they are not isolated from the rest of the New Testament. They are linked with other passages. If we read those passages with the Virgin Birth in mind, as a belief which the authors judged them to be consistent with, data of a non-miraculous kind begin to emerge.

Simply as an instance of what is meant here by linkage, consider the two genealogies of Jesus in Matthew 1:1–16 and Luke 3:23–38. Both are given to prove his descent from David, a requirement of Messiahship, and both trace it through Joseph. Critics have argued that the compilers must have thought he was Joseph's son in the normal sense, because, otherwise, such an exercise would be pointless. Since the pedigrees are given by the same authors who record the Virgin Birth, this argument appears shaky. The question in fact is open, for a reason that is plain when we compare the two, and try to make out how they are supposed to be compatible with each other.

They trace the line from David to Joseph, and thence to Jesus, by two distinct paths. In Matthew, Joseph's father is Jacob; in Luke, Heli. Nearly all the names are different, back to David himself. This crux is resolved by the imprecision of Jewish relation-words. Relationships by adoption or marriage were not always distinguished from ties of blood. The word 'son' in Luke 3:23 ('Joseph the son of Heli') could mean for example 'stepson', on the presumption that Jacob died and Joseph's mother remarried, her second husband, Heli, being of David's house by a different lineage. But it follows from this that in the eyes of at least one genealogist, sonship included adoptive sonship. If that could apply to Joseph it could apply also to Jesus. He could count as a descendant of David through Joseph as foster-father, and still be born of a virgin, the unique Son of God. The words 'as was supposed' in Luke 3:23, even if interpolated, are further proof that a line so traced, without paternity by blood, was held to be valid. Greek legend supplies a parallel. Though Alexander was begotten by Zeus, he still counted as a descendant of Heracles through his official father Philip.

Thus far, the genealogies do not seem to add anything about Mary. But now let us press the Virgin Birth doctrine a little harder. How are we to take Paul in Romans 1:3, when he says that Christ was 'descended from David according to the flesh?' If his words are given their full weight, adoptive descent through Joseph is not enough. Whether or not Paul himself believed in the Virgin Birth, Romans was admitted as a true and canonical work by Christians who did. Apparently, therefore, Mary herself had a Davidic pedigree. If the New Testament is not to be self-contradictory, hers is the only 'flesh' which Paul can be referring to. It is a large addition to our idea of her. Yet as soon as it is proposed, we begin to see other grounds for it. One is Joseph's absence from Mark. The author knows that if Jesus is the Messiah he has to be a descendant of David, and in 10:47–8 Bartimaeus addresses him as such. But this Gospel never mentions the man Joseph through whom, elsewhere, the Davidic lineage is traced. It seems sufficient that Jesus is the son of Mary (6:3). If so, again, she must be a descendant of David herself.[14]

This view is in fact a time-hallowed one in the Church, and a natural conclusion was drawn long ago: that the Luke genealogy is not Joseph's but Mary's. In that case 'the son of Heli' in verse 23 may mean 'the son-in-law' of Heli. The compiler brings Joseph in because he is unhappy about tracing ancestry through the mother – it could expose Jesus to a charge of illegitimacy – and wants a male succession without a break. But the ancestors back to David are the wife's, not the husband's.

What has this manoeuvre achieved? It has shown that by bearing the Virgin Birth in mind, we can say something about Mary which may quite well be true and is not supernatural at all: that she claimed Davidic ancestry. The New Testament alone might take us no further. If, however, we look outside and see how her virginity was actually understood by the Church, we plunge into deeper waters. As far back as we can trace it the Christian consensus seems to have been that she was not only a virgin when she conceived and bore Jesus, but a virgin totally, for the rest of her days. She had no marital experience, ever. Joseph was simply a companion. To retain her integrity after motherhood, Christians enlarged the miracle. Through a divine privilege, they claimed, the birth was painless and her body was unaffected.

The last notions are speculative and need not detain us. The rest is important. Catholics still maintain that Mary had no sexual relations after the Birth. That tenet is reputed to be a popish innovation, but it is not. It is implied in an apocryphal work composed during the second century AD, the *Book of James* or *Protevangelium*. This is worthless as history, but it attests the belief, and it is cited on the subject of Mary's condition by Origen, who wrote early in the third century. There is no trace of a different opinion among the orthodox faithful till about 383, when Helvidius, who thought Mary bore other children afterwards in the normal way, was pounced upon by St Jerome and sternly rebuked.[15]

Surely, this time, we really are dealing with an added legend inspired by prudishness, and useless for extracting knowledge from the New Testament? Mary's perpetual virginity is not only unmentioned by scripture but (one might judge) at odds with it.

'Purity' of course was apt to be an obsession with early Christians, and they were reluctant to think of Mary as ever being a sexual object. On the other hand it is doubtful whether a sexless view of her could have imposed itself against notorious facts, such as the existence of a swarm of great-grandchildren. All we can do is test the ground, and see what does emerge from the New Testament if her virginity is assumed to mean perpetual virginity.

The first impression is that the attempt is futile, because it cannot mean that. Matthew 1:24–5 informs us that Joseph 'took his wife, but knew her not until she had borne a son', i.e. Jesus. The natural inference is that he did afterwards. In Luke 2:7 Jesus is Mary's 'first-born', a term hinting at more children later. That hint is strengthened by references in all four Gospels to his brothers, and in two of them to his sisters. One of the brothers, James, is mentioned by the Jewish historian, Josephus, as 'brother of the so-called Christ'.[16] All these texts are explained easily (or so it seems) by supposing that after the one Birth, Mary lived normally with her husband, and that this was understood by Christians throughout apostolic times.

Catholics offer replies to the objections. It looks suspicious that they have to use several different arguments to rebut one simple proposition which would, alone, cover all the data. Still, let us suspend judgment.

With the 'until' verse, it is claimed, the Greek conjunction carries no implication that the event did take place afterwards. The Old Testament supplies a few parallels. In Genesis 8:7, we are told that Noah's raven 'went to and fro until the waters were dried up from the earth', with no suggestion that it stopped when they were. In Psalm 110:1, which Matthew himself quotes, the Lord says 'Sit at my right hand, till I make your enemies your footstool'; he does not imply 'then get up and go away'. In Isaiah 42:4, also quoted by Matthew, God's servant 'will not fail or be discouraged till he has established justice in the earth'; will he fail or be discouraged as soon as he has? Knox renders Matthew 1:25 with the paraphrase 'he had not known her when she bore a son', and this is probably fair.

The 'first-born' text is easier to dispose of. It refers to the child's status under the Law of Moses, which enjoined a ritual mentioned by Luke himself (2:23), and laid down rights and duties whether or not any further children followed. Two Jewish religious writings have the phrase 'first-born and only-born', and a tomb inscription contemporary with Christ records that a young woman died in giving birth to her first-born child. Here, obviously, there were no more.[17]

The trouble is that with Mary, to judge from the allusions to Christ's brothers and sisters, there were. It is on this problem of the Holy Family that the issue finally turns. The results of pursuing it to the end are surprising.

How did the Church cope with it? In the first place, by falling back – as in the genealogies – on the vagueness of Jewish relation-words. The *Protevangelium* explains that Joseph had children by a previous marriage; in other words the brothers and sisters were half-brothers and sisters. But after some hesitation, most Christians rejected even this answer. They held out, and in the Catholic Church they still do, for an entirely celibate couple. Joseph was not a widower and never had any children. Jesus's 'brothers' and 'sisters' are really cousins.[18]

Surely this at least is mere fantasy, concocted by rather repellent minds, and irrelevant to the New Testament and the people in it? Not so. The more closely we study the idea, the more seriously we have to take it. In the Greek of the Gospels, the word used for 'brother' is *adelphos*, which does normally mean a full brother by blood. But the Gospels are based on the words of Jews speaking Aramaic, with its Semitic lack of precise and suitable terms. The Greek translation of the Old Testament, the Septuagint, uses *adelphos* several times where a relationship is not actually fraternal, because the Hebrew of the original has no word for it. In Genesis 14:14 and 16 Lot is Abraham's 'brother', in 29:12 and 15 Jacob is Laban's 'brother', though they are nephews; and in 1 Chronicles 23:22 *adelphos* is used for 'cousin', as the Catholic view of Jesus's relations requires.

That view is at least viable, then. It has one immediate point in its favour. When Jesus is dying (John 19:25–7) he tells John to treat Mary as his mother and look after her. If the 'brothers' and 'sisters' are her own children, why can she not be looked after by one of them? Why is she alone? The 'brothers' have been mentioned in the same Gospel. So it is not out of the question that the Catholic view does preserve what the first Christians believed about the family. Let us see if that hypothesis leads to a plausible picture.[19]

5

Christ's four 'brothers' are – with minor spelling variations – James, Joses or Joseph, Jude or Judas, and Simon. His 'sisters' are anonymous; since the word 'all' is used, there are at least three (Matthew 13:55–6; Mark 6:3). James is that 'brother of the Lord' who later heads the Church in Jerusalem, and figures in Acts. He is credited with the epistle placed after Hebrews. Jude returns to view also with a shorter epistle of his own, introducing himself in the first verse as 'a servant of Jesus Christ and brother of James', words which might imply that Jesus was not Jude's brother in the sense that James was.

Now a James and a Joses (or Joseph), true brothers credibly the same as the two who head the quartet, appear in Mark 15:40. They are sons of a woman named Mary . . . but she is not the Virgin. Described as the 'other Mary', she accompanies Jesus and witnesses the Crucifixion and Resurrection. She is seen fleetingly in Matthew 27:55–6 and 61; in Mark 15:47 and 16:1; and in Luke 24:10. The Fourth Gospel's account of the same events adds a further detail (19:25).

Standing by the cross of Jesus were his mother, and his mother's sister, Mary the wife of Clopas, and Mary Magdalene.

The wife of Clopas – in Latin, Cleophas – is the 'other Mary' again, the mother of James and Joses. But does the sentence refer to three women or four? Linguistic usage would favour three. The second comma should go. We should read 'his mother's sister Mary the wife of Clopas'. It thus turns out that Jesus's 'brothers' James and Joses are quite arguably sons of his mother's sister, therefore cousins indeed. With these two granted, the rest follow. Would the Virgin have had a sister with the same name as herself, another Mary? St Jerome thought she had. An apocryphal book falsely ascribed to Matthew says that when the Virgin left home at an early age, her parents had another daughter and gave her the same name – Mary II, so to speak. But a likelier explanation is that the two Marys are sisters-in-law.

These are clues with a solid interest, and we have been guided to them by the doctrine of Mary Ever-Virgin and the irrefutability principle: the rule that Christians did not affirm anything blatantly contradicted by obvious facts, so that if they affirmed this doctrine, there must be a way of showing that the brothers and sisters are compatible with it. The wife of Clopas supplies that way. Armed with her clues, we can put together a picture of the Holy Family which has actual advantages over the 'rational' one that would regard Jesus and all the rest as simply children of Joseph and Mary. By starting from the doctrine and not otherwise, we can reach a point where we need not despair of giving the mother of Christ a sort of biography.

To a certain extent this reconstruction is a matter of taste, though the end product will always be, in substance, the same. My personal taste inclines me to begin with the Heli of the Luke genealogy.

He is a citizen of Nazareth, proud of his descent from King David, with a house rather more opulent than most. Here he lives with a son, Clopas, and a daughter, Mary the Virgin. Into the neighbourhood comes the young carpenter, Joseph, descended from David by another line. His family home is in Judaea, away to the south, but the death of his father Jacob has turned him adrift. Heli more or less adopts him and gives his blessing to a marriage with Mary: thus Joseph becomes, in effect, Heli's son, though Clopas of course retains his rights as the heir. While the couple are in Bethlehem Mary gives birth to Jesus.

After their return to Nazareth, reduced to poverty by much wandering, Joseph is not equal to setting up a home of his own. As his work – largely on buildings – takes him away a great deal, Mary and the child stay in the house of Heli, and Joseph does so himself when he is with them.

Clopas is still there, and on Heli's death he is master of the house. He has married another Mary, and over the years they produce seven children, James, Joses, Simon, Jude and three daughters. All the children including Jesus grow up together, eat together, play together. In the town's eyes and each other's, they are all brothers and sisters. Joseph dies through illness or accident. Jesus, however, is old enough to continue the carpentry, and he and his mother are allowed to stay on.

Here is the family tree, worked out strictly from the traditional axiom of Mary's marriage with Joseph being for ever unconsummated. [20]

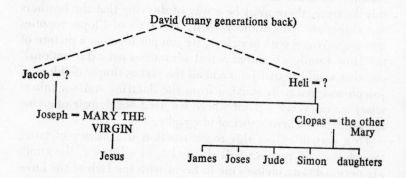

This holds everything including the two genealogies – one through Jacob, the other through Heli – and gives Mary Davidic lineage, so that no trouble arises over Romans 1:3, or her husband's absence from Mark. It also fills in a helpful background. With Joseph a landless man, it is easier to see how he can be portrayed in Matthew (as he is) taking Mary and the child to Egypt and staying away for years. Back in Nazareth he had only a temporary lodging, and now he has no property of his own to attend to. His only belongings are the tools of his trade, so he can travel light. Uprooted and impoverished by the long journeys, he never does become independent in Nazareth, and when he dies he leaves nothing. By the time of Jesus's ministry he is only dimly recalled as 'that poor young man from the south that Heli was so good to', and Jesus is thought of by the locals as Mary's son rather than his.

Though Jesus must apparently have been Joseph's heir, the Gospels never give an impression of his possessing anything. He has plied his trade for a while, and that is all. The tools are his sole inheritance and he has no home of his own (Luke 9:58). If the house is Clopas's, we can see why not. It is all too painfully easy to picture Joseph's widow being reduced to a poor relation with the merest niche in the household, best provided for after her Son's death by removal to the home of his friend John.

If plausibility is not a strong enough argument, this view of the family has a more cogent merit. It solves a recognized problem, the problem of James and his status in the Jerusalem Church. Jesus's 'brothers', according to the Fourth Gospel (7:5), did not believe in him. But the words may apply to some of them only; or one, at least, may have had a change of heart. Paul at any rate counts James as an apostle a few years later. In Galatians 1:19, recalling his first visit to the Jerusalem Christians and Peter, he says: 'I saw none of the other apostles except James the Lord's brother.' He may be using words loosely, but he seems to say it again in 1 Corinthians 15:7, where he tells how the risen Christ 'appeared to James, then to all the apostles', a sentence parallel with 'he appeared to Cephas' (Peter), 'then to the twelve' a few lines before. James's quick rise to leadership is a puzzle indeed if he was not previously what Paul says – an apostle, a close follower of his amazing relative.

Can he be fitted in as such? The lists in the Gospels give two apostles called James. One is the son of Zebedee and brother of John. The other is a James who is distinguished from him in Christian tradition as 'the less' or 'the younger'. If we adopt the proposed scheme of the Holy Family, or something like it, we can identify this James with the Lord's 'brother'. In Mark 15:40, where the other Mary is mentioned with two of her sons, James is actually dubbed 'the less' or 'younger'. It is the same epithet given to the apostle.

This equation is not a modern guess. Their identity is, and has always been, standard Catholic belief. It avoids the need for three apostles called James – two in the Gospels and a third, the Lord's brother, in Galatians, making the total thirteen instead of twelve. It also explains how the brother rises so rapidly in the Church after Christ's death: he was with him during the last phase of his life, one of the fellowship.

The only real obstacle is that the second James in the apostolic lists is called the son of Alphaeus, not Clopas. The normal Catholic answer is that Alphaeus and Clopas may be two names of the same man. Similarly Matthew is also Levi, Bartholomew is also Nathanael, Peter is also Simon. 'Alphaeus' is a Greek version of the Jewish name Halphai or Chalpai (*ch* as in 'loch'), which means 'successor' or 'heir', and is a plausible name for an eldest son, one who would inherit a house, for instance. But we may be able to do better. It has been argued that 'Clopas' is a Greek transliteration of the 'Chalpai' form, so that the two names are the same. In Hebrew it is 'Halphai' and comes through to the Synoptics as Alphaeus, in Aramaic it is 'Chalpai' and comes through to John as Clopas.[21]

The whole story therefore seems watertight, and it is deduced, I repeat, from the doctrine of Mary Ever-Virgin. What happens if we take the 'rational' stance instead? We shall have a different Holy Family, living in Joseph's house.

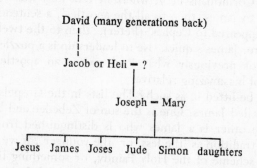

But is this really so rational? It enmeshes us at once in a web of difficulties, all of which the Catholic view avoids.

To begin with, it leaves the other Mary dangling, endowed by an odd coincidence with another James and Joses who are apparently first cousins of these. Joseph's absence from Mark becomes a riddle again. As a solid householder, even deceased, he ought to be mentioned in 6:3, and without him Jesus is not descended from David. Joseph's freedom to roam, his heir's lack of a house or property, his widow's lack of sons to take care of her in a Gospel which (on this showing) has twice mentioned them, all become harder to comprehend.

As for James, he is a nightmare. There have to be at least three Jameses, two being apostles, the third being the Lord's brother but not an apostle. In that case the apostle James the less, son of Alphaeus, is almost imperceptible; Paul's words have to be fudged; and the rise of the Lord's brother in the Jerusalem Church, after indifference during the Lord's lifetime, must be consigned to mystery.[22] If rationality rejects the Clopas-Alphaeus equation, as papist wishful thinking, we need four Jameses: (1) the apostle James the greater, son of Zebedee; (2) the apostle James the less, or younger, son of Alphaeus; (3) the Lord's brother, who, though described as an apostle, is not; and (4) the son of the other Mary and Clopas, who is called 'the less', yet cannot be the same as (2) because Clopas is not the same as Alphaeus.

So by following in Catholic footsteps, we attain an end which may disturb. The Catholic view of Mary leads to a story which – in all respects but the central miracle itself – is much easier to accept, makes much better sense, than the one suggested by a 'rational' view. Yet critics have urged, with some justice, that the story would never have been worked out if Catholics had not been so doggedly resolved to explain everything without impugning the sacrosanct virginity. Must we confess that special pleading in support of a miracle gives better history than reason?

There is no need to state the issue like that. We can conclude, fairly and soberly, that faith in the miracle has supplied Catholics with a key (whether or not they deserve it) because the family did more or less conform to the miraculous pattern. Mary and her husband belonged to a large household with another, related couple in it. Jesus was her only child. He seemed strange and different, but passed as the brother, in the approximate Jewish sense, of a medley of her nephews and nieces under the same roof, children of the other couple. These included James, who became a disciple. So, if less closely, did James's mother.

It was an early belief of Christians that Mary conceived Jesus miraculously while a virgin and had no conjugal life afterwards either. This belief was not fantasy in a void. It was the account they gave of a known family situation. They were aware, of course, that such things do not normally happen, but there was nothing specific (such as an elder offspring, or a marked physical resemblance of Jesus to Joseph) to refute this exception in Mary's case, divinely ordained. For those who knew the family history it was at least *as if* the belief were true; it was, to repeat our word, irrefutable.

That is as far as impartial history can venture. If the belief actually was true – if the Virgin Birth actually happened, setting this child apart as human-yet-more-than-human – then history cannot comment. If, on the other hand, it was a false interpretation imposed on the facts, then history can ask what suggested it. Mere prudery, or an attempt to cover up a scandal, seem inadequate to inspire such a doctrine or secure general assent. The logic of the 'Son of God' concept (p. 57) may have been enough. Or there may have been some hint, though hardly an obvious one, from Jewish scripture or pagan myth. Very few myths, however, are directly relevant. The only figures with any interest as antecedents are those offered by Egypt and Egyptian Judaism, the Anath-Neith-Wisdom complex of deity. As mother and virgin, and still more as perpetual virgin, Mary does have affinities in that quarter. Moreover, the Egyptian themes appear in her cult later. She becomes Queen of Heaven like Anath. She is the paradoxical daughter of her divine Son, as Neith is. She is assimilated to Wisdom in her liturgy, and in Byzantine and Russian mysticism. Later we may be able to develop these insights.

To revert, however, to her earthly career. It is now plain that a strong, well-knit tradition of Jesus's family was preserved for many years after his death. The Gospel writers are not much concerned with it except as it impinges on their main story, but various bits which they have heard are coherent and credible. The harmony of the data is convincing because it is not obvious, not contrived. It is casual, devious, backhanded. We have to work hard to find it, but it is there to be found. The documentation of Mary and her kinsfolk is something we can build upon. It is more than fantasy. Fantasy would not fit together — not like that.[23]

Chapter 4

MAGNIFICAT

I

Mary is coming into focus. We have formed ideas about her background and setting, and her relationships to various people. Can we now move forward at last, and give her a life-story or anything like one? If we can, how far does it explain or warrant the Catholic cult of her? It is through the Church, one would naturally assume, that any awakening of Goddess-motifs must have occurred. But without the first steps, we are not ready even to think about the later ones.

Mariology (to use the Church's forbidding term) has never claimed that a Life of the Virgin can be written. Attempts have been made by nuns who relied on visions, but without adding any facts that stand up as history. Such things are religious fiction, no more. In any case an account of Mary in herself, not primarily as Mother of Christ, would go against the normal devotional grain. As Cardinal Newman put it, 'the glories of Mary are for the sake of her Son'. That is a theologian's statement of an issue which can be stated without theology. The Church has placed the emphasis in a certain way. Mary, it has affirmed, is important beyond all knowing; yet Christ, not she, is at the centre. If we wish to understand her more deeply, the effort to imagine her in herself is futile. Scripture never presents her thus, nor indeed does any other authoritative source. The one method of any value is to reflect upon the story of Christ from her point of view, and in terms of what it implies about her.

Catholic practice enshrines this attitude in the Rosary.

Correctly employed, the Rosary is a device for meditation on two levels. The person who says it repeats the 'Hail Mary' prayer (an expanded version of texts in Luke) over and over again, keeping count with the beads. That mechanical action steadies the mind for meditation on the themes of the exercise, most of which are Gospel scenes where the Virgin figures – first the Annunciation (i.e. Gabriel's message); then the Visitation (i.e. the meeting that follows between Mary and Elizabeth); then the Birth; and so on. The principle can be transposed into history. Catholic piety has been right to at least this extent, that in essence there is no other way of approaching Mary. The question is whether even this can take us beyond the bare text, and unlock a biography or quasi-biography.

Most Protestants would maintain that it cannot, that such meditation may draw morals but will never extend the facts. The choice certainly looks discouraging. If we do not want pious romance about Our Lady, is the sole alternative a full stop? Perhaps not. We have seen how a doctrine defining Mary's motherhood, the perpetual virginity, leads to fresh insights and unsuspected answers. They are valid even if the doctrine is nonsense, because they are *there*; they are implicit in aspects of the record which the doctrine fits in with, and can throw into relief.

Suppose then that we continue to follow Catholic thinking and find out where it takes us. If we survey the Gospels Rosary-style – that is, from Mary's point of view, and in terms of what they imply about her – can we make her a credible personality, with a life-story and a role in Christian origins? And if so, do that personality, that life-story, that role, confirm the view of her which underlies her cult in the Church? It may be objected that this is question-begging. If we start by thinking on Roman lines we are bound to reach Roman conclusions. But I do not think this is so. We can accept – we must – that the logic of her cult, as expressed in the Rosary and elsewhere, is the only logic that stands a chance of yielding anything positive. We have yet to see what happens if it is pursued without the bead-teller's preconceptions. The results may be orthodox. On the other hand they may place a query over the cult itself; not the negative Protestant query, but a more searching one.

2

The Gospels have no incident in Mary's life earlier than the Annunciation. However, Gentile Christians who studied them soon began to demand more, and to draw inferences from them reaching backward in time. The chosen vessel of the Lord's Incarnation *must*, they thought, have been specially prepared. She was not simply a young woman of good character who happened to be on hand. Story-tellers willing to supply the demand proceeded to do so. Legends of the Virgin's own birth and childhood, stemming out from the canonical data, were getting into writing within a lifetime of the Fourth Gospel.

Most of them can be found in the Greek *Book of James* so-called. Its other title the *Protevangelium* was invented in the Renaissance by Guillaume Postel, who introduced it to western Europe. It was composed in stages during the second century, and was known in some form to two early Fathers of the Church, Clement of Alexandria and Origen.[1]

The part of it that leads up to the Gospel events tells the following tale. A wealthy Jew named Joachim had a wife, Anna. For a long time they were childless, but at last an angel told Anna that she would bear a famous offspring, and Anna vowed it (whether a 'him' or a 'her') to the Lord's service. In due course Mary arrived. She could walk at the age of six months. When she was three, her parents brought her to the Temple in Jerusalem and she danced on the altar steps. She became a Temple maiden and lived in the precinct, receiving her food from an angel's hand. On her attaining puberty the High Priest Zechariah resolved that she must leave, and sought a guardian for her. He wanted a widower who would not transgress the proper limits of guardianship. Joseph the carpenter was singled out by a heavenly sign. He protested: 'I have sons, and I am an old man, but she is a girl.' However, Mary was entrusted to him and went to live in his house. During his absence on building work, the Temple priests asked her to spin some scarlet thread for a new curtain. Just as she was beginning, Gabriel appeared and told her she was to be the mother of the Saviour Jesus. Her pregnancy caused the scribe Annas to accuse Joseph of seduction, or a clandestine marriage, but he had to withdraw the charge. Mary remained always intact, the birth of Jesus making no physical difference to her.

This version of her youth has inspired many variants and sequels. It proves the antiquity of the Ever-Virgin belief, and supplies an explanation, if not the one Catholics finally settled upon, for Christ's 'brothers'. It is the source of the names popularly given to Mary's parents, St Joachim and St Anne, though if the Luke pedigree is hers, resort must be made to the two-names-for-the-same-man escape route. Also it is the reason for Joseph's frequent portrayal in art as much older than his wife.

But it is not history, and there is very little reason to suspect genuine tradition behind it. The author gives himself away by his gross ignorance of the setting. He pictures his characters as members of a village community of 'Israel' where all are close neighbours. Furthermore, no young maidens were attached to the Temple. At the time when Mary would have been there, Herod the Great, King of Judaea under Rome's aegis, was carrying out a grandiose rebuilding of the whole structure; the Wailing Wall is the last remnant of it. The idea of a little girl in residence, with workmen trampling around her and gigantic blocks of stone rumbling past, is simply comic. Other absurdities are not worth going into.

Even as scriptural romance, this first part of the *Protevangelium* is feeble. The author's knowledge of the Gospels is sketchy, or perhaps he has only read them in spurious versions, which weaken his credit when his story is compared with the approved ones. He makes Joseph a guardian, not a husband even in name. He ignores the testimony of Luke that the Annunciation happened at Nazareth. He takes Zechariah from the same Gospel but wrongly calls him High Priest. Excusably St Jerome denounced this book as a fabrication of heretics, apocryphal nonsense, idle dreams.[2]

Still, if we use the Gospels better than Pseudo-James does, we can infer a little about the prelude. Mary's year of birth, for instance, is not beyond all conjecture. It depends on her Son's and must be reached by counting back from his. Notoriously the Christian era has a mistaken starting-point, fixed by the monk Dionysius Exiguus, with very imperfect information. Matthew 2 puts the birth of Jesus before the death of Herod, probably two or three years before; and Herod died in 4 BC. Luke 2:2 says the birth coincided with a Roman census 'when Quirinius was governor of Syria'. A census was held under Quirinius's governorship in AD 6, which was long remembered for causing a revolt (Acts 5:37). It cannot be the same. The Greek is ambiguous, and may mean that Christ was born during the census preceding the famous one under Quirinius. However, an inscription proves that Quirinius held office in Syria before, about 8 BC. Therefore the census allusion, though not (as was once thought) incompatible with Matthew, is too uncertain for guidance.[3]

A more tempting clue is the belief of Jewish astrologers that the Messiah would be born at a conjunction of Saturn and Jupiter in Pisces. Such a conjunction took place three times in 7 BC – on 29 May, 3 October and 4 December – and could have inspired Messianic hopes for a child born then. Unfortunately the belief cannot be documented early enough. On various grounds, however, 7 BC does appear to be a good choice. Since Jewish girls were married at about fourteen, we have, allowing for nine months of pregnancy, 22 BC or thereabouts for Christ's mother. The Church observes her birthday on 8 September.[4]

Her place of birth is unknown. A number of authors say Jerusalem, but not on any serious grounds. More likely she was native to Nazareth, a descendant of immigrants who moved into southern Galilee after its conquest by the Jewish king Aristobulus I, eighty years earlier. Nazareth is a small town on a hillside, colourful in spring with numerous flowers. The house where Mary lived with her parents (and her brother Clopas, if that theory is right) would have been very plain, stone-built, rectangular, thick-walled, slit-windowed; extremely cluttered and scantily furnished. A Jewish girl's education, apart from its practical household side, was largely a basic course in the Torah – that is, the teaching of Moses and the prophets, plus rabbinic comments. Mary's family doubtless attended the local synagogue, and heard preachers speak of the heir of David who would come to establish Israel as an eternal kingdom.

Marriages in general were arranged by the parents, and solemnized, except among the rich, without much ceremony. The nature of Mary's marriage with Joseph has been a theologically vexed question. Catholics have maintained, and some still do, that her protest when told she is to bear a child ('How shall this be?') is due not to the immediate circumstances but to her having taken a vow of virginity. There is no basis for this but a wish to make her a model for celibates. The Jewish celibates of her day, such as the Essenes, lived apart in communities of their own, and it is doubtful whether any such group enrolled women. Moreover, if Mary had taken such a vow, why did she marry? Marriages kept sexless by choice are not unknown to the history of religion, but they belong to the Hindu world rather than the Judaic. A major modern example is Gandhi, and even he did not take his vow of continence till after he had fathered four sons. A similar decision by Joseph and Mary, made in awe after the birth of Jesus, is perhaps within the bounds of belief. A vow in advance is not.[5]

Have we any idea what Mary was like, simply as a visible human being? An eighth-century monk named Epiphanius gives us quite a detailed description.

> She was grave and dignified in all her actions. She spoke little and only when it was necessary to do so. She listened readily and could be addressed easily. She greeted everyone. She was of medium height, but some say she was slightly taller than that. She would speak to everyone fearlessly and clearly, without laughter or agitation, and she was specially slow to anger. Her complexion was of the colour of ripe wheat, and her hair was auburn. Her eyes were bright and keen, and light brown in colour, and the pupils were of an olive-green tint. Her eyebrows were arched and deep black. Her nose was long, her lips were red and full, and overflowing with the sweetness of her words. Her face was not round, but somewhat oval. Her hands were long, and her fingers also.[6]

Against this must be set a denial by St Augustine, who lived much earlier, that anyone knew what Mary looked like. Yet certain features of the portrait agree with the only other clue, which, if it illuminates her at all, does so via the same logic as always — her relationship to her Son. In this case, her literal relationship. The clue is the Holy Shroud of Turin. This much-publicized relic is a strip of cloth bearing markings which, in photographic negative, become a curiously impressive image of Christ, as he might have looked after being taken down from the cross.[7] Several sculptors have worked from the image to reconstruct him in the round, and one tried ingeniously to reconstruct Mary as well. He argued that if she was Jesus's only human parent, all his physical heredity came from her. So they must have been very much alike, and we can picture her as a feminine version of the man in the Shroud: above average height, with a longish face and a calm, reposeful beauty. Whatever the value of the logic, imagination can dwell happily on its outcome.

3

Jesus's double birth-narrative starts in Luke. If that Gospel's opening chapters are to any extent historical, Mary herself must be the main source. Perhaps the author (let us call him Luke for convenience) met her in person. But the style of the chapters is more Semitic than his own usually is, and that difference, plus the poetic form of several speeches, makes it likelier that he is using a kind of saga current among her younger associates. Textual analysts have gone so far as to call this narrative the Gospel of Mary, and to trace its transmission and editing by two other women and a converted Jewish priest.[8]

Luke sets the scene with a preface about the forerunner of Christ, John the Baptist. This is the linked story already glanced at, which introduces Mary's kinswoman Elizabeth. She is married to the priest Zechariah. They are elderly and childless, and Elizabeth is understood to be barren. However, when Zechariah is burning incense in the Jerusalem Temple, the angel Gabriel appears with the promise of a son. Zechariah is to call the boy John.

'He shall drink no wine nor strong drink,
and he will be filled with the Holy Spirit,
even from his mother's womb.
And he will turn many of the sons of Israel to the Lord their
    God,

and he will go before him in the spirit and power of Elijah,
to turn the hearts of the fathers to the children,
and the disobedient to the wisdom of the just,
to make ready for the Lord a people prepared.'

The priest is incredulous, and Gabriel tells him he will be struck
dumb till the prophecy is fulfilled. Soon afterwards his wife does
conceive.

Luke's object in this preliminary tale, with its echoes of others
in the Old Testament, is to show that John the Baptist – a well-
known popular preacher with followers of his own – was
strictly Jesus's destined precursor and never a leader in his own
right. John apparently did hail Jesus as the Messiah, but his final
attitude was doubtful, and Luke is anxious to stress the Christian
view. The sentence about Elijah is another echo, this time of
Malachi 4:5–6.

Behold, I will send you Elijah the prophet before the great
and terrible day of the Lord comes. And he will turn the
hearts of the fathers to their children and the hearts of
children to their fathers, lest I come and smite the land with
a curse.

Jews connected the 'day of the Lord' with the Messiah's advent.
A man to whom this text was applied, as Luke applies it to John,
could not be the Messiah himself. He had to be, precisely, a
forerunner, and the significance of whatever he did would
depend on a greater sequel.

Next Luke turns to the origin of that sequel, the Annunciation
itself. The difficulty with this, and with all the stories of Jesus's
birth and infancy, is not so much over the stories themselves –
we can put them in a 'rational' form if we so desire – as over their
relation to the rest of the Gospels. In essence they are about a
minor Messianic excitement during Herod's last years, occasioned
by a child born at that time. Why not? Visions or astrological
reckonings may well have caused such an excitement. It could
even have been inspired by the Roman census. Pious Jews
regarded census-taking as wicked, on the strength of 1 Chronicles
21. The acquiescence of Herod, a ruler who professed Judaism,

could have been construed as a sin inviting the advent of the true King as a divine judgment.

What we are asked to believe, however, is that this child to whom expectation pointed reappeared thirty-odd years later and turned out to be, in literal fact, an astounding person and a credible Messiah. The foresight or insight alleged to have been shown at his birth, and even before, would seem to be either frankly supernatural or most unlikely. The birth-stories, therefore, look like legends devised after Jesus's lifetime, as they were for Zoroaster and others, to make him unique from the beginning. This view of them is much easier to maintain than the corresponding view of the main Gospel narratives, because it is less open to the retort that the Christians' enemies never offered any rebuttal. By the time of publication the birth-stories would have been very hard to rebut, with every contemporary dead and no records available.

To such an opinion, nevertheless, the Annunciation itself is fatal. It takes a little thought to see why, and we must study it again from a different aspect. Gabriel visits Mary about six months after his visit to Zechariah. The traditional date is 25 March, Lady Day, nine months (the duration of pregnancy) before Christmas. Christmas itself, however, is only a commemoration and not a serious birth-date, and Lady Day may rather carry a hint of spring and the renewal of life. Since Mary leaves 'with haste' for the south, the event perhaps belongs in a season when she would not have been needed for any regular task, such as helping in the fields. On this ground May has been suggested. The astrological theory would point to a date nine months before one of the Saturn-Jupiter conjunctions in 7 BC.[9]

When the angel comes to her she is at Nazareth, doubtless in the home of her parents, and just betrothed to Joseph. She is about fourteen, and despite Pseudo-James and artistic fancy, he is not likely to be much over twenty-five. In the eyes of custom and law they are, in in effect, married, but they are not yet living together and she is still a virgin.

Her dialogue with Gabriel has a feminine quality. However externalized in vision or apparition, it is a Jewish girl's daydream of becoming the mother of the Messiah. Believers may add, an 'inspired' or 'true' daydream; that does not alter its quality. She conceives her Son – according to theologians, at the instant of consenting to do so – and her daydream is on its way to realization.

But here is what Gabriel says of Jesus.

'He will be great, and will be called the Son of the Most High;
and the Lord God will give to him the throne of his father
   David,
and he will reign over the house of Jacob for ever;
and of his kingdom there will be no end.'

There is not a word here, as there is in Matthew, about a mystical saviourship from sin. Jesus is to be the Son of God (that is repeated a few lines later), he is to receive the throne of David, and he is to reign for ever. The promise makes Jesus the anointed monarch of Jewish national hope, and not demonstrably anything else. 'For ever' could refer to his dynasty rather than himself. The title 'Son of God' might be thought a major addition, but this is far from certain. Jews may have imagined the Messiah as 'Son of God', in some not very well defined sense, quite apart from Christianity. Matthew 26:63 and Mark 14:61 suggest that they did.[10]

One of the angelic phrases must be paused over specially. Gabriel promises that Jesus will reign, not over 'the Jews' or 'Israel', but over 'the house of Jacob'. Jacob was the patriarch whose twelve sons, according to Genesis, founded the twelve tribes. The new name 'Israel' which God bestowed on him passed to the whole body of the Chosen People. David ruled them all, but after the reign of his son Solomon they split apart. The Jews of Mary's time were descended from the southern tribes of Judah and Benjamin, with a sprinkling of Levites. Some lived in the Holy Land, many more were scattered through various countries. They counted themselves as 'Israel' and as representing the whole Chosen People. However, they had not forgotten the northern tribes, which had been deported (for their sins) by the Assyrians and, apart from stragglers, had never returned. The hated Samaritans had a northern strain in their ancestry, but were excluded from the community as bastards and heretics. According to current Jewish belief the true Lost Tribes still kept their identity in some Asian land beyond the Euphrates.

It was hoped – largely on the basis of Jeremiah 31:7 ff. and Ezekiel 37:15–28 – that the Anointed, the heir of David, would be God's agent in bringing them back reconciled to him, and would unite them with the Jews, thus restoring the original, greater Israel.[11]

To speak of Jesus as destined to reign over 'the house of Jacob' is thus a heavily-charged hint. Jacob was the father of all twelve tribes, therefore the promised kingship is over the Lost Tribes as well as the Jews. This idea looks to a royal, even imperial Messianism, and seems to have persisted in Jesus's family. The Mary stories drawn on by Luke include a surprising token representative of the lost Israelites, the prophetess Anna 'of the tribe of Asher' (2:36). Jesus himself says that the apostles will sit as judges over all twelve (Matthew 19:28). The epistle ascribed to his brother James opens with a greeting to the twelve tribes dispersed through the world, whatever precisely he means by that.

Gabriel's phrase 'the house of Jacob' confirms the general drift of his promise. And this promise would not have been invented in this form when Luke was written, because it had already been falsified. Christ's ministry and death had not fitted the Jewish Messianic pattern, and the Church had dismissed it. The Annunciation could now only be squared with Christian doctrine by awkward 'interpretation'. Luke wrote it thus because its wording was already fixed and could not be tampered with. It must date from before the Crucifixion at the very latest, and the source may well be much earlier, in Mary's genuine remembrances and convictions – convictions that pointed to a royal Messiahship and to nothing else.

If some version of it was actually applied to her Son's birth, the rest of the birth-stories have a tolerable logic. They are based on traditions of the brief Messianic stir which her vision caused. Yet we still have the problem. Setting aside the simple appeal to miracles, is it to be believed that the hope attached itself so perceptively to the right child, one who was later able to measure up to it and then transcend it?

The ultimate riddle is of course Jesus's origin. If he was conceived through some unknown exception to the order of nature, we have no idea what it was or what its genetic consequences would have been. It could have aroused awestruck hopes and also produced a genius who seemed to fulfil them. Who can tell? But on the purely human level, Jesus's career has an aspect too easily overlooked – the family aspect. Right at the beginning, Mary's relationship to Elizabeth makes the herald John the Baptist a cousin of some sort, another remarkable man from the same stock. The family aspect is hinted at negatively also. We are not told who Mary is living with when Gabriel visits her (the Heli-Clopas household, however plausible, is an inference only), but when her condition is disclosed, we would expect it to get her into trouble with those around her: with parents, brothers, sisters. They would want reassurance at least as much as Joseph does. Yet nothing at all is said about this. Whatever has happened, the tradition suggests a family willing to acquiesce in it from the outset, and (some of them) to do more than acquiesce later.

The eventual involvement of Jesus's 'brother' James, and his mother's sister or sister-in-law, carries on an earlier rallying of kindred and acquaintance: Mary's, it would seem, not Joseph's. Jesus begins his public life by going to his cousin John for baptism; the first outsider to join him is a follower of John's, namely Andrew; Simon Peter, who becomes the chief apostle, is Andrew's brother and is drawn in by him; while another founder-member, Nathanael, lives at Cana where Mary has important friends (John 1:35–42, 49; 2:1 ff; 21:2). Christ emerges from what at least could be a long-standing group centred on his mother.

Accidents of heredity, plus the right climate in the home, do sometimes produce astonishing families. The Bachs are the classic instance. It would not be too unlikely for a woman member of such a family to have a correct intuition about the calibre of her offspring. Furthermore, once the notion was planted, a process of grooming might ensue. Grooming cannot turn a commonplace boy into a Christ – or a Bach, or an Einstein; but in the intensely conditioned Jewish milieu it could have fostered qualities which would have remained dormant in other boys. We can speak, with due caution, of a prophecy helping to create its own fulfilment. As a matter of fact Jewish scripture supplied the model for a prophetic family, even a Messianic one – Moses, Aaron and Miriam in Exodus. The relationships were different, but reflections on the prototype-Mary, the Virgin's namesake, could have suggested two further parallels: Jesus as the new Moses, liberator, prophet, and lawgiver of the Messianic covenant; John the Baptist as the new Aaron, introducing him to Israel (Exodus 4:27–31).

So we move on. After hearing the angel, Mary sets out to visit Elizabeth, who lives in a town in the Judaean hill country to the south. It is unnamed, but cannot be very far from Jerusalem, since Zechariah is a priest of the Temple. An apocryphal Ethiopic book[12] makes Mary relate that she had no early symptoms of pregnancy and was unsure what was going on till her stay with her older relative. There is at least a glimmer of insight here. Even after 'How shall this be?' and the angelic reply, the story has a sceptical tinge. Gabriel mentions Elizabeth's condition as confirming his message; Mary makes the visit to see for herself, and check that the Annunciation was truthful. She is cautious. She is also independent-spirited, a quality shown in another way by the journey which she now undertakes. What, we may ask, about Joseph? He does not go with her. He does not even seem to be there. Absence at work is the simplest answer. It is one of the few happy inspirations in the *Protevangelium*.

On arrival, Mary greets Elizabeth and gives her some notion of what has happened. Elizabeth replies: 'Blessed are you among women, and blessed is the fruit of your womb! And why is this granted me, that the mother of my Lord should come to me?' The impending birth of the Promised One is now accepted by both. Luke portrays Mary putting her delayed conviction into a song, which is called the *Magnificat* from its first word in Latin.

'My soul magnifies the Lord,
and my spirit rejoices in God my Saviour,
for he has regarded the low estate of his handmaiden.
For behold, henceforth all generations will call me blessed;
for he who is mighty has done great things for me,
and holy is his name.
And his mercy is on those who fear him
from generation to generation.
He has shown strength with his arm,
he has scattered the proud in the imagination of their hearts,

he has put down the mighty from their thrones,
and exalted those of low degree;
he has filled the hungry with good things,
and the rich he has sent empty away.
He has helped his servant Israel,
in remembrance of his mercy,
as he spoke to our fathers,
to Abraham and to his posterity for ever.'

It has echoes of the Psalms, and the speech of Hannah in 1 Samuel 2, and – significantly – the triumph-song of Miriam. But it is a splendid thing in its own right. If the *Magnificat* is authentic, Mary was a true poet; and though she probably did not compose it on the spot, she may well have done so later. The left-wing, subversive tone is not to be overlooked. God's Anointed will surely be an overthrower of earthly powers, not a mere successor.[13]

She stays with Elizabeth and Zechariah for almost three months, long enough to help at their son's birth. By now her own pregnancy is certain and she must confront Joseph, who, presumably, is back in Nazareth waiting for her. This is where Luke intersects Matthew. Perhaps, after all, no confrontation occurs. Matthew is vague – Mary is 'found to be with child' – and very probably news has reached Nazareth from the south. Joseph's thoughts of dissolving the marriage are ended by the angel's explaining to him in a dream. The first two chapters of Matthew contain no fewer than five instances of guidance in dreams. In four of them the dreamer is Joseph. He is given to dreaming instructively like his namesake in Genesis, and most of his decisions are reached by that route. Apart from his being a carpenter and a 'just man', that is almost the only personal touch.

With his wife it is different. We may consider that these stories cannot be taken literally, in detail. They are supernatural, they are written long after the events with religious objects in mind, they are moulded by conventions and precedents. Yet I think Mary does begin to emerge as a person: as a young woman – still very young indeed – with a marked character and a definite hope.

Elizabeth produces her son. Zechariah, who is still dumb and conversing by signs, writes on a tablet: 'His name is John.' He has acknowledged, at last, the validity of his vision. His tongue is freed and he utters a hymn of blessing, like Mary. He foretells that the boy will 'go before the Lord to prepare his ways'. Six months later, at Bethlehem, Jesus is born.

4

That birth and its sequels are the most mythical-looking episodes in the Gospels. Bethlehem, David's city, is near Jerusalem and a long way from Galilee. The birth has an air of being invented to fulfil Micah 5:2, a prophecy which Matthew quotes, or rather adapts:

> And you, O Bethlehem, in the land of Judah,
> are by no means least among the rulers of Judah;
> for from you shall come a ruler
> who will govern my people Israel.

We are told that Joseph had to go there for the imperial census. In itself this is not very convincing. Furthermore, all the events that follow seem open to a major objection. They imply, not merely the Messianic expectancy which might have gathered round a particular child, but an instant and widespread interest which is too facile. Shepherds at Bethlehem run to see him; the old people Simeon and Anna, waiting in the Temple for Israel's deliverer, recognize the baby as the one they are waiting for; wise men come from the east; Herod orders a massacre of male children, trying to destroy the threat to his dynasty.

There are further stumbling-blocks. The shepherds' vision of angels, however beautiful as a story, is daunting as history. So are two other facts: that the Persian god Mithras was also adored by shepherds at his birth; and that the Indian god Krishna also escaped a Massacre of the Innocents.

On the first point, Bethlehem, the theory of an afterthought is not as impressive as it looks. In the time of Christ, and even when the Gospels were written, the Jewish hope of a Messiah was more a matter of popular faith than of defined, text-citing orthodoxy. It congealed in dogma only among later rabbis, whose views in detail cannot have affected the New Testament. Before then, Jews generated a mass of guesswork in which the notion of Bethlehem as the proper birthplace was at most only one among several, and not outstanding.

Many thought the Messiah had already come, but was waiting to declare himself. Some said he was in Rome, some in the north. Some expected him to appear out of nowhere. It is far from certain that a specific Palestinian birthplace, at Bethlehem or anywhere else, would have been an advantage to a claimant. In one of the few Gospel passages where Jesus's origin is mentioned during his ministry, it does not tell in his favour but against him. Jews who are looking for a wholly mysterious Messiah resist one who has a definite background. 'We know where this man comes from; and when the Christ appears, no one will know where he comes from.'[14]

We need not be too afraid, therefore, of accepting that Jesus really was born in Bethlehem, whether Mary was brought there because of a census or for some other reason. Moreover, to locate the event near Jerusalem is to have a key to the main difficulty, and it is in keeping with the impression which may already be forming. Here again, surely, is the family aspect. All these stories are about a state of affairs which is credible in substance on a single assumption: that Zechariah and Elizabeth, having made up their minds about their young relative's pregnancy, have been talking. They live near Jerusalem themselves. They are people of standing. Zechariah is on the Temple staff. The birth of their own son, John the future Baptist, has excited a community edified by the story of Abraham and Sarah. Because of them, the family's Messianic hope is already planted – a hope of the kind that can harden into predictions and even plans. Simeon and Anna, who watch and wait in the Temple, are well-known characters there, and Zechariah tells them who to look out for. In such an atmosphere a spread of rumour among the peasantry and farther afield, even as far as the morbidly suspicious Herod, is not too hard to credit. Luke partly testifies to it (1:65). Granted always the basic proposition, that the Gospels show us a family which really did see a Messianic future for the child born to one of its members *from the beginning*. The idea that Mary's pregnancy was extraordinary would have been reason enough. We have glimpsed other possible causes in dreams, visions, astrology.

Bethlehem is a small town on two hills, five miles south of the capital. Over the centuries it has been noted for its vineyards and honey. In Christ's time it was smaller still; John 7:42 calls it a village. Matthew simply mentions the birth without enlarging on it, Luke gives details. His account of the couple's arrival at an inn, and their removal to a stable because the inn is full, is too familiar to need any comment. Except perhaps this, that the word 'stable' is never used. Mary puts the child in a manger, but she is not in another building, she is in a cave adapted for housing animals. When the Empress Helena planned to build a church at Christ's birthplace, local Christians identified the cave for her. Today the Church of the Nativity stands above an underground room about forty feet long, with a silver star marking the reputed manger.

Luke does not tell us the time when the birth occurred. The *Protevangelium* puts it in the daytime, and inserts a miracle with an odd science-fiction flavour, a halting of the universe. Joseph is made to describe it:

Now I Joseph was walking, and I walked not. And I looked up to the air and saw the air in amazement. And I looked up unto the pole of the heaven and saw it standing still, and the fowls of the heaven without motion. And I looked upon the earth and saw a dish set, and workmen lying by it, and their hands were in the dish: and they that were chewing chewed not, and they that were lifting the food lifted it not, and they that put it to their mouth put it not thereto, but the faces of all of them were looking upward. And behold there were sheep being driven, and they went not forward but stood still; and the shepherd lifted his hand to smite them with his staff, and his hand remained up. And I looked upon the stream of the river and saw the mouths of the kids upon the water and they drank not. And of a sudden all things moved onward in their course.[15]

The same book adds that Mary was examined at once by a midwife, and certified intact. Luke has nothing like this; the canonical Gospels are free of the physical curiosity that comes later. He goes straight on to the shepherds' visit at night. Local knowledge of the Messiah's advent is attributed to their spreading the news (2:17–18) – a further hint, at least, that local knowledge existed and news was spread. Mary 'keeps all these things in her heart' and ponders them.

After eight days the child is circumcised and given the name Jesus. A month after that, his parents take him to Jerusalem to be presented to the Lord in the Temple, as prescribed by the Mosaic Law. Their offering is the poor person's offering of two doves. It is here that they meet Simeon, to whom it has been revealed that he will not die till he has seen the Christ. He is waiting for them, and takes the child in his arms and blesses God. His words are given in the form of a canticle like Mary's and Zechariah's, the *Nunc Dimittis*.

'Lord, now lettest thou thy servant depart in peace,
according to thy word;
for mine eyes have seen thy salvation . . .'

Turning to Mary, he adds a prophecy:

'Behold, this child is set for the fall and rising of many in Israel,
and for a sign that is spoken against
(and a sword will pierce through your own soul also),
that thoughts out of many hearts may be revealed.'

The venerable prophetess Anna – of the tribe of Asher, and therefore representing the lost members of Israel – is also present. She too greets the infant as the One promised, and talks about him afterwards to anyone who will listen (2:38). Whatever Zechariah may have been doing, Anna has launched a rumour capable of worrying Herod, whose palace is less than half a mile away.

That is the end of the birth-stories in Luke. The natural reading of the text is that Joseph and Mary went straight home to Nazareth. However, the equally famous events of Matthew 2 can only be fitted in before their return. If Luke's source was a Mary-saga derived ultimately from the Virgin herself, it must have been laconic at this point. Perhaps Matthew reveals why.

Wise men from the east, it will be remembered, arrive in

Jerusalem looking for the new-born 'King of the Jews'. They have seen his star and come to pay homage. Herod is alarmed, and consults priests as to where the Christ is to be born. Their reply, citing Micah 5:2, is 'Bethlehem'. He asks the wise men to go there and inquire. Guided by the star, they find the child and offer him gifts, then leave for their own country without reporting back to Herod. Joseph has a dream warning him of danger, and takes Mary and Jesus to Egypt. Unable to identify the menacing child, Herod assumes he is still in Bethlehem, and orders the killing of all male children in the town who are two years old or less. After Herod's death Joseph brings his family back from Egypt, but Herod's son Archelaus is now reigning, and they go to Nazareth and settle, Galilee being outside his jurisdiction.

As far as Herod is concerned, the story is in character. His victims were many. In 7 BC he killed two sons of his own on suspicion of a conspiracy. The slaughter of the babies at Bethlehem, probably few in such a small place, would have been an easy and minor crime for him. It need not be assumed that he is unaware of the Messianic rumour before he hears it from his exotic visitors. What disturbs him is the proof that it has spread far enough to interest such important men. A rival King of the Jews, even an infant, could become a focus of subversion and cause trouble with Rome. The priests' confident answer to his question about the birthplace is not credible at face value. But it makes good sense if their colleague Zechariah has already been speaking of the child born in Bethlehem, and citing Micah in support. They are telling Herod the current form of the rumour. The result is dreadful: they give him a target, and cause a massacre.[16]

The wise men and their star raise an interesting issue. 'Star' may mean 'astrological portent' and refer to the conjunction of Saturn and Jupiter, or some other Messianic signal. However, the motif cannot be pressed, since the 'star' does not behave astronomically (2:9). As for the wise men – not kings and not necessarily three, despite Christian legend – they are usually regarded now as magi or priest-sages, attached to the Zoroastrian religion of Iran. This was related in some obscure way to Judaism, which borrowed several of its doctrines. But it is not clear why any magi should have been interested in a 'King of the Jews'. In view of various hints, already glanced at on pp. 83–4, it may be we have a tradition here about envoys of the Lost Tribes of Israel, who were drawn from their home beyond Euphrates by the spreading Messianic report, and came to offer their allegiance. When Matthew was written the Church no longer cared about a reunion of Israel, and the meaning of the tradition was forgotten.

Less speculative is the implied picture of Mary's life at this time. The wise men visit her at Bethlehem in a house, not an inn or a cave (2:11). Joseph seems to have gone back there after the presentation in the Temple and tried to settle in the south, perhaps because it is his home ground. Herod's notion that the child may be as old as two suggests a fair interval between the Birth and the Flight to Egypt. Joseph and Mary are in Egypt a year or so and come back about the middle of 4 BC, but the risk of trouble with Herod's heir Archelaus upsets any plans for further residence in Judaea. After some wavering, and another dream, they return at last to Nazareth. In Matthew Nazareth has not been mentioned till now. The reason alleged for their deciding to live there is an otherwise unknown prophecy about Christ being a 'Nazarene'. This is far-fetched and confused. They go because Nazareth is the home of Mary's people, who adopted Joseph as an honorary member before, and will again. The haven is badly needed. Years of exile have left him too poverty-stricken to set up on his own.

Such is Matthew's account of the sequel to the Birth, and its sheer painfulness tells in its favour. If it is combined with Luke's, we have a consistent picture of Mary's early ecstasies turning gradually sour. The simple daydream of her child being king has led to a threat of divorce, to a bewildering hubbub all around her, to peasants bursting in on her after a comfortless confinement, to a frightening prophecy about a sword piercing her soul, to upper-class foreigners arriving whom she is too poor to welcome; and then, more grimly, to involvement with politics, to homelessness and destitution in a strange land, and to the murder of other women's children who might have been hers. Did the couple pass through Bethlehem on their way back from Egypt? and did any bereaved parents recognize the stranger who had brought so much misery? Christians who reflect devoutly on the 'life of Our Lady' seldom consider the burden of grief and guilt which their beliefs imply for her, at the age of seventeen or so, if she had the least sensitivity.

But a problem has quietly dissolved. The early chapters of Matthew and Luke, it is often claimed, are so different and overlap so little that it is absurd to treat them as history; they are simply irreconcilable collections of legends. Certainly the wording of Luke 2:39 makes it very hard to fit in the whole of Matthew 2 between 'when they had performed everything according to the law of the Lord' and 'they returned into Galilee, to their own city, Nazareth'. Yet the narratives interlock, and the story which both imply of Mary's passage from joy to sorrow is – for her – one story. Moreover, as soon as we grasp this, we can see a possible reason why the overlap is so slight and the events of Matthew 2 are missing from Luke. If Luke used a version of Mary's own reminiscences, it is all too humanly comprehensible that this should have said nothing of Herod or Egypt. Her friends heard only, or chiefly, of earlier and happier scenes. She was unwilling to dwell on the darkest phase. It may be that those traumatic ordeals caused her to thrust the angelic vision into the back of her mind and even doubt it.

5

Life at Nazareth is resumed. On the proposed view of the family, it becomes a crowded turmoil with four adults (Clopas, Joseph and the two Marys) and at least eight children, all 'brothers' and 'sisters' together. Joseph, perhaps, goes out to work on a building project at Sepphoris three miles away, launched about this time by Herod Antipas, the ruler of Galilee.[17] Mary has the tasks of a Jewish housewife in a small country town – grinding flour, baking, cooking, raising vegetables. She makes her own clothes, which are plain and homely: essentially a wide-sleeved ankle-length gown, with a cloak over it that can cover the head, and simple ornaments. There is no special reason to imagine her wearing blue, as so often in art.

Jesus, in the words of Luke, is growing and becoming strong, and the favour of God is upon him. The apocryphal 'Infancy

Gospels' seek to improve on this. We are solemnly told how, at the age of five, he made clay sparrows that came to life and flew away; how another child, who jostled him in the street, dropped dead; how he struck slanderers blind; how, at eight, he sowed a handful of wheat and reaped a harvest that fed all the poor of the neighbourhood; how he stretched a wooden beam which his father had made too short; how he was rude to a well-meaning man who tried to teach him the alphabet. The precocious little god of these fables is often detestable. Few of them do Jesus any honour. Few add anything, even fiction, to the story of his mother.[18]

Matthew tells nothing more about him till he is grown up, nor do Mark and John. Luke has the one famous glimpse at the age of twelve, when his parents take him to Jerusalem for the Passover, which they attend annually. Afterwards they start for home, but he stays in Jerusalem without their knowledge. They look for him among travelling friends and relatives, and then return to the city. For three days they search. Belatedly they try the Temple, and find him in a group of rabbis, listening and asking questions. Mary says (and this is the only dialogue between them in the Synoptic Gospels): 'Son, why have you treated us so? Behold, your father and I have been looking for you anxiously.' Jesus replies: 'How is it that you sought me? Did you not know that I must be in my Father's house?'

His parents 'do not understand'. It is a strange statement after what has gone before. If we are still getting Mary's testimony here, the impression is that she had almost succeeded in effacing her youthful hopes. Gabriel said, twice, that Jesus would be the Son of God, yet now when he confirms it himself, she fails to make the connection. The canonical Gospels have no further boyhood incidents. So why this one? Did she recall it vividly, and speak of it in later life, because on reflection it revived her belief? Luke repeats the phrase about her 'keeping all these things in her heart' which he employed after the Birth. It suggests a renewal. Ten years earlier, very probably, the sequels of that event caused her to recoil, and anticipate Mary Shelley in wishing that her child might be like other people. The Temple incident proves that he is not: there must have been something in it after all.

To quote Luke again, he grows in wisdom and stature, and in favour with God and man. Also he is obedient to his parents. The family is changing. Zechariah and Elizabeth are dead. Joseph dies also, perhaps through an accident at work. Still, the promise was made to Mary, and taken up by her kin, not Joseph's. Clopas's wife and her son James are beginning to be impressed by Jesus, even while living under the same roof, and even while he quietly learns his trade as a carpenter.

Somewhere between the Temple incident and the beginning of his public career, Mary recovers full faith in him. This is to be inferred because we presently find her taking a leading role in his first Messianic act, the miracle of Cana, and even urging him to it. But at whatever point the faith revives, we can hardly admit a return to her adolescent ardours. Not after the squalors of Egypt, not after the massacre at Bethlehem, not in the grinding humiliation of day-to-day life in somebody else's house. With the well-schooled Jewish mind suggested by the *Magnificat*, Mary could have reasoned that the Lord's hand *must* be here, that her Son *must* be the Christ indeed, if her various nightmares were to make any sense. But her mature faith as a widow in her forties would certainly have been harder, and more than merely acceptance over again. Above all, if the Bethlehem massacre is a fact, nothing less than a sort of expiatory dedication could have silenced the reproach. Henceforth her Son has to be special, he has to be the saviour of Israel, if he and she are to justify the agony they have caused already.

There is more here than psychological speculation. However mythical the slaughter of the children may seem (and I do not forget Krishna), it helps to account not only for the little more we are told of the Virgin's actions, but for a strand of early Christian thinking which is traceable in the New Testament and related to her. It is more useful as fact than it looks.

In the first place, if it happened, somebody would have observed at some point that Moses was rescued from a similar massacre, with the aid of Miriam, and that this event set him on the road to his triumphant dealings with the Egyptian court and the salvation of Israel. To a devout Jewish woman, an annual Passover pilgrim, such an argument would have been powerful in suggesting the hand of God at work. It would also have underlined the parallel her own name evoked, confirming her as the new Miriam of a new God-inspired family, with her Son as its Moses.

And why stop there? The evidence suggests that for some reason, and very possibly for this reason, Mary's circle undertook a searching of scripture which led to a much weightier prophetic discovery. It may shed an oblique light on Jesus's notorious 'lost years'. The approach is roundabout. We must begin by reverting yet once more to the Annunciation. Gabriel salutes Mary with a word of greeting which is translated into English as 'hail'. No one knows what it was in the original language. But Luke's Greek version, which is the source of the English, uses the word *chairé*. Given its full weight, *chairé* means 'rejoice'.

The promise of the Messiah is thus linked with what Jews understood to be the same promise in Zephaniah 3:14–15 and Zechariah 9:9. We glanced at these texts in Chapter 1, together with several more sharing a common factor.

> Sing aloud, O daughter of Zion;
>   shout, O Israel!
> Rejoice and exult with all your heart,
>   O daughter of Jerusalem! . . .
> The King of Israel, the Lord, is in your midst;
>   you shall fear evil no more.
>
> Rejoice greatly, O daughter of Zion!
>   Shout aloud, O daughter of Jerusalem!
> Lo, your king comes to you.

The angelic salutation makes Mary herself the Maiden Zion. Through a millennial travail, Israel has evolved to a point where she stands embodied, virginal as Jeremiah foreshadowed, ready at last for the Lord's advent. Mary is Israel-as-a-whole, or rather the faithful remnant, focused in Her through whom the Messiah is now about to come.[19]

Luke's key-word *chairé* testifies to this idea among Christians of his time, and it is probably present in another New Testament passage, of which more hereafter. However, he does not spell it out, nor does anyone else. We may ask who did, and where it started, and when. Did the original wording of the Annunciation, before Christianity, carry the same hint? and was it expounded to make Mary a prophesied figure, and confirm her vocation, before her Son entered the public stage at all? If we turn back to another of the Old Testament's 'virgin Israel' texts, we find it occurring in a passage which is not only related to the Annunciation but is a recognized seed-bed of Christian thinking, a passage that *was* read as prophesying (among other things) the Bethlehem massacre and the Messianic work of Jesus. But more interesting still, one verse seems to date the original reading of it in this sense to a time before its citation by Christians, a time before Jesus's public career, in a phase of family preparation.

Two chapters of Jeremiah to be specific, the thirtieth and thirty-first, foretell the glorious days to come, and exhort the 'virgin' to take heart and be ready to play her timbrel . . . like Miriam. They refer as Gabriel does to 'Jacob' and to the future Davidic king (30:9, 10, 18; 31:4). Towards the close (31:31–4) comes the Lord's majestic pledge of a 'new covenant'. This was taken up by the Church and applied to Christ; from the Christian point of view, it became one of the most important of all Messianic prophecies. It is not, however, the only part of this chapter to surface again in the Christian setting. A little before it, in verses 15–16, we read:

> A voice is heard in Ramah,
>   lamentation and bitter weeping.
> Rachel is weeping for her children;
>   she refuses to be comforted for her children,
>   because they are not.
> Thus says the Lord:
> Keep your voice from weeping,
>   and your eyes from tears;
> for your work shall be rewarded.

Matthew 2:18 cites the first of these verses as foreshadowing Herod's massacre.

The new covenant itself is fifteen verses farther on:

Behold, the days are coming, says the Lord, when I will
make a new covenant with the house of Israel and the house
of Judah.

Not like the covenant which I made with their fathers
when I took them by the hand to bring them out of the land
of Egypt, my covenant which they broke, though I was their
husband, says the Lord.

But this is the covenant which I will make with the
house of Israel after those days, says the Lord; I will put my
law within them, and I will write it upon their hearts; and I
will be their God, and they shall be my people.

And no longer shall each man teach his neighbour and
each his brother, saying 'Know the Lord', for they shall all
know me, from the least of them to the greatest, says the
Lord; for I will forgive their iniquity, and I will remember
their sin no more.

The Christian fulfilment of this promise can be fixed, because
Christ is said to have instituted the new covenant at the Last
Supper (1 Corinthians 11:23–5, and corresponding Gospel
texts). The importance of the passage is such that the whole of it
is transcribed in Hebrews 8.

So, on the reading of Jeremiah 31:15–34 as prophetic of Jesus,
verse 15 is fulfilled in Herod's time, and verses 31–4 are fulfilled during Jesus's ministry. The chronological order is right.
What about the part between? In 21–2, God says:

> Consider well the highway,
>   the road by which you went.
> Return, O virgin Israel,
>   return to these your cities.
> How long will you waver,
>   O faithless daughter?
> For the Lord has created a new thing on the earth:
>   a woman protects a man.

Here is the symbolic figure whom Luke shows to have merged
with Mary. As Israel she is in some sense the Lord's bride
(verse 32). As Mary she fits in extremely well. In verse 15 we

have the massacre; in 16 the Lord is saying, 'Take heart'; in 21–2, after Herod's death, he summons Mary back from Egyptian wanderings to her task in her own country; and in 31–4 comes the new covenant which is to arise from her Son's mission. If the passage is read straight through, the chronological sequence holds.

Jeremiah 31:15–34 is thus a connected utterance with three points of Christian contact. But no known Christian does actually connect the three, or discuss the passage as a whole. In the New Testament we seem to be getting only fragments of a full commentary. It is as if the Annunciation, in its original form, drew attention to the chapters of Jeremiah; as if someone interpreted 31:15–34 in terms of the massacre, the flight and return of Mary, and the work of Jesus; and as if that interpretation came through to the New Testament piecemeal. But when was the interpretation first worked out?

It fits most naturally not into the period of Christian preaching but into a much earlier time before Christ's public activities, when his mother had regained her faith, and speculation about his destiny was gathering round him in a small circle of friends and relatives. The reason lies in that odd verse 22: 'The Lord has created a new thing on the earth: a woman protects a man.' This is the English of the Revised Standard Version. The literal meaning is 'a female shall surround a male', but there may be an error in the Hebrew and commentators have been vastly perplexed. Other would-be renderings include 'a woman shall compass a man' (King James), 'frail woman becomes manly' (Moffatt), 'weak woman is to be the protectress of man's strength' (Knox), and 'a woman turned into a man' (New English Bible). The gist is that in the dawning of the new age, a woman – presumably the virgin addressed – is to assume a male role, i.e. a commanding one; or perhaps more specifically, that her strength will buttress an individual man. Either reading would give a background for Mary's attitude as it shows dimly in the tradition of Christ's first 'sign', the Cana miracle. Either would have been irrelevant and unthinkable later, with Christ standing alone at the centre of the Church's faith. [20]

6

Whatever the truth about this prophecy, the family threads do begin to twitch. The other boy, Elizabeth's John, is now adult and active. He has been living in the wilderness where the holy men of Israel go (Luke 1:80), but now he emerges on the bank of Jordan east of Jerusalem to baptize, preach and warn.

With John the Baptist at least, we can break out of the Bible into non-Christian history. Josephus gives an account of him, as a man of high character who attracted large audiences. He baptized with water to cleanse the body and to wash away 'some sins'. Such lustral practice was habitual among the Essenes. These and other communities of Jewish ascetics are known to us not only through Josephus but through the Dead Sea Scrolls. John seems to have been a loosely affiliated hermit rather than a full member of any group, but their texts shed a vivid light on him. The monks lived where he did, in the fearful mountainous wasteland near the Dead Sea. They fasted, studied the scriptures in bare cells, and observed rules of daunting strictness. They regarded most other Jews as backsliders and themselves as the true Israel, a faithful few, the Sons of Light purifying themselves for the coming kingdom. Though their whole mode of life was based on the Messianic vision, there is no evidence that the Qumran group or any other picked out a Messiah. That step was left to John the Baptist, a maverick prophet not subject to communal restraints.[21]

The growth of Jesus's own vocation is beyond conjecture. It is simplest to imagine him developing in the family context, and plying his trade. His mother tells him about his portentous origin. His other relatives argue, but listen, and show respect. Readings at the synagogue cause debates, rabbis offer interpretations of texts. The process takes many years. He is no longer a youth. But pressure to declare himself does not build up until his cousin John becomes famous, haranguing crowds beside the river, disclaiming the title of Christ himself, foretelling the advent of someone greater, and urging the people to prepare. 'Repent, for the Kingdom of Heaven is at hand.'

What encouragement has John had from his kinsfolk in Galilee? What is the role of the Galilean Andrew who travels south and becomes his disciple, but is ready, as soon as Jesus arrives, not only to join him but to produce a brother who has also come south (John 1:35–42)? We can only guess. But at Nazareth, clearly, Mary is treasuring the angel's remembered word. The King is about to be shown to Israel.

Chapter 5

THE HEART OF THE LABYRINTH

I

Jesus duly enters on his career. The event is hard to date. John the Baptist has been preparing the ground for some time; he is well known and is becoming, or soon to become, a nuisance to the authorities. Luke assigns the beginning of John's activities to the fifteenth year of the reign of Tiberius. Tiberius succeeded Augustus as emperor in AD 14. John, therefore, demarcates an uncertain period from 28 or 29 onwards. It may have been two or three years, with Jesus coming on the scene neither immediately after the beginning nor very close to the end.

Luke says he was about thirty. It is difficult to make him much less than thirty-five. Such a late start would be surprising today, but not in that Semitic setting. There is no need to make his 'lost years' a portentous mystery, no need to imagine him in an Essene monastery, or wandering through Tibet. Mohammed was forty when he took his first hesitant steps toward proclaiming Islam. Age conferred prestige. Luke, a Gentile addressing Gentiles, values it less and prefers an approximation downwards. During his ministry Jesus is best pictured (in keeping with the Holy Shroud) as in his middle or late thirties, physically vigorous, with a very mature manner. Some of his Jewish critics say he is 'not yet fifty' (John 8:57) – 'fifty' rather than 'forty'. Mary, meanwhile, is still far from aged, and it is legitimate to imagine her, in her more inspired moments, as not looking very much older than her Son.

He takes the stage as a public figure when John baptizes him, saluting him as the One foretold. After the baptism he retires into the wilderness of Judaea. There, in a fiery light which burns away everything but God and man, he wrestles with his vocation and resists promptings to betray it. Then he assembles his first disciples, one of whom, Nathanael of Cana, calls him 'King of Israel'. Most of these events are described in at least three Gospels. But the actual start of the Messianic adventure, the first 'manifestation of his glory', survives in the Fourth only: almost as if the Synoptics were uneasy about it, and censored it out in the light of later developments. It takes place when he is back in Galilee, and it involves Mary as the other accounts of the period do not.

We are bound to ask whose testimony this Gospel gives us. The name at its head is that of the 'beloved disciple' John, who is present at the Last Supper and therefore the same man listed elsewhere as an apostle, the son of Zebedee. It speaks of him in the third person. Near the close (21:24) is a sentence which confirms that he is the source, or reputed source, but also reveals another hand besides his. 'This is the disciple who is bearing witness to these things; and we know that his testimony is true.' The implication tallies with critical judgment as to date. The Fourth Gospel was completed somewhere about AD 100. A papyrus fragment in a Manchester library proves that it is not very much later, but it is not much earlier either. At its date of composition, John son of Zebedee is unlikely to have been alive. The other long work ascribed to him, the Apocalypse or Revelation, is in a different and cruder style. Hints from early tradition offer a satisfactory answer – that in the Fourth Gospel we do have the apostle's recollections in old age, but they have been written out, polished, and expanded at leisure by some-one else. The erratic movement, the shifting of events out of sequence (2:14–16 is the outstanding case), the apparent passing-over of major events because the Synoptics have dealt with them already, all fit in with the picture of an aged man reminiscing and an amanuensis of genius building up notes into the extraordinary book we now have.

The Fourth Gospel is not meant to be taken literally at all points. It is the sovereign instance of that crucial process within the Church, the struggle to cope with the impact of Jesus Christ, to explain and expound. The voice we hear in it is not always insisting 'This happened', but rather, 'This is what it was all about'.[1] Yet the author draws on memories of actual events. If we allow that the beloved disciple was at least a main source, there is a possibility that here, as with Luke, we have information originating from the mother of Christ. She is said in this same Gospel to have lived in John's home after the Crucifixion, and if she did, she can hardly have been entirely mute.

It thus carries peculiar weight that the Johannine account of Jesus's first 'sign' brings her in not merely as a witness but as an active participant. She comes to a wedding feast at Cana, which is a small town in the higher country of Galilee. Jesus is invited too, and comes separately with several disciples, including, it seems, the local man Nathanael. The wedding feast in fact has the air of a rendezvous, and it leads up to a miracle strangely unlike the ones Jesus performs later.

While festivities are still in progress the wine runs out. Mary says to her Son, 'They have no wine.' Plainly this is his cue to do something, but he demurs. His reply is a brusque, rather cryptic sentence which has been variously translated – 'O woman, what have you to do with me?' or 'what is that to me and to you?' or at its mildest, 'why do you trouble me with that?' He adds: 'My hour has not yet come.' In Greek the word 'woman' was a polite mode of address with no tone of contempt or irritation, and he uses it elsewhere to Mary Magdalene and others; but spoken to one's own mother it would have been unusual and far from warm, and so would its Aramaic equivalent.[2]

Commentators have toiled over this exchange. Augustine concedes a mystery in Christ's attitude to Mary, and mentions heretics who inferred from the Cana speech that she was not his mother at all. The best Augustine can do is to argue that as the impending miracle is a divine act, to be performed as and when the Son of God chooses, the purely human Mary is being dissociated from it.[3] This is unconvincing, because she is very decidedly not dissociated. Without answering Jesus directly, she orders the servants to do whatever he tells them. Since they are not hers to order, some prior understanding must be presumed. They gather round her Son for instructions, and he is driven to act. He tells them to fill six jars with water, each holding more than twenty gallons, and then to draw from them. The liquid taken out is no longer water but wine, and the bridegroom is praised for keeping his best vintage to the last.

What is seldom remarked upon is that the amount is monstrous and absurd. No credible number of guests could have finished it on top of the rest. It would have required a long, conspicuous, largely useless fetching-and-carrying, even if the house had its own well, as is most unlikely. More is intended by the story than a mere refill. Whatever we care to think of as literally 'happening', the point of the sign is clear. Jewish Messianic tradition supplies the key to it. The new age was to be an age of plenty, and Israel's royal saviour was to usher it in with a great feast for his people. Cana supplies a feast ready-made; Jesus is expected to prove who he is by enlarging it to huge proportions, with wine enough for a multitude.[4]

He makes this concession to the popular image, but he makes it hesitantly. The fact that he only complies because his mother has refused to take 'no' for an answer is destined to inspire many prayers to her down the centuries. Afterwards he moves to Capernaum, where a lodging has been found which will become his headquarters. So far the company is united. Mary and his 'brothers' go with him as well as his disciples (John 2:12). When he is settled, the relations apparently return to Nazareth and the disciples remain with him. Capernaum is beside the lake of Tiberias, in the upper Jordan valley. The Galilean plateau falls away sharply to the lake, and the western fringe with its little towns is green and kindly. In this small, intimate area, among peasants and fishermen, Jesus elects to stay for most of the time, though with many sorties outside. He begins teaching and heal-ing. But now, from his mother's point of view, something definitely goes wrong. The regal career promised in the Annunciation, and briefly confirmed at Cana, is crumbling.

Humanly speaking, why? I think we see a crisis here that was repeated, though with immeasurably less grandeur and tragedy, in the life of a messiah of modern times. His history is well known and sheds a backward light on the Gospels.

Shortly before the First World War, Annie Besant, the head of the Theosophical Society, adopted a Hindu boy. A colleague had assured her that this boy, Jeddu Krishnamurti, was a rare spirit destined to be the next World Teacher, on a level with Buddha and Christ himself. After legal wrangles with his father the Theosophists succeeded in building a movement round him, the Order of the Star in the East. They obtained the use of a Dutch castle as headquarters, and groomed him for his mission. He grew up in that atmosphere. But in 1929, with impressive integrity, he refused the crown and dissolved the Order. It is worth stressing, as a further sidelight on the story of Christ, that his sponsors had been right when they discerned unusual gifts in him as a child. He did not lapse into nullity but moved off on a path of his own, with a doctrine of spiritual self-reliance which many have valued, Aldous Huxley among them. What he did disavow was the arrogance of being a leader such as Annie Besant intended, with a movement behind him which he could not honestly approve.[5]

Krishnamurti's break with her was in part the outcome of an experience a year or two earlier, which had convinced him that although he was a teacher, he was not the teacher she meant him to be. This was wholly serious and free from the tragi-comedy of the public fiasco. If we put the Gospels together, we find Jesus arriving at the Cana wedding fresh from an experience of the same type. The Fourth Gospel, which describes Cana, does not mention this. The Synoptic writers, who do mention it, say nothing of Cana. They want to portray Jesus as carrying on from his experience with an undeviating logic. It has a special interest as being the only Gospel episode for which (in essence) Jesus himself must be the source — having been without human companions at the time.

The episode of course is the Temptation. It fits in between his baptism by John and his coming to the wedding. We are told how, when alone among the hills by the Dead Sea and hungry from a prolonged fast, he was approached by the Devil with three proposals: that he should feed himself by turning stones into bread; that he should cast himself down from the pinnacle of the Temple, trusting in divine power to save him; and that he should become king of the world in exchange for an act of homage to Satan. His triple refusal routed the tempter.

Now these things which he rejects in the Temptation story are the very things which popular opinion looked for from the

Messiah – material welfare, stunt-type wonder-working, Jewish world power. He decides that the leadership expected of him is wrong, and turns it down. But a few days later, when he rejoins Mary at Cana with no chance of an explanation, she wants to launch him with a 'sign' far too closely akin to the diabolic feats he has just condemned. Turning water into wine is not very different from turning stones into bread; and turning it into a much greater amount than the party needs is a Messianic stunt. He acquiesces, but a cloud has slipped across the sky.

The miracles he is portrayed working afterwards are in another spirit altogether. If they are pure mythology they are still the mythology of a different outlook. Most of them are concerned with healing, either physical or mental. Even when he feeds the five thousand, the emphasis is on charity and com-passion, and there is no colossal excess, only a modest tidying-up of left-overs. Even when he walks on water he does it at night, not in the daytime to amaze onlookers, and he comes to help his disciples in their boat.

After his relatives have left him in Capernaum he confounds their hopes more and more flagrantly. He teaches and heals and exorcizes without progress. He talks in apocalyptic tones of the coming kingdom, but makes no political move to match his words, and resists attempts to force his hand. The summons to the Lost Tribes beyond Euphrates is deferred indefinitely. His kingdom seems to imply, or to presuppose, a transformation of human nature which his audiences fail to grasp. He accepts that he is the Christ, but tells the apostles not to say so in public, and claims a unique relationship with his heavenly Father which is no part of their Messianic idea. They find it all bewildering, and press him about 'restoring the kingdom to Israel' up to the very last moment (Acts 1:6). But they, at least, persevere in making what sense of him they can, and only Judas is lost beyond recall. With his earlier circle it is not so.

His brothers – some, at any rate – are sceptical, and he holds aloof from them. When they go to Jerusalem for a Jewish feast he tells them he is not joining the pilgrimage, and then goes by himself (John 7:2–10). Only James becomes an apostle.[6] John the Baptist has been imprisoned, and reports that reach the prison cause him to waver and have misgivings (Matthew 11:2–6). He sends Jesus a message: 'Are you he who is to come, or shall we look for another?' What an admission! The answer which the messengers have to take back is not wholly reassuring:

> Go and tell John what you hear and see: the blind receive their sight and the lame walk, lepers are cleansed and the deaf hear, and the dead are raised up, and the poor have good news preached to them. And blessed is he who takes no offence at me.

Offence is already being taken. Rumours are spreading that Jesus is insane (Mark 3:21; John 10:20), and that this caster-out of devils is possessed by a greater devil himself. Friends or kinsfolk try to place him under restraint, though the plan comes to nothing. Thus far Mary has not re-entered the story. Now she does. Jesus is at his lodging in Capernaum. The room is packed with listeners. His mother and his brothers arrive at the door and send in a message asking him to come outside. Luke tells us (8:19) that they could not get in because of the crowd. Space, however, would surely have been made for the Master's relations, and Mark places the visit so soon after the attempted putting-away that the effect is disturbing. It is strengthened by the fact that Jesus stays where he is in the middle of the crowd, and declines to come out.

> He replied, 'Who are my mother and my brothers?' And looking around on those who sat about him, he said, 'Here are my mother and my brothers! Whoever does the will of of God is my brother, and sister, and mother.'

He is putting first things first, of course; yet the impression of a slap is hard to avoid. After making his point he may well have spoken with them. An outright refusal would have been a declaration of war. But the split is showing.

A further incident, given only in Luke 11:27–8, tends to confirm it. A woman says to Jesus, 'Blessed is the womb that bore you, and the breasts that you sucked!' He retorts, 'Blessed rather are those who hear the word of God and keep it!' In that oriental setting, the words of praise must be understood as praise of himself rather than his mother. Unavoidably, however, they do evoke her. Christ's answer again puts first things first. Beyond that, it is ambiguous. He could mean: 'True, but not because of the blood-relationship, which is nothing; rather because she does hear the word of God and keep it.' Or he could be drawing a darker contrast, hinting that she has heard the word and not kept it. Much would depend on manner. An actor might convey the first nuance by smiling, speaking gently, gazing thoughtfully into space; the second, by hardening his features, pausing an instant, then looking the woman in the eye and speaking sternly. We have no way of telling. Yet in the light of that remark in Capernaum, the second alternative is a shade too arguable for comfort.

Up to now Jesus has only once tried to teach in Nazareth, among people who have known him from childhood (Luke 4:16–30). That encounter began well and ended badly, with a physical attack. After his family's approach to him at Capernaum, he returns their visit and goes to Nazareth again. Again some of its citizens are briefly stirred, but the contempt born of familiarity triumphs. They do not relish the son of Mary being such a celebrity. Matthew says he 'did not do many mighty works there, because of their unbelief'. The earlier and franker Mark says that he could not.

From here onward, Mary almost vanishes. The Synoptics have nothing further. The Fourth Gospel speaks of her that one more time, at the Crucifixion: Jesus addresses her as 'woman' again and commits her to the care of John. Otherwise all four are silent. It is a sad petering-out after such rapturous beginnings. Has the near-failure among her friends and neighbours driven her into total withdrawal? We are left to imagine her waiting unhappily in Nazareth, while the atmosphere of the house grows colder towards her, and Jesus marches open-eyed to the doom he foresees. James is with him, and so is the other Mary. But at the end, the Virgin only rejoins her Son in time to see him put to death. Simeon's prophecy is fulfilled. The sword has pierced her soul.

2

After that moment of utter darkness, the light creeps back. Christ's rising from the dead and his ascension into heaven – whatever meaning we give to those events – restore the disciples' faith and revive the hopes of the family. The risen Lord has a nucleus of believers, and his mother and brothers join with the apostles in prayer. That parting glimpse of her is in Acts (1:14), a book ascribed to Luke. Computer analysis supports identity of authorship with the Gospel. The man who wrote of the Virgin and the angel could not quite ignore her.

But the last thing to observe about her recorded earthly career is a glaring absence. Something happens, or rather fails to happen, in the stories of the Resurrection. These are notoriously confused, and we have six to puzzle over, not simply the Gospel four, because Acts begins with another, and Paul gives a list of the risen Lord's appearances in 1 Corinthians 15. Putting them all together we have a varied series. He appears to Mary Magdalene and the other Mary, his mother's sister; to all the apostles at sundry times and places; to two men on the road to Emmaus; to a gathering of 'more than five hundred brethren'. He shows no bias against members of the family. His brother James is specially visited (1 Corinthians 15:7), and the other Mary is in the Magdalene's company a moment after the first meeting of all. *But he never appears to his mother.* When the women report that the tomb is empty, John sees for himself and then goes home – to the Jerusalem lodging where Mary herself now is. What does he tell her? Does she come out to look? The blank is complete.

This is no hypercritical quibble. Christians have been aware of the gap for many centuries, and it has worried them. Some have suggested that Mary was among certain 'other women' who are mentioned at the tomb in Luke 24:10. Some have suggested that she was among the five hundred in Paul's account. The most that such wishful thinking can offer is an argument of the 'must have' type.[7]

The only speculation with any interest arises from a crux in the Luke Resurrection. Jesus is described as appearing to the apostles on Sunday, telling them to remain in Jerusalem, and parting with them the same night. That, at least, is the natural reading. But in Acts 1 the same author's summary of the same events agrees with the others in putting a long interval – forty days, no less – between Resurrection and Ascension. The forty days can only be fitted into his Gospel after verse 43. Whatever his text formerly said here, if anything, has vanished. A single speech of Christ is left to sum up. This hiatus occurs in the only Gospel that has much to say about Mary. If a passage has been lost, and it still did not mention an appearance to her, the silence is even more pointed. If it did, or indeed if it introduced her in any way, its loss hints at censorship. For some reason her role in the story was theologically awkward. She was not wanted.

Speculation aside, the sixfold canonical version stands. Mary of all people does not share in the experience that revives the disciples and creates Christianity. Whether the Resurrection is fact or vision or hallucination, daydream or myth or fraud, the Lord's own mother, the holy Virgin through whom he was made man, is excluded from it.

She fades from credible record. Her nephews James and Jude rise in the Church, she herself is nowhere. It is commonly assumed that she stayed in Jerusalem with John. Since he moved to Ephesus, or is reputed to have done so, fanciful biographers have made her go there with him, and die there. But by the likely time of his move she would have been very old, perhaps too frail to travel. Dates mentioned for her death range from the thirties to the sixties of the first century: in other words there is no evidence on the subject. History supplies nothing more except for one remarkable, probably true statement. To which we shall come.

Meanwhile let us take the full measure of the problem looming ahead. As the Christian era rolls onward, the Church proclaims its unwavering fidelity to the Gospels. Yet it also develops a worship of Our Lady, Mother of Christ, which the Gospels entirely fail to justify. Not only does this happen, it happens with almost no protest. We took note at the outset (pp. 8–9) that her Immaculate Conception and her Assumption are not in scripture. But where, even, is the rest of her Catholic image?

As grounds for the cult, the Church has taught that she was unique among human beings for her sinlessness and fullness of grace; that her divine Son had a special and lasting care for her; that conversely, she was closer to him than anyone else, loved him with a profounder love, and indeed was entirely at one with him, even to the extent of mystically sharing in his redemptive work. She is said, furthermore, to be in some sense an epitome of the Church, and spiritual mother of all the faithful.[8]

These are ideas which may fairly be tested against the words of scripture, and the support for them is negligible.

The Gospels furnish no evidence that Mary was of rare virtue, at least by conventional standards, let alone that she was sinless. Only one of them, Luke, goes so far as to say that she found favour with God, and she shares that honour with other biblical figures, some of them far from impeccable. The Catholic translation of Gabriel's greeting to her, 'Hail, thou who art full of grace', proves nothing except in the light of doctrinal afterthoughts. Also it involves a series of assumptions about the text. In Luke's Greek the phrase is a play on words, *chairé kecharitomené*. This may correspond to a Hebrew original with a similar echo, but then again it may not; Luke may have treated the original freely for the sake of his word-play. St Jerome rendered the Greek into Latin – far from literally – as *ave plena gratia*, which is the basis of the English. But even the Latin is at two linguistic removes from Gabriel. It is surely far-fetched to insist, not only on an inspired original, but on two inspired translations, ending up with a phrase which is not equivalent to Luke's but *may* support the doctrine of Mary's sinlessness.[9]

As for virtue in a positive sense, the entire case rests on her consent in Luke 1:38, her willingness to comply with God's purpose and bear his Son. Catholic writers and preachers revert to this again and again. It is an act of sovereign importance, yes. But surely any Jewish woman who had such a visitant with such a marvellous promise, and believed in him, would have done likewise? Mary is contrasted favourably with Zechariah because, though both have doubts, she finally accepts the message and he does not. Given acceptance, however, consent seems a foregone conclusion. In any case Gabriel does not ask if she will do it. She has no real chance to refuse.

To turn to the next point, there is no sign that Jesus did have a special and lasting care for her. No proof is ever offered but two passages in John. At the start of his ministry he performs the Cana miracle for his mother's sake, and at the end, on the verge of death, he appoints a foster-son to give her a home. Since his tone at Cana is scarcely cordial, the whole idea, scripturally speaking, hangs by the single thread of John 19:26–7; and this is utterly, crushingly outweighed by his not appearing to her after the Resurrection.

Nor, to look from the other side, does she seem specially close to him, or conspicuously loving. When he is twelve and slips away in Jerusalem, she assumes casually that he is somewhere in the party, and starts for home without checking. She takes a day to find that he is missing, and three to run him to earth. His comment that she ought to have looked at once in 'his Father's house' means nothing to her, despite the angel's words. Luke gives no direct dialogue between them after this incident, and Matthew and Mark give none at all.

The Gospels do not tell us – nor do Acts or the Epistles – anything of Mary's later life, or her death. She never even begins to be a spiritual mother of the faithful in general. The text which Catholic authors cite here is John 19:26–7 again – 'woman, behold, your son' and 'behold, your mother' – on the ground that the beloved disciple stands for the whole of Christ's flock. But the saying seems too personal to bear a symbolic load of this kind, and nothing happens afterwards to confirm the reading. At the single gathering which Mary attends after Christ's departure, she does not preside. Indeed, on the strict theological premiss that the Church did not exist as such till Pentecost, there is no certainty that she even belonged to it. The frequent assumption that she was present at Pentecost herself is not proved by Acts, unless the word 'all' in 2:1 refers to all the believers and not only the apostles.

So far as scripture goes – taken at face value, not even critically dissected – Mary's glory as Virgin Mother of the Divine Son is all over when she is barely out of childhood herself. The rest of her life is a long-drawn tragedy of fluctuating and eventually fading hope, with a hideous climax and then near-silence. She inspires more sympathy than words can express. But surely it is a mere intrusive fantasy to construe her grief at the foot of the cross as a willed mystical sacrifice, a spiritual offering, making her Co-Redeemer with Christ.

Catholics object, quite fairly, to Protestant demands that everything must be proved from the Bible. With the Marian cult as with other things, such as papal supremacy, they invoke tradition. But even tradition must, supposedly, have some kind of biblical support. Outside the Marian field, it always has. Inside, it has not. Catholic logic, impartially pursued, does not lead to a Catholic conclusion. To treat the Gospels with respect, and think of the Virgin in relation to what they tell us of Christ, does not in the end justify her cult. Various passages up and down the Bible may be thought to fit her, once she has been raised to her special eminence; but the ecclesiastical case for taking that step, with its appeal to the Gospels, simply collapses.

Not that it confirms negative Protestantism either. It is going much too far to contend that Mary was of minor importance. As we have seen, she may well have been very important indeed, consciously preparing the way, working through family and friends, even trying (for a short time) to stage-manage her Son's campaign. But this is not the kind of importance which the Church has claimed for her; and the outcome, in any case, seems to have been estrangement. Christ diverges from his mother. If he is divine and infallible she is in the wrong, and badly in the wrong. She stands for something which he refuses to stand for. She builds up – or there is built up round her – a Messianic scheme starting from the angelic message, which he repudiates. He is not the king expected; his kingdom is otherwise. It could be argued that the estrangement is an illusion, caused by the Gospel writers' wishing to play down the role of the family. However, the Catholic case cannot be rescued by alleging such a falsification. If the Gospels are as untrustworthy as that, the whole system totters.

Nor does this inquiry make them appear so. With Mary at least, it seems to me, they cohere strikingly and outline the real tragedy of a real woman. But the Virgin of the Gospels is not the Virgin of the cult. We cannot get from one to the other even through apocryphal legend. Christian legend-spinning is strictly secondary to the far stranger thing the Church does.

It institutes Mary-worship, and then tries to justify it by arguments which could only work if the Gospels supported them . . . and they manifestly do not. Stranger still, though the Bible does offer a footing for the cult, this is never directly used. Even where the Fathers of the Church have a case, they seem to cover their tracks so as to appear irresponsible and subjective. A word that comes to mind is 'compulsion'. Another is 'rationalization'. At a definite stage in the Church's growth, the apotheosis of Mary becomes a necessity. There is no overt logic in this. The Church's reasons come afterwards and are mostly feeble, valid only for those who acknowledge the compulsion.

Where then does the story go from here? The obvious thought is that we are now in sight of a confrontation with the Goddess, the Eternal-Womanly. Surely what happened was that her ancient magic surged in, swept recalcitrant facts aside, and re-enthroned her as Mary, the mother of the dying yet life-giving god under a new name? And this is true. But it is far from being the whole truth. As I remarked before, incantatory repetition of words like 'myth' is no substitute for patiently ascertaining what happened. It is not from outside but from within the Christian tradition (at least in the first instance) that a path to the cult, however broken and tortuous, must be traced.

Chapter 6

A BRIDGE WITHOUT
A SPAN

I

While Mary's worship came to mean many things, it certainly
had its roots in one thing. The only credible point of departure is
her special, divinely-ordained motherhood. Let us recapitulate.
The doctrine was centred on the Annunciation, a prophecy we
can accept as truly pre-Christian, at least in substance. The word
translated 'hail', *chairé*, is Luke's relic of what may once have
been a clearer association of Mary with the Daughter of Zion, the
woman standing for Israel, whom two prophets called upon to
rejoice because her King was coming to her; though with Mary
a new and bold idea has been added – that he is coming through
conception in her own womb.

Once this Daughter-of-Zion motif is recognized, it highlights
other occurrences of the same figure, and shows how other
Marian foreshadowings might have been discerned in the Old
Testament. The most important instance is that address to
'virgin Israel' embedded in Jeremiah 30–31, a long prophecy of
the Davidic king and the new age, which the Annunciation
echoes. Its use among believers in Jesus is attested by the New
Testament fully half a dozen times. The crucial 'virgin Israel'
allusion is in 31:21–2, and could fit Mary, at the end of her
Egyptian exile, with unusual biographical neatness.

It raises, of course, a major question. Does it supply what has
hitherto been lacking, a good 'rational' explanation of the Virgin
Birth doctrine itself? The prophecy looks as if it may have been

first applied to Jesus, not in the Church after his death, but in the family prelude when his public career was still to come. Could it be that the word 'virgin' in 31:21 was read originally as a metaphor only – as referring, perhaps, to his mother's purity of soul[1] – and that Christians afterwards, vaguely aware of some doubt or reticence over his origin, took the phrase in a physical sense? Did they go on to insist that the equivocal 'young woman' in Isaiah 7:14 was also a virgin, and improve the birth-stories accordingly?

I do not offer this as The Truth. It is simply a way, if a way is wanted, of conserving the facts without conceding the miracle. What does matter is that even this 'rational' account still keeps our eyes unwaveringly on the same theme – Mary as the woman embodying the People of God, to whom, and by means of whom, the Messiah comes. That theme in fact is the only bridge from the Bible to her cult.[2]

It is a frail bridge. There is little reason to think that Christians in apostolic times maintained any enthusiasm for such a view of Christ's mother. We can see why they might not have done. If Christ diverged from her, the whole idea would have raised complications; and if the parallel with Moses' sister was seriously drawn, it would hardly have escaped notice that Miriam too considered Israel's leader to be going astray and was disciplined by the Lord for her protest (Numbers 12). But the Mary symbolism retained enough vigour – somewhere, somehow – to carry over to Luke . . . just. Scripturally the whole of her later splendour depends on his word *chairé*, which, in its context, is the one vestigial witness to this view of her. For it is only in the light of this view that there is any real reason to detect her in another New Testament scene, where Gospels, Acts and Epistles are left behind, and imagery of a different sort bursts upon us.

I refer to the Apocalypse or Revelation, and specifically to chapter 12. As with the Fourth Gospel we confront the problem of provenance. This book too is ascribed to John, according to some the apostle, according to others a younger man of the same name. It was certainly written in western Asia Minor, where the apostle is said to have gone – specifically, to Ephesus. Though not much like the Gospel, it has verbal affinities which may be due to the presence of the same mind behind both.[3]

It is a Christian essay in a Jewish literary form. In that age of mingled hope and despair, symbolic visions of world events had been enjoying an eager public for a considerable time. They prophesied mighty wars between good and evil, and divine action to change the world. Revelation, which is much more impressive and better planned than its precursors, is the work of a Jewish convert of genius, whether John the apostle or some other. It seems to have been written – or at least put in its present form – late in the first century. Domitian is emperor, and his persecution of Christians is freshly dramatizing the Church's plight. The seer opposes Christ and Antichrist, the People of God and the People of the Enemy, the Church and pagan Rome, in gorgeous and cryptic language which has exercised commentators and cranks ever since. Revelation is the one book of the New Testament which Calvin never tried to interpret; he said that anybody who tackles it is either mad when he starts or mad when he has finished.

The twelfth chapter alone is so remarkable that an eccentric scholar based a theory of Christianity on it, arguing that this came first and the Gospels came afterwards.[4] The only way to present it fairly is to give it in full (the verses are numbered for future reference).

1 And a great portent appeared in heaven, a woman clothed with the sun, with the moon under her feet, and on her head a crown of twelve stars;

2 she was with child and she cried out in her pangs of birth, in anguish for delivery.

3 And another portent appeared in heaven; behold, a great red dragon, with seven heads and ten horns, and seven diadems upon his heads.

4 His tail swept down a third of the stars of heaven, and cast them to the earth. And the dragon stood before the woman who was about to bear a child, that he might devour her child when she brought it forth;

5 she brought forth a male child, one who is to rule all the nations with a rod of iron, but her child was caught up to God and to his throne,

6 and the woman fled into the wilderness, where she has

a place prepared by God, in which to be nourished for one thousand two hundred and sixty days.

7 Now war arose in heaven, Michael and his angels fighting against the dragon; and the dragon and his angels fought,

8 but they were defeated and there was no longer any place for them in heaven.

9 And the great dragon was thrown down, that ancient serpent, who is called the Devil and Satan, the deceiver of the whole world – he was thrown down to the earth, and his angels were thrown down with him.

10 And I heard a loud voice in heaven, saying, 'Now the salvation and the power and the kingdom of our God and the authority of his Christ have come, for the accuser of our brethren has been thrown down, who accuses them day and night before our God.

11 And they have conquered him by the blood of the Lamb and by the word of their testimony, for they loved not their lives even unto death.

12 Rejoice then, O heaven and you that dwell therein! But woe to you, O earth and sea, for the devil has come down to you in great wrath, because he knows that his time is short!'

13 And when the dragon saw that he had been thrown down to the earth, he pursued the woman who had borne the male child.

14 But the woman was given the two wings of the great eagle that she might fly from the serpent into the wilderness, to the place where she is to be nourished for a time, and times, and half a time.

15 The serpent poured water like a river out of his mouth after the woman, to sweep her away with the flood.

16 But the earth came to the help of the woman, and the earth opened its mouth and swallowed the river which the dragon had poured from his mouth.

17 Then the dragon was angry with the woman, and went off to make war on the rest of her offspring, on those who keep the commandments of God and bear

testimony to Jesus. And he stood on the sand of the
sea.

The dragon at least is given a plain meaning. As a monster
he has deep roots in Babylonian myth, but here he is Satan, the
'ancient serpent' of Genesis through whom man fell (verse 9).
The child whom he vainly seeks to destroy (Herod's massacre
again?) is the Messiah, Christ, the world's destined overlord.
The author foreshortens Christ's earthly life, passing straight
from his birth to his ascension into heaven. Who then is the
woman? She is more complex. Her meaning lies in the long-
accepted female personification of the People of God. Several
Christians during the early centuries explain her as standing for
the Church. They are right in principle, but most of them over-
simplify. She is the 'Jerusalem above, our mother' of Galatians
4:26, and she extends through both the Old and New Testa-
ments.

At first she is Israel before Christ, and her twelve stars are the
twelve tribes, an image recalling Joseph's dream in Genesis 37:9.
As dimly foreshadowed by Jeremiah and Micah (see pp. 24 and
25 above), she is in labour to produce the Messiah and eventually
does. Through him the old Jewish community gives place to the
new Christian one; God's people are now the Christians, and
the woman becomes the Church, the new Israel, with no break
in continuity. Her stars are not only the tribes but the apostles,
a correspondence that recalls words of Christ himself ('You
who have followed me will sit on twelve thrones, judging the
twelve tribes of Israel', Matthew 19:28). In verses 13–17,
after Christ's departure from earth, the dragon turns against
the woman and 'the rest of her offspring'. That is, he inspires
persecutions of the Christians, beginning presumably with those
in Acts and growing more savage with those of Nero and
Domitian.

So far so good, but visions and allegories are apt to have
several layers of meaning. Since this woman gives birth to
Christ, we may wonder *prima facie* whether, on a different
level, she is also Mary. Verse 2 clashes with the orthodox
notion that the birth of Jesus was painless; but that particular
verse may not apply to Mary, or perhaps the notion had not

yet taken root at the date of writing. If she injected a completely distinct idea, she would complicate the text too much. But she does not. As we now know, she *was* the Maiden Zion, *was* the female Israel-personified, in whatever tradition Luke caught hold of. To discern her in the apocalyptic woman is only to carry on its logic. The woman's vaguer symbolism as the old Israel comes into focus (so to speak) in the actual Israelite mother who gives birth to the Messiah and marks the transition. Then it broadens out again into her symbolism as the new Israel, the Church.[5]

To admit the Virgin here is to be well on the way to finding a basis for her worship. She is cosmic and glorified. She is personally triumphant over the Devil. Not only does she represent Israel, she passes into a figure of the Church and is mother of the faithful indeed, 'her offspring'. If we are looking for a hint at the Assumption, there it is, poetically at least: she is in heaven as in her own place when the vision unfolds. If we are looking for reminiscences of the many-faced Goddess . . . well, the divine child has no father. The woman bears him alone, like Neith.

Most of what was needed seems to be here in the Bible after all. But there is one drawback. When we move forward and look for these ideas in the Church Fathers, they are not there. After three centuries or so the Mary cult begins entering the life of the Church, yet it enters, apparently, from nowhere. In all that time its sole scriptural credentials have never been mentioned. No early Christian author does point to Mary as Maiden Zion, or read Zephaniah or Zechariah as prophetic of her. No early Christian author does say the relevant things about the apocalyptic woman. She is scarcely ever mentioned, and when she is, the approved view seems to be that she is simply an image of the Church.[6]

The mystery is deeper. A few authors write *as if* these ideas had already been worked out and were familiar, *as if* the twelfth chapter of Revelation had already received its Marian gloss. They give us inferences from it in that spirit. Yet they never acknowledge it as the source. Vital events for the future of Christian doctrine seems to have happened, but they have not happened in orthodox circles, or if they have, the tracks have

1.   Detail from *The Creation of Adam,* by Michelangelo. God's left
arm embraces the female figure of Wisdom, who appears mysteriously
in late Jewish scripture, with a background of Goddess-worship.
Christian liturgy applies the texts about her to Mary.

2. *The Annunciation,* by Botticelli. In earlier medieval art, the angel Gabriel is portrayed standing. Here he kneels. By Botticelli's time, Mary has become the highest of all God's creatures, queen over the angels themselves, even in her earthly life.

been covered. Where written evidence fails, the habitual Catholic appeal is to oral tradition. This, however, is something harder to define than tradition.

2

In reviewing what Christians do say about Mary during those centuries, the first fact to grasp is how many of them say nothing, or very little. Modern Mariologists seldom bring this out. They show her presence in various texts but not her absence in others. By quoting Justin Martyr and Irenaeus, who mention her, they make it appear that she was much thought of; by not quoting Clement of Rome, Hermas, Polycarp, who give them nothing to quote, they leave their readers unapprised of a silence.

So far as any discussion of her occurs, most of it is very much as the Gospels would lead us to expect. Marian ideas which they do not warrant do not appear, or appear only sketchily, disputably, and without emphasis. Mary is the Virgin Mother of Christ with the stress on Christ, whose divine nature the miracle proves.

The only point worth pausing over is that several details given by the earliest writers are not quite in harmony with the Gospels.[7] Thus Ignatius of Antioch, about 110, says in a letter that when Jesus was born . . .

A star shone in heaven brighter than all the stars. Its light was indescribable and its novelty caused amazement. The rest of the stars, along with the sun and moon, formed a ring around it; yet it outshone them all.

This recalls Matthew but is by no means the same. The outshining of the sun and moon is an injudicious rhetorical flourish, yet even without that the story is different. A few decades later, Justin Martyr deals with the Virgin Birth at some length, comparing it with pagan myths such as the birth of Perseus. Several times he seems to have Matthew or Luke in mind, yet something is always just a little wrong. Although he mentions the Magi, he puts their visit before Joseph's first dream; and

E

although he quotes the Annunciation, he makes Gabriel say that Jesus will save his people from their sins . . . which is conspicuously not what Gabriel says. No Father of the Church cites the birth-stories exactly as we know them till Irenaeus, about 177. The Virgin Birth is plainly a strong tradition taking various forms, not a fiction foisted on Christianity by Matthew and Luke and then merely copied from them.

In Irenaeus himself, and for more than a hundred years after him, the miracle remains focused on Jesus and not on Mary. Christians of this period are arguing with heretics who dissent from it on one side or the other, claiming either that Jesus was born like anyone else, or that he was a kind of divine phantom never born in the flesh at all. The Virgin Birth is opposed to both views, and Origen, in the first half of the third century, makes it clear that the doctrine is well known among pagans as a Christian tenet. Mary is not merely the Virgin but the Ever-Virgin; that too is made increasingly clear, and never called in question by any orthodox Christian.[8]

By the fourth century Christians have said all they have to say about the Virgin Birth in its implications for Christ. They now begin to think of it in relation to Mary.[9] Their interest is less exclusively in the advent of God's Son, rather more in the virginity of the mother, and her marvellousness in her own right. But they are wholly retrospective. They look back on the event and enlarge on it – mainly, it must be confessed, to draw morals about the virtue of shunning sex.

Within the Church, these reflections go on through a period equal to the whole time from Queen Anne to the present without even beginning to set Mary up as a living object of worship, as a hearer of human prayers, or as anything more than a revered figure of sacred history. In that context her cult simply never dawns, and the stress on her early rather than her later life suggests an awareness that the accounts of her Son's maturity supply little evidence for her closeness to him, and little material for her praise.

There are a few anticipatory gleams of the glorification that is still far off, but they are puzzling. Justin Martyr, in a panegyric composed about 155, praises Mary as the Second Eve who cancelled the doom brought by the first.

[Christ] is born of the Virgin, in order that the disobedience caused by the serpent might be destroyed in the same manner in which it had originated. For Eve, an undefiled virgin, conceived the word of the serpent, and brought forth disobedience and death. But the Virgin Mary, filled with faith and joy, when the angel Gabriel announced to her the good tidings . . . answered: 'Be it done unto me according to thy word.' And, indeed, she gave birth to him . . . by whom God destroys both the serpent and those angels who have become like the serpent, but frees from death those who repent of their sins and believe in Christ.

Irenaeus takes up the theme.

For as Eve was seduced by the word of an angel [that is, a fallen one] to avoid God after she had disobeyed his word, so Mary, by the word of an angel, had the glad tidings delivered to her that she might bear God, obeying his word. And whereas the former had disobeyed God, yet the latter was persuaded to obey God in order that the Virgin Mary might be the advocate of the virgin Eve. . . . The guile of the serpent was overcome by the simplicity of the dove, and we were set free from those chains by which we had been bound to death.

So also Tertullian, and Origen, though briefly.[10]

These paragraphs, as they stand, are somewhat far-fetched. The authors are turning over an idea which they hold on other grounds than the Annunciation story itself. It might appear that a hint has been taken from Paul in Romans 5:12–14 or 1 Corinthians 15:22 – 'As in Adam all die, so in Christ shall all be made alive.' But the step from Christ as Second Adam to Mary as Second Eve would have been unthinkable. Eve was Adam's wife, not his mother. To place Mary in this relationship would have been, for the orthodox, a factual outrage and worse: it would have re-evoked the Goddess with her son-spouse, Cybele with Attis.

Christians did in fact steer clear of the Pauline texts. The one that emerges as a basis for the Eve-Mary linkage is, at first sight, curious – Genesis 3:15. After the Fall, God says to the serpent: 'I will put enmity between you and the woman, and between your seed and her seed; he shall bruise your head, and you shall bruise his heel.' The woman must be Eve, since no other exists. But the speech came to be read as a Messianic prophecy. The seed of the woman, destined to bruise the serpent's head, was Christ; and her meaning (so to speak) was completed by Mary. That continued to be the Catholic view. In the words of a modern commentator: 'As the final fulfillment of the prophecy of the "seed" is verified only in Christ, so "the woman" who bore the seed is finally fulfilled in the Blessed Virgin.'[11]

The impression, surely, is that this obscure verse cannot be the source of the idea and does not even support it convincingly. In fact it is only mentioned after Mary has been established as Second Eve without it. The real scriptural basis can only be the vision we have already encountered, Revelation 12. Here the woman, through her child, does triumph over the 'ancient serpent', who recalls Genesis in plain terms (verse 9). In an intelligible sense she is Eve over again, assailed by the Devil but with a happier outcome. To see Mary in her would be to see Mary as the Second Eve.

It has been cogently urged that somebody must have done so. Apart from Revelation there is no passage in scripture which would suggest casting her in that role. Some have argued that Genesis 3:15 inspired the apocalyptic imagery. But even if it really was in the background, it was only through the imagery it inspired that Mary could have been brought into such a forced-looking relation with it. Whether or not Genesis 3:15 belongs here, it seems wholly plausible that the authors who launch the Second Eve theme should have drawn it from the apocalyptic source. Justin was converted at Ephesus, where Revelation was published and Johannine traditions lingered on; he even quotes 12:9, though in another connection. Irenaeus was a native of the same area and a disciple of Polycarp, who was a disciple of John himself. Yet the riddle remains. We cannot catch Justin or Irenaeus or any other early Christian associating the woman of the Apocalypse with Mary. Those who speak of the Virgin as the Second Eve, defeating Satan, never cite the chapter where alone she may be judged to appear in that capacity. The idea presupposes a train of thought which has been suppressed.[12]

Another motif to glimmer on the horizon is Mary's symbolism of the Church, and in that sense – not yet in her own person – her motherhood of all the faithful. Irenaeus detects such a symbolism vaguely in her 'pure womb which regenerates man unto God'. Tertullian regards Mary and the Church as both prefigured by Eve, therefore associated. Origen is more curious than either. In one passing allusion, without doctrinal stress, he proposes Mary as mother of the perfected Christian though not of Christians in general. This notion takes the form of a tortuous metaphor in the introduction to his commentary on John.

The Fourth Gospel, Origen says, is the one that brings us closest to the fullness of Christianity. Nobody can fathom it except by becoming 'another John', living close to Jesus and 'receiving from Jesus Mary to be his mother also'.

> For if Mary, as those declare who with sound mind extol her, had no other son but Jesus, and yet Jesus says to his mother, 'Woman, behold thy son', and not 'Behold you have this son also', then he virtually said to her, 'Lo, this is Jesus, whom thou didst bear'. Is it not the case that every one who is perfect lives himself no longer, but Christ lives in him (Galatians 2:20); and if Christ lives in him, then it is said of him to Mary, 'Behold thy son Christ'.

Thus Origen appeals to the incident at the cross which later becomes the classic 'proof' of the spiritual motherhood.[13]

Coming from a man of immense learning and intelligence (even Bertrand Russell gives him two and a half pages in the *History of Western Philosophy*), this is strangely circuitous and strangely pointless. Why bring Mary in at all? Why not simply say that the Christian who aspires to understand John's Gospel must become like him, in perfect unity with Christ? For some reason Origen wants to introduce the Mother as standing in a special relationship to the mystical communion of believers, even though the thought is obscure and is never followed up afterwards in his works. The passage is his involved rationalization of an idea that is already current and has commended itself to him. And the single text which offers a real basis for it, yet goes unmentioned, is not this one but the same which alone supports the Eve idea: Revelation 12. By Origen's time, it seems, somebody has discerned Mary in the woman of the Apocalypse and thus made her a figure of the Church, with Christians as her children (verse 17). But Origen has either not heard of this or chosen to keep silence. When a version of the symbolic motherhood finds its way into his writing, it is awkwardly imposed on a text which does not prove it and would not, to an unprompted reader, suggest it. Yet this is the text which the Church later invokes. Again a more natural train of thought is presupposed; again it seems to have been suppressed; and it is the same one as before, the Marian reading of Revelation 12.[14]

For the present we can only note such behaviour as a hint at matters undivulged, and pass on. The idea of Mary as the Second Eve, helps to endow her, over the years, with further attributes. 'It is this theme,' says the Jesuit Paul F. Palmer, 'that is developed with ever-unfolding variations in what may be called the Church's symphonic hymn to Mary.' To some extent at least Father Palmer is right, but he fails to underline the extreme slowness and deviousness of the process.

Till well on in the fourth century, the only 'variation' that calls for comment is the belief defined long afterwards as the Immaculate Conception – Mary's absolute sinlessness, her freedom even from original sin, as the chosen vessel without a flaw. Her title as Second Eve may be regarded as part of the ground for it, because she cancels the First and is, as it were, Eve-without-the-Fall.

The Catholic case for the antiquity of this belief is negative. The earlier Fathers never say in plain terms that the Virgin could not go wrong. On the other hand, one senses a mounting hesitancy among them to say that she ever did. For whatever reason a notion of her impeccability can be seen making its way among the faithful. Hippolytus, early in the third century, compares Christ to the Ark of the Covenant made of incorruptible wood, and this wood, in his figurative sense, means 'the Virgin and the Holy Spirit'. But the belief contends against a nagging awareness of what the Gospels suggest and the Church later has to explain away, Mary's estrangement from Jesus. Irenaeus finds fault with her 'untimely haste' at Cana, and accepts that Christ did reprove her. Tertullian questions whether she believed in him at all. Origen thinks that although she did, her faith wavered at the end. John Chrysostom accuses her of trying to domineer and to 'make herself illustrious through her Son'. Commenting on Matthew 12:46–50 (the Capernaum incident mentioned on p. 109), he argues that Jesus is being kind and might well have spoken more harshly of his relatives – 'This is not my mother, nor these my brethren, because they do not do my will.'

In spite of Chrysostom, and in spite of the lack of any positive statement, Mary's sinlessness gains ground in the faith of the Church. About 415 Augustine sums up the consensus attained by then. No one however holy, he says, has been without sin, with the exception of the Virgin Mary. She alone was pure.[15]

Yet throughout most of this development there is no inkling of the cult which is to absorb and develop such honours. Orthodox writers devise new ways of thinking about the Virgin. They give her an exalted part in the salvation of man. They hold her up as a theme for meditation. But she remains a figure of the past, one to think about indeed, but not to engage in dialogue with. They do not enthrone her as present Queen of Heaven, or as a living intercessor with God. Nor do they make her a demi-goddess herself.

The origin of the cult still escapes us. Nevertheless we are not quite empty-handed. Through the first three or four Christian centuries we have a sense of things unsaid, omitted, excluded from the orthodox picture. Those who speculate about Mary seem to be borrowing from another context, where she was seen in the apocalyptic woman, the woman whose children are Christ and all his people, and whose thwarted enemy is the ancient serpent. They borrow, yet they disavow, even at the cost of leaving their thoughts foundationless, propped up by texts which are unequal to the load. The Marian logic seems to have been pursued in some school of thought which the Fathers owe a debt to but will not acknowledge. This may also have been the source of the doctrine of Mary's sinlessness, which no Father even mentions, yet which exerts a slow and successful pressure against adverse evidence.

The natural guess is that we ought to look for some popular movement or heretical sect, from which Marian ideas seeped into the mind of the Church. Can we find it?

3

A popular movement might be expected to show itself in popular legend. Among rank-and-file Christians there was always a demand for more information about the New Testament characters. It was strongest when concerned with the Holy Family. Ordinary people were more interested in homely detail than they were in the exploits of apostles and preachers. Yet here the Gospels were tantalizing. They gave enough to provoke questions, seldom enough to settle them. Story-tellers who professed to know more found a ready audience. Their talents, however, were selective. Like some of the Fathers, they seem to have been aware that the family side of Christ's adult life had an unhappy quality. Most of the legends that survive dwell on the early years, when he was still a child or unborn, and his mother's future looked bright before her.

We have already seen in Chapter 4 what the *Book of James* or *Protevangelium* has to say. It testifies to the early belief that Mary was not only a virgin when she conceived but a virgin always, even immediately after giving birth. It also proves that popular legend, however apocryphal, could infiltrate orthodoxy. Mary's alleged parents, Joachim and Anne, were enrolled among the saints. Her absurd childhood in the Temple under a vow of virginity, with Joseph an old man appointed to be her guardian, was accepted with only slight modification as factual. The *Protevangelium* was a main source for an even wilder book, supposedly written by Matthew as a supplement to his Gospel, which was faked about the ninth century, and supplied medieval artists and poets with most of their uncanonical stories of the Virgin's youth.[16]

A theme much favoured by other fanciful minds was the Flight into Egypt. Egyptian Christians loved to enlarge on this. They described incidents of the journey and assigned them to exact locations, such as Matarieh, where a spring of fresh water (a rarity in that country) burst forth for the Holy Family's refreshment, and a sycamore grew to shade them. An Egyptian legacy to the whole Church was a legend linking the Flight with the story of the thieves crucified alongside Jesus. One was said to have been a Jew, the other an Egyptian. They robbed the Holy Family, but the Egyptian took pity and restored the meagre loot. It was he who repented on the cross thirty years later and was promised paradise (Luke 23:39–43). The tale is a curious adaptation of the motif of long-lost friends and relatives and surprising reunions, so dear to playwrights of the later Greek theatre, their Roman imitators, and their successors well into the Victorian era.[17]

To point this out, however, is to define the essence of the matter. Such stories are not theological or devotional but romantic. Even where they centre on Christ himself, as in the 'Infancy Gospels', the utmost they do is to portray him working miracles – some rather charming, some repulsive – at an earlier age than the New Testament admits. These infancy legends, like the writings about the Virgin Birth, tend as time passes to dwell more on Mary than on her child. Thus, while he is still a baby, she works miracles herself by allowing the sick to touch his clothes or to sprinkle themselves with water he has been washed in, whereupon they are healed. But there is no tendency to raise her above humanity, and there are no forays into doctrine or exegesis.[18]

It may be added that the same is true of her first appearances in art. They are in simple Roman catacomb paintings. The oldest are open to doubt precisely because they are so purely human. We cannot be certain that the subject is Mary at all. She seems to confront us in a fresco in the cemetery of Priscilla, dating from the first half of the second century. Very rough and blurred, and almost monochrome, it shows a robust-looking mother holding a baby in her arms. Beside her a man stands pointing. He has usually been explained as Isaiah drawing attention to the Virgin foretold.

This catacomb has another, clearer picture, painted about a hundred and fifty years later. It depicts a serious-faced young mother suckling her infant. She wears a white robe with a purple border, the dress of a Roman lady. Again her identity is not certain. More nearly proved is a fourth-century fresco portrait in the Caemeterium Majus. Here Mary is full-face with the Child in front of her. She is dark, with strong eyes and somewhat heavy features, anything but ethereal; a Mediterranean peasant type, though with a rich necklace betokening importance. Apart from an affinity of hair-style, this Virgin has no likeness to the previous one. The artist is not working in a tradition, whether authentic or fictitious. His Virgin is bare-headed, whereas in most subsequent art her head is covered. Also he makes her an Orante, that is, she is in the ancient posture of prayer, her arms spread and her hands raised. She is not being prayed to, or inviting it; she is praying herself.[19]

So much for the simpler faithful, their stories and their pictures. Christians of a more intellectual cast composed fiction of their own. Here the prospect of Marian deviation may seem better, because, undoubtedly, some of them did flirt with the paganism around them, and were more exposed to the irruption of pagan themes – Isis-worship for instance.

One zone of contact was the propaganda of the Sibylline Oracles.[20] The original volumes known by that name were collections of verses, supposed to have been uttered by a long-ago prophetess, which were kept in Rome and consulted in times of crisis. When these were destroyed by fire, a government attempt to reconstitute the collection produced 'Sibylline verses' by the thousand. The frenzy of forgery continued for many years. Some of the most adroit forgers were Jews who made the Sibyl foretell a Messiah. From the late second century onwards, Christians were publishing the Jews' work in improved editions. Their new Oracles contained direct 'prophecies' of Christ, and bits of the Gospel history purportedly seen in vision by the Sibyl.

The authors have enough knowledge and skill to give them a faintly pagan air. The Sibylline Christ is a divine child who ushers in an age of renewal, as in Virgil's mysterious Fourth Eclogue. However, while the Virgin Mother is mentioned, she never sounds like a goddess or has any attributes taking us clearly outside the Gospels. When Gabriel speaks to her she undergoes a rapid surge of conflicting emotions:

Terror and surprise
Seized her at once as she heard, and she stood
In trembling, and her mind was filled with fear,
Her heart leaped at the messages unknown.
But she again was gladdened, and her heart
Was by the voice cheered, and the maiden laughed,
And her young cheek blushed, merry with the joy;
And she was spell-bound in her heart with awe.

Mary's laughter is pagan, not Jewish. But it is also human, not divine.

In those centuries, however, the major paganizers were Gnostics. It is among these, or under their influence, that we might really hope to find Mariolatry. In the eyes of such churchmen as Irenaeus, Gnosticism and heresy were synonymous. According to Irenaeus the father and founder of all heresy was Simon Magus, the Samaritan magician in Acts 8:9–24, who accepted baptism but thought he could buy spiritual power for money. Several forms of Gnosticism branched out from his teachings. Some of them were independent systems rather than heresies. Most, however, made use of Christian ideas, though with a different bias. The religion-building of orthodox Christians was always, in essence, an attempt to interpret Christ; Gnostics started by working out a religion and then fitted Christ into it, with whatever mangling they found necessary.

These systems were complicated. They deployed vast arrays of hitherto unheard-of celestial powers. Gnostic masters drew on pagan philosophy and mythology, and while they also drew on the Bible, they twisted it without mercy. Gnosticism of every school was cliquish, and closely akin to magic. It taught salvation through knowledge (in Greek, *gnosis*) rather than faith or works. Knowledge, furthermore, did not mean knowledge in general but *secret* knowledge, confined to initiates; and salvation meant employing it to realize one's true spiritual nature, and soar upward into a select heaven. The world of matter was despised as hopelessly evil. The God of the Old Testament had created it, as the Bible said, but he was a fallen being. True deity was far above him. According to some schools the serpent of Genesis was an envoy of light. Gnostic contempt for the material world extended to the body, which was a mere trap for the spirit. One inference was that all sex-relations and the production of children were to be viewed with disfavour.

Some apocryphal Christian books show touches of Gnostic influence, or, at any rate, wander into similar dubious fairylands. Their authors invent grotesque visions and divulge secrets unknown to scripture. Or they betray Gnostic attitudes, such as a morbid hyper-spirituality denouncing sex as such, even in marriage. Where virginity has a value still higher than Paul gives it, we might expect to find new thoughts about the Virgin herself.

We do, but the harvest is not abundant. To begin with, there are obstacles over dating. Several of the books are too late to have had anything to do with the origin of the Mary cult. Sometimes it can be proved, even with late ones, that older versions existed or that older ideas are filtering through. But in the texts that might tell us something, Marian motifs are infrequent.

Those that do occur are bizarre. Two are in pseudepigraphic writings – that is, works falsely ascribed (like the Sibylline Oracles) to persons living long before, who were thus made to 'prophesy' Christ. The *Ascension of Isaiah*, which may have been composed about the same time as the Fourth Gospel, denies that Mary gave birth at all in the vulgar material way of women. Her baby, it declares, simply appeared in front of her. She was amazed, as well she might be. (Further stories in the same vein inform us that the infant materialized out of light, and that he was weightless, never needed cleaning, never cried, and had adult intelligence: a real science-fiction monster.) In the *Odes of Solomon*, written before 150, Mary does give birth. However, she does it not only without pain – by now an accepted Christian belief – but 'as if she were a man, of her own will'. The phrase suggests the primeval mother Neith.[21]

After these two items, most of the eccentric Marian matter is preserved in Coptic, the language of the Church in Egypt and Ethiopia. Coptic literature includes a *Discourse on Mary* ascribed wrongly to Cyril of Jerusalem, who lived in the fourth century. This quotes a 'Gospel to the Hebrews' as telling how, when Christ willed to become man, his Father summoned 'a mighty power in the heavens which was called Michael', and 'the power came down into the world and it was called Mary, and Christ was in her womb seven months'. Here the Virgin herself incarnates a celestial power, but it seems to be impersonal, and its name is confusing. Pseudo-Cyril disapproves of the doctrine and the alleged Gospel, which, being lost, cannot be checked or exactly dated. But he himself is favoured with a revelation that is more bewildering still. The Virgin comes to him in person from whatever heavenly mansion she occupies. Having spoken of her childhood and family, she goes on: 'I am Mary Magdalene because the name of the village wherein I was born was Magdalia. My name is Mary of Cleopa' (i.e. Clopas). Therefore she was all three of the Marys at the foot of the cross; or they were all the same, a kind of female trinity; one hardly knows how to put it.[22]

Somewhere this esoteric notion seems to have been traditional. There are three pieces of writing that remedy Mary's absence from the Resurrection by expanding it to bring her in, and two of them do it by equating her with the Magdalene in the garden scene (John 20:11–18). They are both Coptic. One is a fragment only. The other is a more copious *Book of the Resurrection of Christ by Bartholomew the Apostle*. This gives pride of place to the Bartholomew known also as Nathanael, and may derive from a lost Gospel once ascribed to him. Though it is not itself older than the fifth century, the source-'Gospel' is mentioned by St Jerome in the fourth and may have been earlier.[23]

The *Book of the Resurrection* is scrappy, muddled and fantastic. When Mary – that is (on the face of it) the Magdalene – is at the empty tomb, Christ appears 'on the chariot of the Father'. He addresses her as 'Mary the mother of the Son of God', and she replies, 'Son of God the Almighty, my Lord, and my Son'. He hails her with a long series of titles of praise, mingling Christian and Gnostic terms. Being warned not to touch him, as in John 20:17, she says: 'If indeed I am not permitted to touch thee, at least bless my body in which thou didst deign to dwell.' He does so, and departs in a great company of angels. When he appears again in Galilee he comes 'to console the apostles and Mary', but we hear no more of her.

Another book which may give us bits of the same lost 'Gospel' is *The Questions of Bartholomew*, composed in Greek, and translated, after a longish interval, into Latin and Slavonic.[24] It takes the form of a series of dialogues and visions. The apostles, with Bartholomew as their spokesman, are talking to the risen Lord. In at least two episodes Mary is present.

When she appears first they are in a place called Cherubim or Chairoudec or Cheltoura (readings vary), described further on as 'the place of truth'. At this point Christ is not with them. Bartholomew wants to question Mary about the mystery of the Incarnation: 'Let us ask her that is highly favoured how she conceived the incomprehensible, or how she bare him that cannot be carried, or how she brought forth so much greatness.' When Peter and John hesitate, Bartholomew puts the question himself. She answers: 'Ask me not concerning this mystery. If I should begin to tell you, fire will issue forth out of my mouth and consume all the world.' They insist, however. So Mary stands up and 'spreads out her hands toward the heaven', as in the early picture of her. Having uttered a prayer in twenty-two unintelligible words, wrongly said to be Hebrew, she sits down again and requests four of the apostles to sit close, because she fears that the disclosure will have deadly effects on her.

Then she tells a story of her early life in the Temple (the *Protevangelium* legend), describing how on a certain day 'one in the likeness of an angel' came to her with bread and a great cup of wine. He ate and drank, and so did she, and the bread and wine were as before. He said: 'Yet three years, and I will send my word unto thee and thou shalt conceive my Son, and through him shall the whole creation be saved. Peace be unto thee, my beloved, and my peace shall be with thee continually.' After which he vanished from Mary's sight. . . . The story gets no further. Before she comes to her actual conception, fire issues from her mouth. Jesus appears and says: 'Utter not this mystery, or this day my whole creation will come to an end.'

It is a strange scene, with no parallel anywhere else. The thought is that the full secret of the Incarnation is known only to Mary, in whose womb it happened. The bread and wine are the elements of the Eucharist, which, in Catholic doctrine, are the body and blood of Christ; but the suggestion here is that Christ came to earth in that form before he came as a human being, and entered his mother by a communion. The twenty-two cryptic words, the great cup, and the blinding revelation of God-made-man which the apostles approach but do not achieve, all foreshadow a more famous theme of irregular Christianity, the Holy Grail. But the key is missing.

The second Mary scene in this book occurs on the Mount of Olives. Peter urges her to question Jesus about 'the things that are in the heavens'. She demurs, saying it is for Peter to ask. Her reason is unexpected.

'Thou art the image of Adam: was not he first formed and then Eve? Look upon the sun, that according to the likeness of Adam it is bright, and upon the moon, that because of the transgression of Eve it is full of clay. For God did place Adam in the east and Eve in the west, and appointed the lights that the sun should shine on the earth unto Adam in the east in his fiery chariots, and the moon in the west should give light unto Eve with a countenance like milk. And she defiled the commandment of the Lord. Therefore was the moon stained with clay and her light is not bright. Thou therefore, since thou art the likeness of Adam, oughtest to ask him: but in me was he contained that I might recover the strength of the female.'

The sting of her speech is in the tail. Mary as Second Eve is here, in effect, the special saviour of women, with a possible reminiscence of Jeremiah 31:22 (p. 100) above. Peter argues that she has 'brought to nought the transgression of Eve' and may properly inquire on celestial matters. However, the dialogue stops there. Bartholomew forestalls them both with a question about the Devil.

In these pseudo-Gospels and kindred books we are certainly catching glimpses of something. Like the works of the Fathers, they hint repeatedly at a corpus of Marian doctrine outside the mainstream. But there is little overlap and little enlightenment. They fail to explain what the Fathers say themselves, or what happens afterwards when the cult develops. No Marian school of thought is as yet in sight. Still, Gnostic influence is present, though it may be neither direct nor extensive; and other apocryphal books where it is absent add no more. Can we make any progress by turning from the Christian apocrypha to the teachings of avowed Gnostics?

It is sometimes more or less assumed that the Gnostics invented Mariolatry and the Church adopted it. This is a mistake. Though the Virgin had a place in their systems, it was a very humble place and far removed from the regions of light. They did re-introduce the Eternal-Womanly in a form linked with Judaism, but not so as to encourage Christians to cast Mary in the same role.

Simon Magus, the heresiarch himself, took the first step. It was more engaging than some of the later Gnostic exercises. He went about with a prostitute named Helen whom he had picked up in Tyre, and he made dazzling claims for her. There was, he taught, a celestial being called Sophia – i.e. the Lady Wisdom of Proverbs and Ecclesiasticus by her Greek name – who had suffered a 'fall' and was condemned to a series of earthly lives. She had been Helen of Troy and sundry other women, and she was now Simon's companion, rescued by him from a nadir of degradation, and set on a pathway back to glory as *Kyria* or heavenly Queen. His followers set up statues of the pair of them as Zeus and Athene. While the later Gnostics lost interest in Helen, they enlarged on the theme of that immortal Sophia who had dwelt in her body. In effect Sophia became a version of the Goddess, but a fallen version, with an unlovely mythology placing her well below the summit.

Even when some Gnostics involved her in the birth of Jesus, even when some connected her with a primordial entity called the 'Mother of Christ', they never did it in a way likely to inspire a Christian cult of Mary. They were talking about entirely different things. In any case Gnosticism was damnable heresy and Helen was an unsavoury precedent. The most Gnosticism can do is draw attention to motifs that were current in speculative circles. It never shows us the 'Marian school of thought' even in embryo.[25]

4

By the middle of the fourth century Christianity had entered a fresh phase. Thanks to the Emperor Constantine it had ceased to be persecuted and become the state religion. The Council of Nicaea, held in 325 under his aegis, had published the Nicene Creed, which (among much else) re-affirmed Christ's birth from the Virgin Mary. Nicaea built that miracle into the ideology of the Roman world. It now had an altered stress already remarked upon. The focus was no longer on Christ-as-miraculously-conceived, it was on Mary-as-miraculously-conceiving, and as still pure and intact after giving birth. Eusebius, Constantine's right-hand man in Church matters, adverted to the theme in a speech praising the Emperor. 'Why is it impossible,' he said, 'that she who was with child of the Holy Spirit should be, and ever continue to be, a virgin?'

With hindsight we can see the Nicene developments fixing the ground-plan for Mary's worship. The reason was eloquently explained by Newman. His words, however, require a preface.

The Gnostics who theologized Wisdom were reviving, in their own narrow field, a debate which Christians held to be closed. Nicaea was prompted by what they thought to be its final eruption, at any rate within the Church. Long before Christ, it will be recalled, the Lady Wisdom was projected by Jewish anguish at the remoteness of God. She was then a holy intermediary between Above and Below, a created being indeed but the first of all, God's primal utterance and chief agent in his work. Hers were the law, harmony and beauty of the cosmos. In the words of the Wisdom of Solomon (8:1), she 'reached mightily from one end of the earth to the other, and ordered all things well'. As she had spoken through Moses and made her home in Zion, the Chosen People had access, in her, to all they needed to know of the divine counsels. The Lord could be transcendent so long as Wisdom stayed within reach.

Fear of so seductive a demi-goddess impelled pious Jews to treat her as an allegory of the Torah. In Ecclesiasticus 24 Ben-Sira, or an interpolator, explains at the end of the Wisdom rhapsody: 'All this is the book of the covenant of the Most High God, the law which Moses commanded us.' But even those who said so had to give the Torah a mystical meaning, setting it up as a kind of supernal pattern or order prior to the universe, which Moses merely expounded when the time came.

That idea had further potentialities. Presently the philosopher Philo, an Alexandrian Jew influenced by the arch-pattern-maker Plato, executed a manoeuvre that seemed to dispose of the demi-goddess entirely. The essence of it was that he changed her sex. In his hands Wisdom was depersonalized to a merely symbolic status. The qualities that had given her so much character were transferred to a male power, the Logos or Word, hovering in metaphysical interspace. For practical purposes he absorbed and supplanted her. Like the Wisdom of the apocryphal books, Philo's Logos was the first of created beings. Like her, he was God's agent in making everything else. Like her, he was the cosmic order. Like her, but with a new linguistic point, he spoke to mankind through the 'word' of scripture. Apart from gender the main difference was that he was more sharply defined. Wisdom had been a shape-shifter. She could sometimes be taken virtually in the normal sense, as a human quality only barely personified. The Logos could not. He was more abstractly conceived, yet he was more consistently a being.

Philo's theories were never popular with his fellow-Jews, but they supplied Christians with a method of interpreting Christ, and this was what Nicaea was chiefly about. An affinity between Christ and Wisdom – or the Logos – began to emerge in Christian thought between AD 70 and 90 in the Epistle to the Hebrews. The Wisdom of Solomon (7:26) had called Wisdom 'a reflection of eternal light, a spotless mirror of the working of God, and an image of his goodness'; and in Hebrews (1:3) Christ was said to 'reflect the glory of God and bear the very stamp of his nature'. Not long afterwards, the author of the Fourth Gospel adopted Philo's Logos in plain terms. 'In the beginning was the Word. . . . The Word became flesh and dwelt among us.' Thanks to that amazing preface, the Divine Son became the Logos and the 'true' or male personal form of God's Wisdom, coming down from heaven as Jesus. But the language applied to him continued, as Philo's did, to echo descriptions of the feminine antetype. His Johannine title still recalled her if mutedly, since she had been in effect God's 'word' herself in Ecclesiasticus 24:3, 'coming forth from the mouth of the Most High'. He was co-creator as she had been: 'he was in the beginning with God; all things were made through him.'[26]

Likeness of language, however, did not prevent a profound change of concept. Convinced that the Son was wholly one with his Father, Christians moved the Logos upward into the Godhead itself as the co-equal Second Person of the Trinity, incarnate in Jesus, but eternal and uncreated as Philo's Logos was not. The primary business of Nicaea was to define that doctrine more precisely. The heretic Arius had shifted the Logos downward again to the level where Philo placed him first. Arius maintained that the Son was a created being, prior to all others indeed, greater than all others, but not God as the Father was God. In effect Arius re-affirmed Wisdom but as a male being instead of a female one, intermediate between Above and Below, and appearing in human form as Christ.

Nicaea condemned him. The Council's decrees declared the Son to be Very God and no less. They saved the Incarnation as an event in history, God truly becoming man, the heart of Christian belief . . . but at a price. The Son's establishment in the Triune Godhead tended to give him the same remoteness that had troubled Yahweh's worshippers long before. It renewed the sense of a gulf between earth and heaven. Granted, he had come down among humankind, but it was all very long ago now. He had soon returned to the Father and for three centuries no mortal eye had seen him. Even when Arius was not only anathematized but dead, a feeling persisted that his instinct had not been altogether at fault. A living semi-divine intermediary *ought* to exist. There was a cosmic gap which such an entity *ought* to bridge. Arius's view of Christ lingered on for some decades in the Roman Empire, with backing in high places, and missionaries carried it beyond the frontier. But there could be another answer, consistent with the Nicene Creed. The Lady Wisdom — in a new guise and under a new name — could be summoned back, and co-exist, at her own level, with the wholly deified Logos.

On this let Newman now be heard. He argues that Arius's idea of Christ as a demigod only, though dismissed by the Church, started an irreversible train of thought. The status proposed for him and rejected, or something like it, came to be allotted to his mother instead.

The Arian controversy . . . opened a question which it did not settle. It discovered a new sphere, if we may so speak, in the realms of light, to which the Church had not yet assigned its inhabitant. . . . Thus there was 'a wonder in heaven': a throne was seen, far above all created powers, mediatorial, intercessory; a title archetypal; a crown bright as the morning star; a glory issuing from the Eternal Throne; robes pure as the heavens; and a sceptre over all; and who was the predestined heir of that Majesty? Since it was not high enough for the Highest, who was that Wisdom, and what was her name, 'the Mother of fair love, and fear, and holy hope', 'exalted like a palm-tree in En-gaddi, and a rose-plant in Jericho', 'created from the beginning before the world' in God's counsels, and 'in Jerusalem was her power'? The vision is found in the Apocalypse, a Woman clothed with the sun, and the moon under her feet, and upon her head a crown of twelve stars. [27]

As his quotations show, Newman knows very well where materials for the cult lay ready to hand. Mary could be raised skyward through assimilation to the woman of the Apocalypse, and to the resplendent Wisdom of Ecclesiasticus 24, so long as the latter process kept close to scripture and avoided the taint of Gnostic myth. We might add today that the Virgin had an allure of her own because of the abiding need for a female power, for the Goddess in fact, whom a rigidly male Trinity excluded. (Heretical attempts to improve the Trinity by changing the sex of its Third Person, the Holy Spirit, had not been successful. [28])

But this, I repeat, is hindsight, and it leads only to a half-truth. The pressures, the yearnings, the potentialities were there. They helped to prepare a milieu in which the cult could unfold. But they did not produce it; not directly or in them-selves. The plain fact is that within the Church, through four or five decades after Nicaea, neither the panegyrics of theologians nor the fancies of legend-weavers actually did exalt the Virgin further, or make her a living mediator whom the faithful could pray to. As yet there was almost nothing to work upon. Materials for the cult existed, but Christianity had not thus far taken the slightest notice of them. If the Fathers saw Mary in Revelation 12 they had never said so, and they had never connected her with the figure of Wisdom.

The Marian matter in Christianity was as we have seen, a miscellany. It comprised the New Testament passages about her, some pious reflections on them, a medley of legends, and various weird fancies and speculations. There was no coherence in this, no direction, no tendency towards an apotheosis. No quasi-divine personality had even begun to coalesce. Therefore, while the 'new sphere' might indeed be visible in the 'realms of light', the Church was not yet ready with an inhabitant to assign to it.

Nor could it rapidly become so. Nicaea did begin to define a Marian tendency, and this was not a tendency to promote but to reduce. The reason lies in a change in the Church's attitudes to holy people in general, dead and living. Before Nicaea, under recurrent threat of persecution, the ideal Christian was the martyr; and by the third century, Christians had begun praying to martyrs and seeking their intercession.[29] That practice could be justified from the Bible, since in Revelation 6:9–11 it was implied that the martyrs were in God's presence, aware of events below and able to petition the Throne of Grace. Mary was not included in this first scrupulously restricted cult of the saints, because there was no tradition of her being a martyr.

She fitted, however, into a new class of saints which the age of Constantine raised into favour. With persecution ended, the ideal Christian was no longer the martyr but the ascetic. Lacking opportunity, he did not shed his blood for the Faith, but he suffered for it by his own choice. Monasticism, known to the Jews but not hitherto adopted by Christians, was fast spreading through the Church. First in Egypt, then in other parts of the East, a growing army of men and women opted out and withdrew under vows to cells and communities, or into total seclusion within the home. Asceticism meant honouring virginity, if it was chosen as a way of life, and obviously Mary was the queen of all virgins. But deceased ascetics were not yet prayed to as martyrs were; and neither was she. Instead she was held up as an inspiration, and lessened, not deified, in the process.[30]

A minor document of the Council of Nicaea shows how.

> A wise virgin resembles Mary. . . . Mary never saw the face of a strange man, that was why she was confused when she heard the voice of the angel Gabriel. . . . She withdrew all by herself into her house, being served by her own mother. But when she went to her mother she could not tell her a word about her condition, because she had sworn to herself not to tell anyone in this world anything at all about it. She sat always with her face turned towards the east, because she prayed continually. Her brothers wanted to see her and speak to her, and she did not receive them. For the angels came many times to her; they observed her singular way of life and admired her. She slept only according to the need of sleep. . . . When she put on a garment she used to shut her eyes.

This dreadful portrait is sheer fiction, composed without regard for the Gospels to make Mary a *consecrated* virgin, a virtual nun and a pattern for nuns.

Such for the moment was the orthodox trend. Athanasius, Arius's strongest opponent, took up the imitation-of-Mary theme a few years later in an address to religious virgins in general.

> She did not want to be seen by men. . . . She remained continually at home, living a retired life. . . . She generously distributed to the poor what was left over from the work of her hands. . . . She prayed to God, alone to the alone, being intent on two things: not to let a bad thought take root in her heart and to grow neither bold nor hard of heart. . . . Her speech was recollected and her voice low. . . . She was not afraid of death, but rather was sad and sighed every day while she had not yet crossed the threshold of heaven.

Though Athanasius does not make her quite such a little monster of piety, he still makes her essentially little – drawn in and cramped, so to speak, by her own miraculous motherhood. Orthodoxy was narrowing down, focusing on her early life and on a single aspect of that. Christians were still free (at least in places) to censure her behaviour later, when perhaps 'bad thoughts' had taken root after all; John Chrysostom did. The young Mary continued unscathed, but as an enshrined example, no more. The Council had doubtless opened a gap between earth and heaven, but despite Newman, its by-products and sequels disqualified the Virgin from filling it.

5

Is that really so surprising? Today one can talk casually of Christianity being paganized, and polytheism returning through worship of Mary and the saints. But because this did in some degree happen, it is too easy to forget the weight of resistance, and shrug off the problem of its ever having begun. If the Church eventually turned its Virgin into a new Isis or Cybele, the reason was not that churchmen drifted absent-mindedly into doing so, but that some positive Goddess-making factor – some factor which has thus far escaped us – was stronger than their will not to do so.

For three hundred years Christians had rejected paganism and all its ways with utter revulsion. Many had undergone torture and death at the hands of pagan powers. To contaminate the Faith from that source would have been not merely error but treachery, a betrayal of the martyrs. Gnostics might attempt fusion, loyal Christians did not. If they meddled with paganism at all it might well be to take the offensive, as in the matter of the Sibylline verses, rather than make concessions. Christ was worshipped as a Mystery-cult saviour, or something like one, only because that view of him was embedded in scripture. He had suffered and died and risen, and St Paul had expounded those events. Even here Christians were so rootedly anti-pagan that although some admitted the likeness, they ascribed it to diabolic agency: Satan had faked pseudo-Christs, such as Attis and Osiris, to weaken the claims of the true one when he came. Heathen deities in general were demons – in other words, fallen angels opposed to God. The persecutions confirmed their reality and malice. It has been shrewdly remarked that during Rome's long decline, almost the last thinking believers in the old gods were their Christian enemies. A pagan might laugh at

Apollo as a fable. A Christian would shudder at him as a malignant spirit. [31]

To speak glibly of paganization, and the installation of Mary as quasi-Goddess, is a sleight-of-hand which evades the difficulties. In a sense it happened, but how? Where scripture did not supply the basis it did with Christ – or, at any rate, was not construed as doing so – there was no way it could *just* have happened, however propitious the climate might be in theory.

No Christian who valued his salvation would have identified Mary with the fiend Isis, and no bishop would have condoned the practice. Once her apotheosis had taken place, she could attract Isis motifs to herself as she presently did in art and legend, piecemeal, disguised. [32] But the starting-point had to be further back, in a development not against the grain of Christian tradition. Moreover, the quasi-deification of a woman was specially and peculiarly against the grain, because of Simon Magus and Helen. The woman for whom the thing had already been done was the harlot mistress of a Samaritan sorcerer. That episode had been put on record by Christian authors and firmly condemned.

Nevertheless, all the barriers crumbled. They crumbled because they were undermined from within and broken from outside. We have seen how the Fathers witness to Marian thoughts, Marian teachings, in some quarter that was influential yet never acknowledged. Whatever its nature, the pressure from that quarter increased till Christianity altered. The process began quite suddenly and was completed within a lifetime. Mary was enthroned in the heavens. She came to be hailed as a living power, an intermediary between Above and Below, an object of adoration.

We not only find this to be so, we even find her endowed with attributes claimed by Simon for Helen. She, it will be recalled, was Wisdom passing through a series of incarnations. Despite that deterrent, Mary did come to be associated with Wisdom: Newman, in the passage quoted, is not indulging in rhetoric but transcribing the Church's own language. If we move forward in time, to take a look at this, we may well have the same puzzling impression that something started outside the official fold and was then adopted, or partly so, within it. In the words of a more recent author, Louis Bouyer:

What is perhaps the most remarkable point in this application of Wisdom texts to the Virgin is the spontaneity with which it seems to have happened. One cannot cite any great theologian as having proposed it. But we discover it in the liturgy, both eastern and western, as the object of a tacit agreement, of a universal instinct which was not the product of intellectual speculation but rather an incitement to it.

Bouyer is not referring to some obscure fancy, but to the very public fact that when Mary acquired holy days of her own, the Wisdom texts were woven into the scriptural readings for them.[33]

Stranger still in view of the scapegrace Helen, we get hints that Mary has had other earthly lives. These fade out after a pronouncement against reincarnation in 553, but they cannot quite be ignored. Peter Chrysologus, Archbishop of Ravenna and a saint of the Church, has this to say in a sermon preached before the middle of the fifth century:

Mary is called Mother. And when is Mary not a mother? 'The gathering together of the waters he called seas (maria)' (Genesis 1:10). Was it not she who conceived in her single womb the people going out of Egypt, that it might come forth a heavenly progeny reborn to a new creation, according to the words of the Apostle: 'Our fathers were all under the cloud, and all passed through the sea. And all in Moses were baptized, in the cloud, and in the sea'? That Mary might always lead the way in man's salvation, in her own right, she went with a canticle before that same people, whom the generating waters had brought forth to light.

Here the Mother of Christ is mystically the waters, a true Goddess-touch. But she is also her namesake Miriam, the sister of Moses, singing her song of triumph after the safe passage of Israel out of Egypt. Peter's images blend into one another and cannot easily be reduced to mere metaphor. Later, Irish Christians regard St Brigit as the Virgin returned to earth.[34]

It is worth taking this glance ahead to grasp the immensity of the change between Athanasius and Peter Chrysologus. The Marian advent was not a device of the hierarchy. It was not an irruption of Gnosticism. Bishops and intellectuals took it in charge once it had clearly happened, but the impulse came from elsewhere. A force outside the recorded life of the Church gathered strength, bore down resistance, and carried Mary aloft into the place prepared for her, where she was crowned by public acclaim as a democratic heroine. A date can be fixed for the bishops' endorsement of her cult: it is 431. However, the events of that year only set the seal on a process which had begun about sixty years before.

We have one document of the change near its point of origin. One witness gives a glimpse of the thinking which had gathered round Mary for three centuries, had impinged on the Church without greatly affecting it, but now moved in to triumph. The witness is Epiphanius – not the Epiphanius who described Mary's appearance, but an earlier, more distinguished figure, whose information about her is better grounded and highly intriguing.

Chapter 7

THE SEVENTY-NINTH HERESY

I

Epiphanius was born about 310, at Besanduk in Palestine. His parents were Christians and veterans of persecution. Reared in that atmosphere, he showed a single-minded religious vocation from an early age. He learned all the languages he needed for the full study of scripture, and joined a community of monks in Egypt. According to his own (much later) account, beautiful Gnostic women used to lend him books and attempt to win him over. True to ascetic form he went off and told the bishop. Returning to Palestine in his twenties, he was ordained priest and founded a community of his own at Eleutheropolis. His experience in Egypt had alerted him to the seductions of heresy, and he decided that the Church's worst peril came from Origen, whose intellectual poison he combated throughout the rest of his long life.

At Eleutheropolis he became a sort of oracle for the eastern Church, receiving countless visitors, and picking up rumours and reports from all quarters. In 367 he was elected bishop of Salamis in Cyprus. Popular with the masses for his practical charity, he was less popular with the churchmen whom he was constantly abusing for reading Origen. St Jerome described him as 'a last relic of ancient piety'. His refusal to compromise on what he regarded as the Faith led him into such actions as tearing down a church curtain because it had a picture on it. But it also led him to write a valuable survey of unorthodox doctrines, attacking them from the standpoint of an ancestral Christianity which he knew as thoroughly as any man living.

The *Panarion* or Medicine-Chest, as he called his book on heresy, was written between 374 and 377. It is rude and bigoted, and so far-reaching as to be slightly absurd: it deals with no fewer than eighty heresies, and the definition is stretched to include pagan religions long before Christ; but it embalms many traditions which are otherwise lost to view.

Epiphanius is a staunch upholder of Mary's perpetual virginity. But he draws the line in his zeal for her, and it is illuminating to see how he draws it. Two sections of his book are aimed at two contrary errors. One (Heresy No. 78) is the error of the 'Antidicomarianites' or Opponents of Mary, who claimed that she had sexual relations with Joseph after Jesus's birth. In rebuttal, Epiphanius goes over familiar ground. He then turns to the contrary error of the 'Collyridians' (Heresy No. 79). This is a nickname. Whatever the true title of their sect, it brings us into the presence of something unprecedented, dropping out of nowhere into Epiphanius's tract.

The Collyridians, he explains, are mostly women. He vilifies them as silly, weak, contemptible. Yet according to reports which have reached him they are much more than a local coterie. They began in Thrace and have spread their cult into Upper Scythia. (These, roughly, are the lands to the west and north of the Black Sea.) They have also spread it to Arabia. Nothing is said of any countries between, but the range is impressive, implying a fairly long existence before the time of writing. Wherever Collyridians flourish they have 'assemblies' or 'associations'. And they worship Mary as Queen of Heaven, with a ritual derived from far back beyond Christianity.

They adorn a chair or a square throne, spread a linen cloth over it, and, at a certain solemn time, place bread on it and offer it in the name of Mary; and all partake of this bread.

The ceremony goes on for days. Epiphanius denounces it with bitter scorn. The word 'Collyridian' itself is a sneer. It is coined from the Greek *kollyris*, which is found in the Greek version of 2 Samuel 6:19 and means a little loaf or roll. The bishop is oddly close to calling these women Holy Rollers.

He says what almost any Church spokesman would certainly still have echoed without reservation: 'Let the Father, the Son and the Holy Spirit be worshipped, but let no one worship Mary.' In leading up to that maxim he makes a tell-tale admission.

> God came down from heaven, the Word clothed himself in flesh from a holy Virgin, not, assuredly, that the Virgin should be adored, nor to make a goddess of her, nor that we should offer sacrifice in her name, nor that, now after so many generations, women should once again be appointed priests . . . [God] gave her no charge to minister baptism or bless disciples, nor did he bid her rule over the earth.[1]

This is a hint that Collyridians are feminists, who resent a Church founded on male supremacy, and look to Mary as their head. Epiphanius warns against women in religion, and aptly recalls the ones condemned by Jeremiah, who made similar offerings to the Queen of Heaven (7:18); in their case, Astarte.

What exactly was this cult, and where had it come from? Was it, properly speaking, a heresy at all – that is, an exaggeration or distortion of a prior orthodoxy? We have seen the difficulty here. Within the Church, up to this time, there has been no trace of public devotion to Mary as a living being who can receive worship, hear prayers, or 'rule over the earth' in even the mildest sense. Since, before Epiphanius, there has been no trace of it, there has been no trace of its getting exaggerated or distorted by heretics. It has not been there to exaggerate or distort. So far as we know, Mary's cult began with these Collyridians, began with her adoration in her own right as a form of the Goddess. It is hard to say when this happened, but a cult so widely spread by the 370s is likely to have originated several decades at least before that. Epiphanius's information may itself reflect an earlier state of affairs when he was at his listening post in Palestine; it is known that his inquiries in the later years of his life were much less active and conscientious.

At any rate, he lifts the curtain for a moment on something more profound than a heresy. We can make sense of it (and perhaps of much else in virtue of that) by accepting his data at face value. What he has caught sight of is not a Christian vagary but another religion, drawn from the same sources, but distinct.

Taken by itself this is a radical notion, and in the light of what we have disinterred it may be even more radical. The 'Marian school of thought' is a ghostly recurrent presence that has proved elusive. Collyridianism, simply as described, is prior to any organized Marian worship that can be proved among Christians. But has it an ancestry? Is Epiphanius merely noting one ritual of an older, more serious Marian religion? Out of his fund of Christian lore, he produces two linked ideas which suggest that he may be. They give him trouble, because he is rather inclined to favour them, but cannot approve the Mariolatrous milieu where they seem to belong. Hence he keeps them apart from his account of the Collyridians, and puts most of what he has to say in the previous section, where he can deploy it more safely against the opposite heretics who reduce the Virgin too far.

Almost casually, he supplies that lack in earlier Christian teaching on Mary – her assimilation to the woman of the Apocalypse, which, once granted, gives a basis for doctrines that seem disjointed and unintelligible: her role as the Second Eve, her spiritual motherhood of the faithful, perhaps her sinlessness. First of all Fathers, so far as written evidence goes, Epiphanius detects her in Revelation 12. But he approaches the topic by a strange path, and introduces it, when he arrives, in a strange form.

He has been reviewing various ideas about Mary's life. One is the belief that she lived in the home of John permanently, went to Ephesus with him, and died there. We have no proof that she did, says Epiphanius. John's looking after her may have been only temporary. We simply do not know what became of her.

If any think I am in error, let them search the traces of Mary in the scriptures, and they will find there no mention of her death, neither whether she died nor whether she did not die, nor whether she was buried or not buried. And then with regard to the journey of John when he set out for Asia Minor, nowhere do we read that he took the holy Virgin with him.

Thus far, one would think, he is merely underlining what ought to be obvious, and warning against legend-spinning. The phrase 'neither whether she died nor whether she did not die' is surely just rhetoric, no more than that. Only . . . it is more than that. He means it. His next move is into mysterious territory. Scripture, he asserts, veils Mary's fate on purpose, so as not to 'perplex minds' by an 'exceeding great marvel'. What marvel? 'I do not dare to say it,' he tantalizingly goes on, 'but thinking about it preserve silence.'

After hovering in the same style for a few lines more, he comes to Revelation 12 and his Marian reading of it.

> St John tells us in the Apocalypse, that the dragon hastened against the woman who had brought forth the man-child, and there were given to her the wings of an eagle, and she was taken into the desert that the dragon might not seize on her. This then may well have been fulfilled in Mary. However I do not decide, nor say that she remained immortal; nor either will I vouch that she died.

Further on he reverts to the subject.

> Either the Blessed Virgin died and was buried, in which case she fell asleep in honour, her end was chaste purity and the crown of virginity adorns her; or she was murdered, as it is written: 'And thy own soul a sword shall pierce' (Luke 2:35), in which case she shares the glory of the martyrs and her sacred body, from which the light of the world arose, is venerated; or she remained [i.e. did not die], for it is not impossible for God to do everything that he will. For no one knows her end.[2]

Epiphanius seems to connect Revelation 12, verses 6 and 13–14, with a mystery over Mary's fate; with a disappearance rather than a demise, and a consequent rumour of immortality. His statement that 'no one knows her end' is almost certainly true. It is echoed as late as the seventh century by another bishop, Modestus, who sweeps aside a vast growth of legend to re-affirm that the Church has no tradition of Mary's passing. Nor, when Epiphanius hints at the immortality notion, is he likely to be indulging in mere spur-of-the-moment fantasy. Such a zealous foe of all heresies would not have wantonly sown the seeds of a new one. He has an actual belief in mind (one he has heard, perhaps, in Egypt or Palestine) and he is willing to entertain it. He has to be careful, however, partly because it is strictly unofficial, partly because it is an obvious prop – perhaps even a motive – for the Virgin-worship he deplores.

2

Let us look at his two ideas separately, and then see what it is that relates them.

His citation of St John supplies that image of Mary-in-the-Apocalypse which the Fathers' words seem to presuppose. As it comes into Epiphanius it is too late to be their source. But it takes, in any case, an eccentric-looking form which is not directly connected with what they say. Nor could it have been inferred from them. Nor does it link up with any later development. Catholics have claimed Epiphanius as the first witness to Mary's Assumption. Whatever he has in mind, it is not that. The woman is not caught up to heaven but carried to a retreat in the wilderness, and her sojourn there is for a limited period, though the cryptic time-scale may allow the period to be long.[3]

This paragraph in fact is so curiously 'other', so unlike anything else in the Fathers, that it may well be a fragment of that ancient interpretation outside the Church which they seem tacitly indebted to. It raises, moreover, a valid point which orthodox commentators seldom if ever face. The woman stands for God's people, first Israel and then the Church, and if she is also Mary she is Mary only as representing these. So at least say the commentators. Yet the author does draw a distinction, and it is just here that Epiphanius lays his exegetical finger.

When the dragon threatens the woman, she escapes to the place prepared for her. Having failed with her as with her divine child, he goes away to make war on 'the rest of her offspring', the Christian community (verse 17). But if the woman herself stands for that community, how can he be said to turn from one to the other? How can Christians be still in danger if the woman who symbolizes them is safe? Here the planes of the vision seem to divide. When she flees to the wilderness, it is not easy to explain her in any other way than Epiphanius's, as the Virgin individually. The reference could be to a flight from the early persecutions in Jerusalem. If so, Epiphanius may have hold

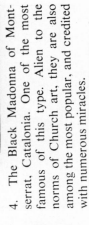

3. Michelangelo's *Pietà*. The Virgin with her crucified Son. So far as the Gospel record goes, this is the last time she ever sees him.
Rome, St Peter's

4. The Black Madonna of Montserrat, Catalonia. One of the most famous of this type. Alien to the norms of Church art, they are also among the most popular, and credited with numerous miracles.
Foto Mas, Barcelona

5 and 6. 'La Vierge
Ouvrante', a painted
wooden figure by a
German artist,
probably fourteenth-
century. When
opened, the
Madonna is seen to
contain the whole
Trinity. (The Holy
Spirit, a dove at the
head of the cross, is
now very faint.)
*Musée de Cluny,
Paris*

of a tradition of the Apocalypse's meaning that has drifted down to him all the way from the first century.[4]

When he puts forward his other special idea, that perhaps Mary never died, the key word is 'remain'. It is the same used in the Fourth Gospel (21:22 and 23) to make the same suggestion about the beloved disciple, John himself. Mary's exemption from death is not an isolated fancy. It fits into a recognized niche in Christian legend.

Notions of physical immortality arose early as a by-product of the delay in the Second Coming. Christians had expected their Lord's return quickly. They thought he had promised that some of his contemporaries would live to see it. The relevant text is Matthew 16:28 – 'Truly, I say to you, there are some standing here who will not taste death before they see the Son of Man coming in his kingdom.' Paul seems to know and accept the promise (1 Thessalonians 4:15–17), and indeed it looks so plain that it drove Albert Schweitzer to a momentous conclusion: Jesus could be wrong. No early Christian would have admitted such a blasphemy. As more and more of the first generation died, attention narrowed down to the survivors. At last it was claimed, by some, that Jesus had made the promise to a specific person, who would be preserved miraculously for as long as required.

A phrase in one of the Resurrection stories caused this belief to fasten on John. He did outlive many of his colleagues, but before the writing of the Fourth Gospel, apparently, he died. As Jesus could not have broken his word, it was resolved that the phrase must have been purely hypothetical, and that is how John's 'remaining' is handled (21:20–3). Even so a rumour persisted that he never actually had died, though he was no longer on earth. Ambrose and Augustine testify to it three centuries later.[5]

It is this belief in an undying contemporary of Christ that surfaces again in the Middle Ages with two fictitious immortals called John Bottadio and Cartaphilus. Both names recall the son of Zebedee ('Cartaphilus' means 'most beloved'), but immortality is conceived now as a penance rather than a blessing. Legend finally transfers it to the Wandering Jew, who spurns Christ from his door on the way to Calvary, and is condemned to live without rest until he comes back. When Epiphanius thinks of Mary as deathless he has, of course, no foretaste of such a grim development. Whatever happened to her was holy.

Though no one else confirms the idea positively, there is one negative fact suggesting that popular thought did favour her immortality; or, at any rate, did draw back from commitment to her death. This is the complete absence, throughout those early generations, of a grave for her – even a reputed grave – and bodily relics. Jerome, writing in Palestine in the late fourth century, mentions various holy sites real and alleged, but no tomb of the Virgin. Such a tomb may have been asserted a little later, but that takes us well into the fifth century, when many ideas were changing. As for relics, Christians hoarded the bones and dust of their holy dead from at least as early as 156, when Polycarp was martyred. Fragments were enshrined as mementoes, and credited with marvellous properties. Genuine relics produced a much larger crop of bogus ones, and the claims extended backward to characters in the Bible. But so far as is known, nothing was ever exhibited that presupposed the corpse of Mary. Invention reached a point where garments of hers were put on show, and drops of her milk. Yet some curb always forbade a claim to her bones, or her dust, or (until a new doctrine altered the situation) her grave. She was not to be thought of as physically dissolved.

So Epiphanius may well preserve an early-planted belief in Mary's 'remaining', due to a query over her end. She might still be on earth in some secret place, she might be in celestial regions, but anyhow she was a glorified being whom God had preserved from death. The question, however, is who precisely propounded this belief and in what form. Martin Jugie, a major authority on Marian doctrines, has argued that it existed simply as a devout opinion commonly held by Christians. Most other authorities retort that the Church, so far as can be made out, always accepted that Mary did die, even though it eventually added that she was revived and assumed to heaven directly afterwards. It is the same pattern as before, at a different level. An idea affects Christianity, in this case popular Christianity, from a source which seems to be outside it and is never acknowledged. [6]

Thus Epiphanius's words suggest that when he condemns the

Collyridians, he is discussing only one aspect of a larger thing, which he has come into contact with at other points: a long-standing Marian religion with beliefs of its own. He knows some of these beliefs and finds them attractive. But as the religion is separate from the Church he cannot give credit or be open, and, in fact, it is hidden by clerical and anti-feminist silence till his own slight lifting of the veil. Christian origins would not preclude such a 'branch' religion. Our survey of the Gospels, showing Mary passing into a kind of detachment, is quite in keeping with the growth of a mythos of her own, aside from the main Christian milieu.

An unanswered question is why Epiphanius connects the two ideas; why his 'exceeding great marvel' puts Mary's everlasting life in the context of the Apocalypse. Remarkably, the Apocalypse gives the answer itself. Epiphanius drops a hint that he has it in mind, but virtually 'preserves silence'. It is there all the same, and a further clue to a definite and early tradition unrecognized by the Church.

The woman of the vision is to be 'nourished' in her desert retreat – the curious word 'nourish' occurs twice – and she is to live there in safety for 1,260 days or 'a time, and times, and half a time'. This is a period of three and a half symbolic years, variously expressed, which John (as we may call the author) assigns to the reign of evil powers. It has already started with the oppression of Christians, and it is to end in some dimly-descried future with the triumph of Christ. John takes the actual duration from Daniel 12:7, where it alludes to a persecution of Jews (by Antiochus) which came to be seen as a mystical prototype of persecutions in general: three and a half years is a period that stands for the reign of evil.

But it is found before the Apocalypse in another context. It comes into the story of the prophet Elijah. 1 Kings 17:1–6 tells how he announced that the Lord had empowered him to bring a drought upon Israel, as punishment for the sins and Baal-worship of King Ahab. When it began, he withdrew by divine command to a place in the wilderness east of Jordan, out of Ahab's reach, and was fed by ravens. The Old Testament does not say how long the drought lasted, but in the New Testament the baleful three and a half years is applied to this too, perhaps because it was a time of persecution as well. Jesus speaks in Luke 4:25 of 'the days of Elijah, when the heaven was shut up three years and six months'. In the Epistle of James we read (5:17): 'Elijah was a man of like nature with ourselves and he prayed fervently that it might not rain, and for three years and six months it did not rain on the earth.' Elijah's miracle is glanced at in Revelation itself (11:6) shortly before the woman appears. When John portrays her going to a safe place in the wilderness prepared by God, and being 'nourished' there as Elijah was by ravens, for a period that matches his drought, he must intend a parallel with the prophet.[7] Again there is sound reason to detect Mary here as an individual. A parallel drawn with one human being implies another.

What then is it? In what sense could Mary be a female Elijah? As a fugitive, if she was. Or with more weight, as the embodiment of the true Israel. In 1 Kings 19 Elijah too sees himself as the faithful remnant of God's people holding out against Baal ('I, even I only, am left; and they seek my life, to take it away'). Though he cannot produce a child as Mary does, he is divinely commanded to anoint a new king, Jehu, who becomes a first sketch for the Messiah and thus a foreshadowing of the child born in Revelation 12.

But in the light of what Epiphanius says, such likenesses are eclipsed by another. To New Testament Jews and Christians, the outstanding fact about Elijah was that he had not died, and never would. He was a man who had strangely vanished and was immortal. The stirring events of his career – his triumph at Carmel over the prophets of Baal, his discovery of God in the 'still small voice', his attack on royal injustice – were of much less interest than his passing, and his existence afterwards. The passing is described in 2 Kings 2:6–18. With his successor Elisha, he goes again to the country over Jordan and is whirled up to heaven in a fiery chariot, leaving his cloak in Elisha's hands. A seldom-emphasized footnote is that Elisha's vision of the chariot is not conclusive. In fact he does not report it at once. Fifty men search for Elijah for three days before they give him up. The crucial point is the disappearance. His earthly end is a riddle, and although God is acknowledged to have taken him, legend leaves his abode imprecise and tells of his coming back to revisit the world.

To sum up, the apocalyptic woman, when we last see her, is a female Elijah; John's carefully-chosen language shows that this is no afterthought of commentators, but a theme present to his own mind at the time of writing, in AD 96 at latest; and the way the idea comes through to Epiphanius suggests that its inspiration was a belief that the mother of Christ, like Elijah, departed mysteriously and was exempted from death. This is Epiphanius's 'exceeding great marvel' and the basis for his cryptic remarks.

So we have, at last, a presence of Mary in Revelation (without prejudice to more canonical ways of finding her there) which is early enough to explain those passages in the Fathers, and indeed much beyond them. To compare her to the harsh Hebrew prophet may seem far-fetched, yet as soon as we have the clue, we begin to notice them together in other places. For whatever reason, tradition vaguely connects them. Epiphanius does so himself in his Collyridian section, saying that Elijah is not to be worshipped 'though he is still among the living' and neither is Mary, though her honour is even higher. He also mentions a strange notion, often found later, of Elijah's perpetual virginity. The only apparent motive for this is a wish to bracket him with Mary.[8] In the Middle Ages the two are often linked by mystics of the Carmelite Order, and, unexpectedly, by Moslems. Here it would be ranging too far to consider how. Enough for the moment that the linkage is a motif which does recur, and that there is no adequate reason for it apart from the parallel which Revelation 12 seems to preserve.

But the parallel's chief basis – Mary's immortality, or rather her non-death – is totally foreign to early Christian statements of faith. Moreover it is unlikely that Christians of the first century would have invested her old age with any miraculous glory. Her absence from the Resurrection tradition would then have been too grave a deterrent. Her deathlessness can only have been a tenet of a school of thought independent of the Church, which could be borrowed from (as by John), but not given any publicity.

The belief itself might well have been enough to inspire such a school. This theme of the human Immortal, the great or beloved figure who is dead-yet-not-dead, gone-yet-not-gone, has a tremendous and proven power over imaginations. Outside the Judaeo-Christian system the most famous is King Arthur, of whom it is said that his grave is not to be thought of, that his end is withheld from mortal knowledge; he is alive in a cave or the Isle of Avalon, awaiting the hour of his return, and myths of the Celtic gods have gone into his making. After him come Barbarossa of Germany, Sebastian of Portugal, and even modern political heroes such as Parnell and Zapata.

But Elijah remains more interesting. To grasp what legend did with him is to appreciate what it might have done with Mary, or (looking at the matter from a different angle) to see how her cultic attributes might have taken shape in a sect where she was reckoned to be undying like him. With Elijah the Bible gives an early stage of the process, no more. It touches on his expected role as herald of the Messiah, which John the Baptist fills in a figurative sense. But the notion of a still-living prophet occurs in the Gospels in other ways, as when Jesus himself is rumoured to be Elijah, and when a bystander at the Crucifixion says 'Wait, let us see whether Elijah will come to take him down' (Mark 6:14–15; 15:36). These are the merest glimpses of a legend that was gaining ground among Jews.

Elijah, it presently declared, was unseen but ever at hand, Israel's guardian and comforter through the weary ages. He was deathless because he had never sinned, and therefore never incurred Adam's penalty. When the Angel of Death did try to claim him, God said: 'He is not like other men. He is able to banish you from the world, only you do not recognize his strength.' There was a combat which Elijah won, and he would have destroyed Death if God had not restrained him. He made his heavenward ascent with the vanquished arch-enemy beneath his feet. Some rabbis believed that he was not human at all, but an angel who had been present at the Creation, and volunteered to live on earth. Whatever his nature, his home was now among the heavenly host, where he welcomed the souls of the righteous and interceded for Israel. Some day he would return in visible majesty to anoint the Messiah and raise the dead. Meanwhile he was not confined to the upper regions. He travelled about the world, often in disguise. He came as a friend of the poor and humble, as a rescuer from peril, as an enlightener of scholars and sages. A picturesque folklore portrayed him doing so.

Judaism in fact made him an intermediary between Above and Below such as many Christians desired after Nicaea. In the fourth century some of those Christians seem to have followed the Jewish lead and invoked the prophet, under his Greek name Elias, to bridge the gulf. In the eastern Church he became 'Saint Elias'. Inscriptions in his reputed cave on Mount Carmel testify to honours paid him from the fourth century to the sixth. Theologians, especially in Syria, expanded him into a giant of mystery and legend, celestial patron of both the active and the contemplative lives, the founder of monasticism and the destined forerunner of Christ's Second Coming. Seventy-five churches in the Byzantine Empire were dedicated to him, and so was the first church built in Russia, at Kiev. [9]

If 'Saint Elias' progressed no further, it was not because Christians felt no need for such an intermediary, but because, by then, they had found a better one in the Virgin Mother. They could scarcely have turned to her as and when they did if they had known her only through the Gospels and the limited homage of the Fathers. There, Elijah had simply no competition from her. But if in Epiphanius's uncharted tradition they were alike, with Mary also going away and passing secretly into another mode of existence, then Elijah shows what she might have become in virtue of that. Deathless, pure, and by inference without sin of any kind; triumphant over the powers of darkness; at home in the courts of heaven, no mere spirit but body and soul complete; an ever-active intercessor and comforter; a friend of individual mortals, close at hand in their earthly pilgrimage – all these words describe the Elijah of legend, yet they also bring us close to the Mary of devotion.

3

We have reached, or almost reached, the limit of history. The next few pages are historical fiction. A cautious flight of fancy seems justified here. If it turns out (as I think it does) that a coherent, credible story can be devised which will account for the whole Marian phenomenon, that story has a claim to be seriously considered: not as proving anything, but as offering arguable hypotheses where they are much needed and in short supply.

The disastrous end of Jesus's Messianic career was agonizing for Mary several times over, and threw her into near-despair. A few days afterwards his disciples, including two members of her family, insisted that they had seen him alive. She was unable to disbelieve but powerless to hope; she had seen nothing herself. To her the Resurrection was not the restoring miracle it was for the others. It was one more riddle. As the weeks passed with further appearances, but never to her, it became a heart-rending riddle. She could see no answer. The Annunciation long ago had surely been true, yet now it was falsified. Her Son was not on the throne of David and was not reigning over the house of Jacob. Yet she clung to the conviction that she had not been deluded, not totally. She needed to reflect and put her world together again. Meanwhile she remained friendly with the disciples, but never attempted to advise them or take a part in their work.

Life in Jerusalem was tranquil at first, and John saw that she was taken care of. After a few years the first persecution broke out. She was nearly sixty, but neither age nor sex was a guarantee against harassment, and John helped her to move away to a country retreat. In going, she had more than a mere escape in mind. Memories of the Baptist influenced her, and so did stories Jesus had told her of the desert communities, of Qumran and the Essenes. If men could go into a meditative retirement, why not women? She took a younger companion with her. It proved impossible to halt there: others joined them, one or two being women who had followed Christ during his lifetime. In his mother's company they felt closer to what they had cared for than they did in the Church.

Mary herself was virtually cut off from the Church. With its ex-tormentor Paul won over, its troubles were temporarily eased, but she stayed where she was and declined to meet the great new apostle. Paul had never known Jesus personally, and to make matters worse from Mary's point of view, he claimed loudly that Jesus had appeared to him after death. (Her aloofness from Paul is the reason why he never refers to her, and, in his praise of virginity, never cites what ought to be his crowning example.)

She realized that the apostles were building up a distinct sect within Judaism and possibly more than that. To define its message they were looking backward over her Son's career and resolving what it had all been about. James was with them to supply biographical background; Paul came and went with controversial ideas of his own. Mary, after her fashion, was sadly trying to unravel the same tangle. But whereas most of the men knew little more than the end, she knew the beginning, and the far-off things which she had 'kept in her heart'.

She talked to her companions about the marriage with Joseph, the dreams and visions, the birth and its sequels. Or some of them. Herod's slaughter in Bethlehem, which she still felt responsible for, was too painful to dwell on. So was the unhappy exile in Egypt. These topics she preferred to avoid. She spoke of the later years too, of the family's immense hopes, and the rabbi who told her she was the prophesied Daughter of Zion, custodian of the whole life of her people. Here too, however, where memory encountered anguish, she became sketchy.

Her companions treasured her recollections. They interwove her own song the *Magnificat* with other songs and stories, some contributed by a woman who had known Elizabeth in her old age. They put together a brief vernacular Gospel of Mary, preserving the Annunciation, despite the facts that now seemed to refute it. For them she was unique, sometimes like a prophetess, sometimes like a Mother Superior, always a tragic and revered figure. She was behind the whole Christian development; none of it could have happened without her; yet she had no place in it. All its leaders, they gathered, had seen the risen Lord, yet she had not. If he had truly come back, why not to her? She was known to be cherishing a dream that their meeting might still take place before she died, bringing peace and enlightenment at last.

In that little circle of hers, opinions about Jesus were divided. Some of the women privately wrote him off as a failure, or worse, a betrayer. Others accepted the Resurrection without knowing what to make of it, and clung to a kind of faith in him. Among the latter there was one who recalled his reputed promise that some person or persons now living would survive to witness his Second Coming. She suggested that whoever else he had meant, he was thinking particularly of his mother. Surely he would not simply let her perish uncomforted? Perhaps he had left her out of his Resurrection only to give her a privilege of her own – preservation from death till he returned in glory.

This idea prepared the community to come to terms with her actual passing, which was mysterious. In her sixties, still healthy and active, she set off on a pilgrimage she was reticent about. Her companions never saw her again. Being well grounded in scripture and rabbinic lore, they quickly drew the parallel with Elijah. Mary was indeed immortal, and she would live on, somewhere, till the Second Coming re-united her with her Son; or he had taken her to himself already, without death.

The community too lived on. It attracted recruits and visitors. Among the latter was Luke, who copied down its miniature Gospel and eventually used this in his own. It gave him material for his first two chapters. He also worked in a scene with a bearing on the Resurrection; but as this underlined Jesus's non-appearance to Mary, in a way that raised doctrinal difficulties, later editors censored it out – leaving a glaring gap in the narrative after 24:43.

Another visitor was John, who had looked in once or twice while Mary was there, and came for a farewell talk with her friends before leaving for Ephesus. The women's Gospel filled in the dialogue at the Cana wedding feast, which he dictated, many years later, to the author of the canonical one that now bears his name. He listened with respect to what they told him about the pledge that someone would 'remain' till the Second Coming. This reminded him of an obscure remark of Christ's which he had heard himself. Later he discussed the alleged promise with his disciples in Ephesus, and some of them applied it to him, a misunderstanding that led to awkwardness when he died.

Both John and Luke noticed that a Marian orthodoxy was taking shape. It drew on the Jewish Bible (there was no other yet) for prefigurings and parallels. In the community, Mary was identified with the Daughter of Zion, the embodied Israel of prophecy to whom the Messiah came. All his followers were spiritually her children, whether they were aware of it or not. Scripture also foreshadowed her in one or two individuals, notably of course the prophetess Miriam, the prototype-Mary, who was the voice of all Israel hailing its God in the sea-miracle and the deliverance from Egypt. Like another representative of God's people, Elijah, Mary had taken refuge from persecution in solitude (though the place was no longer solitary), and like him she had gone away, translated into a secret everlasting life. Luke transmitted a trace of the first doctrine in his Greek wording of the Annunciation, *chairé* and so forth, but he was not interested further. It all sounded very Jewish, and he was a Gentile writing for Gentiles, one of the flood of Pauline converts. John – for whom Mary actually had been an adoptive mother, by Christ's own wish – found the women's ideas more impressive, and wove some of them into the imagery of a work which became the Apocalypse.

The meaning of its twelfth chapter was handed on among his disciples in Ephesus, and elaborated. They pointed out that the scene of the woman with the Christ-child, thwarting the ancient serpent, linked up with Genesis 3:15 and made the Virgin a Second Eve reversing the defeat of the first. They also pointed out that the passage allowed her to be construed as a symbol of the Church, since the woman stood for the new Israel as well as the old, and all true Christians were her offspring. Justin was converted at Ephesus and absorbed the first of these ideas; John's disciple Polycarp explained it to Irenaeus, who began his life as a Christian in the same circle; and both put it into their writings. The second idea drifted through the east and emerged briefly in Tertullian and Origen. But the source was so patently outside the Church that Revelation itself ceased to be mentioned in these connections, and even the related Genesis text was pushed into the background for many years. The two derived Marian notions were thus left hanging in a void.

In the second century AD the Mary community still existed, with a constant coming and going. None of its members now had even met her, but the oldest of them passed on what they had heard from her friends. Some saw her in dreams and visions. Some prayed to her and were persuaded that she heard. Established among them as a female Elijah, she grew to resemble him more and more. Like him – that is, in legend – she was held to be deathless not because of a miracle late in life but because she had been sinless from the beginning, and therefore exempt from the penalty of Adam and Eve. Like him, she had her place in heaven close to God's throne; in fact she was already re-united with Jesus there, without having to wait for his return to earth; but she often returned herself as Elijah did, secretly, to help and sustain those she cared for. The community always kept a seat vacant for her in case she arrived (here perhaps anticipating, rather than imitating, a Jewish Passover custom in Elijah's honour).

Apart from its homage to the Foundress, the group's religion was a Jewish and Christian mélange. Though it attracted Gentile women as well as Jews, it remained more Jewish in spirit than the Church. Such intercommunion as occurred was purely individual. However, the Church's progress had reduced anti-Christian feeling within it, and eliminated the early animus against Jesus. All members now accepted that he was divine and the Saviour, if only because his mother's miraculous privileges seemed to imply it. But they thought of him in relation to her rather than as part of a Triune Godhead.

Theology might have stopped there if the situation had been stable, but it was altering. When the community broke up, as at last it had to, many women initiated into its lore were scattered through Palestine, Syria and Egypt. They seldom aspired to a missionary role. Yet their cult made headway, in protest against the male Trinity and priesthood. It acquired theologians of its own. These were now a necessity of survival. Their writings were few, and were never widely circulated or copied, because, in such a field, women were considered beneath notice. Nevertheless they formed ideas and quietly spread them.

Marianists taught that by bearing the Divine Son, Mary had cancelled the inferiority of women. They recalled the obscure prophecy in Jeremiah 31:22, which had been picked out long ago when she was still contemplating the young Jesus's future – 'the Lord has created a new thing on the earth: a woman protects a man', or 'assumes a male role'. In Mary the strength of the female had recovered. She was greater than the Christian priests, because their supreme mystery, God-becoming-man, was understood only by her in whose womb it happened.

One of these theologians, better read than most of them, took a bolder step. She grasped the philosophical sex conflict which had led from Ben-Sira through Philo to the Fourth Gospel: first the setting up of the beautiful and glorious Lady Wisdom, then her replacement by the male Logos, then the adaptation of the Logos to fit Christ. Rejecting the Christians' male-biased doctrine, she swept the Logos aside as a metaphysical phantom, and restored Wisdom to the place of honour at God's right hand. She pointed out that Christ himself never talked the language of Philo, but did speak of Wisdom as a person and a feminine one at that, saying in Luke 7:35 that she was 'justified' or 'vindicated' by all her children, and counting himself as one of them.

Thenceforward the association of Mary with Wisdom was easier than the association of Christ with the Logos. According to Ecclesiasticus 24, Wisdom was 'established in Zion' and 'took root in an honoured people', i.e. the Jews. It was not hard to assimilate the Daughter of Zion to her. The goddesses Anath and Athene had gone into her making, and while Jews had never been much aware of Athene, some had certainly been aware of Anath . . . who was Virgin and Mother.

Wisdom, this Marianist teacher proclaimed, was the first-born of creation and the Lord's beloved, his helper in his work. That, after all, was in Proverbs as well as Ecclesiasticus. She had dwelt invisibly with the patriarchs (for which see the Wisdom of Solomon, 10) and then in Israel. Over the ages, furthermore, she had taken human form as several Israelite women named Mary. The first was Miriam, long since recognized as, in some sense, one with the Virgin. Wisdom's climactic incarnation, and the only complete one, was of course the Virgin herself. But Mary Magdalene and Mary the wife of Clopas were lesser aspects of her, even though they lived at the same time. Wisdom was present at the foot of the cross as a female trinity. In other words she did befriend her Son through his public ministry, she did witness his Resurrection, but only through secondary guises. As the Mother, she had accepted an inscrutable doom of loss and estrangement.

In this last thought her theologian was influenced by certain myths of the Goddess – for instance Demeter losing and seeking Persephone, Isis losing and seeking Osiris. But it was a matter of influence only, and very vague influence, not borrowing or paganization. The same could be said of the Gnostic echoes in her doctrines. Osmotically, for instance, Simon Magus's story of Wisdom's avatars (culminating in his own Helen-Athene) had an effect. But it was not consciously imitated. It was simply present in the background, and because Marianists were free from the Christians' horror of heresy, the door was not closed to shut such whisperings out.

Wisdom also revived the dim memories of paganism behind her in Ecclesiasticus. She did not, however, revive Anath or Astarte in person. All that happened was that her identification with Mary suggested the rightness of worshipping Christ's mother as these had been worshipped. Jeremiah, the prophet of the 'new thing' wrought through Mary, had also described the ritual of the Queen of Heaven (7:18; 44:15-19), and quoted the retort of the Egyptian Jews whom he denounced for performing it. When they worshipped her, these Jews told him, they were prosperous – 'But since we left off burning incense to the Queen of Heaven and pouring out libations to her, we have lacked everything and have been consumed by the sword and by famine'; therefore, they had returned to her. Perhaps Jeremiah's warning held a concealed hint for the future? Now that a true Queen of Heaven had come, the divine Wisdom in Mary's shape, perhaps it was right to pay such respects to her, to 'make cakes for her bearing her image', to offer one's prayers and tribute with hope of reward.

Thus Marianism acquired its ritual and priestesses. Wherever it flourished, that remembered empty chair in the community reappeared as a throne and received the offerings. The cult brought back a type of religion which had flowered in paganism when Greek women met for the Thesmophoria, and Roman ones for the rites of the Bona Dea. Judaism had never given women any equivalent, nor, as yet, had the Church; a movement known as Montanism had begun promisingly, but its prophetesses had been gradually silenced. The remoter antecedents of such feminine mysteries were in the Dionysus-worship of ancient Thrace, the land of the Maenads, and its was in Thrace that a wandering Marianist apostle found fertile soil, where the cult grew beyond a mysticism of small groups into a religion that attracted notice.

As its devotees travelled and its assemblies gathered in other countries, its ideas spilt over into Christianity in new ways. The denial of Mary's death, for instance, appealed to popular imagination, and discouraged all claims to possess a tomb or relics. Several of the more daring doctrines found entry into apocryphal books such as the Gospel of Bartholomew. For some time the Christian priesthood tried to ignore Marianism as merely a female superstition. If it had been a heresy within the Church, they would have attacked it sooner, but it was outside. By the middle of the fourth century it was branching widely and gaining converts, including a certain number of men. In out-of-the-way regions where the Christian hierarchy did not amount to much – Thrace itself, Scythia, Arabia – it functioned openly and regularly. At last Epiphanius collated reports from those fringe areas and broke the silence. He knew the tradition of Mary's deathlessness, and the meaning of those verses in Revelation drawing a parallel with Elijah; John's apparent endorsement of the belief disposed him to favour it. But the overt Marianist religion was a different matter, and he held it up to contempt (inaccurately) as a heresy, insisting that the Virgin must not be worshipped, and pouring scorn on her priestesses.

The religion as such was not making serious inroads into Christianity. It was not equipped to do so. Yet it posed a subtle threat, out of proportion to its comparative weakness. Mary as Wisdom filled the gap between earth and heaven. She satisfied ancient needs, and fulfilled ancient myths, which her Son could not. There was also a more specific problem. Most of the pagan saviour-gods had retained their link with the Goddess. The Christian Saviour might do all that they did in other respects, and more, but as things stood he could not reproduce this part of the pattern, could not restore the Eternal-Womanly for its completion; and the reason went deeper than anti-pagan animus. Quite simply the Goddess had never been inferior to her male companion, as, in the Church, Mary was to Jesus. When Christians called Mary the Second Eve they fell into a Goddess-shaped trap, because Christ, according to Paul, was the Second

Adam. Taken together, the metaphors evoked the divine son-spouse relationship. But Christianity, as a body of literal belief, had no way of handling it.

The Marianist religion offered solutions. It mysticized the Virgin as well as Jesus, extended her into other lives, saw her on several levels. As Wisdom she was the Lord's delight, his beloved (Proverbs 8:30); and in that role – as indeed in her old guise as personified Israel – she could take over that refractory book the Song of Songs. Without any surrender to paganism she embodied Goddess-motifs. Besides her other affiliations she was akin to Cybele, the Great Mother of the Gods, who still had a hold in parts of Italy. But she was even more than Cybele. She revived the theology of Neith, the primordial Virgin Mother who gave birth to Ra. Mary was not a mother of gods but *the* Mother of *God* . . . a title which, in the Christian Empire, might almost seem to outflank the Trinity.

4

I repeat, the foregoing section is not history. It is fiction, or at most reconstruction. But it is strictly functional. All the imagined Marianist ideas can be seen to appear in Christian forms. Several of these we know already, others are still to come. They cover a wide range of Christian thought and literature. Some are scriptural, some patristic, some apocryphal; some are doctrinal, some popular, some liturgical; one or two of them surface in poetry. When we move forward to Mary's rise in the Church, the impression is still that she has undergone some such development in a setting outside it. The familiar thing goes on happening. We find what seem to be results of the development, we find what seem to be inferences from it, but we never find the development itself. The Virgin's cult in the Church is disjointed, arbitrary, deprived of roots and reasons. That is supremely true of the two dogmas, the Immaculate Conception and the Assumption. But they are not alone.

The key to the change that overtook Christianity is the title Mother of God. This occurs in the one scrap of writing which looks like a direct Marianist product. It is a fragment of a prayer on papyrus, belonging to the third century or possibly the fourth.

The Greek may be translated: 'Mother of God, hear my sup-
plications: suffer us not to be in adversity, but deliver us from
danger. Thou alone . . .' This can hardly be part of a Christian
liturgy, since all liturgical prayers were addressed to God.
Moreover the word for 'deliver' is the same as in the Lord's
Prayer ('deliver us from evil') and places Mary much too close to
divinity. On the other hand the wording does not fit into any
known school of Gnosticism, and although it is not Christian as it
stands, a prayer that echoes it, Sub tuum praesidium, appears in
Christianity later.[10]

'Mother of God' itself, in Greek Theotokos, was admitted to be
a logical epithet by several Fathers. If Christ was God, the Second
Person of the Trinity, then his mother in his human manifestation
was the Mother of God. The title may even have been invented
inside the Church. According to an uncertain witness it was first
used by Origen. Doubtfully also it is cited in Peter of Alexandria,
who died in 311. It is certainly in the writings of Alexander,
bishop of the same city, a younger contemporary; and in those of
Eusebius and Athanasius, whom we encountered in Chapter 6.
Until the latter part of the fourth century it was chiefly current
among Egyptians, though so widely known through their fond-
ness for it that Julian the Apostate made it a reproach against
Christians – 'You never stop calling Mary "Theotokos".' It
was undoubtedly a disturbing way to describe anyone, and in
more recent times it has been too much for Protestants as it was
for Julian. John Bright told Cardinal Manning that after hearing a
priest in Rome say 'Mary is the Mother of God', he fretted over
the sentence for twenty years afterwards, 'almost every day and
often during the night', trying to make sense of it. Perhaps it was
the sheer shock of the paradox that burst the ecclesiastical dam,
less than three decades after Epiphanius's death.[11]

Chapter 8

THE ROAD TO
EPHESUS

I

Though the dam was still holding in the 370s when Epiphanius
wrote, it was beginning to fissure. His onslaught on Mary-
worship came rather late. Even according to his own meagre
data, the Collyridian cult had had time to travel a long way from
its Thracian homeland. Meanwhile Marianism – in some sense –
had started to trickle into the Church. Soon the trickle was to
become a rivulet and then a deluge.

The transitional Christian figure is a poet, Ephraem of Syria.
He was born about 306 at Nisibis in Mesopotamia, then Roman
territory. In 363 Julian the Apostate was killed fighting the
Persians, and the province was ceded to them as the price of a
treaty. An ironic by-product of the last anti-Christian reign was
the Church's enrichment with a remarkable talent. Disliking
Persian rule, Ephraem moved to Edessa in Syria, settled in a cave
overlooking the city, and became renowned as a holy man. The
impression he made was genuine, unaided by official status or
even appearance: he was never ordained a priest, and he was
short, bald, clean-shaven and ascetic-looking. His admirers'
estimate of him was confirmed by his record as a volunteer
administrator of famine relief. His best-known achievement,
however, was the promotion of singing in public worship,
which was rare before his time. Syrian Gnostics had been spreading popular songs with a heretical message. Ephraem (unwilling,
like others since, that the Devil should have all the good tunes)

composed better ones for orthodox congregations. He died in 373.

He was a late developer, but Syria gave him scope, and in the last decade of his life he wrote copiously. His many hymns and poems include several addressed to the Virgin. Their flowery praise strikes a new note in Christianity. Its language should not be pressed too far: as Professor Miegge observes, 'Poetry is always a little beyond theology and its dogmatic responsibility is not to be over-estimated.'[1] Still it is arresting to find Ephraem calling Mary Christ's 'bride' or 'spouse' (thus being the first Christian to clear the hurdle of the Goddess-and-Son relationship, though with a wrench to doctrine), and writing what seem to be prayers to her, implying her power as a living intercessor with God.

Besides enlarging on the Second Eve theme, and on her sinlessness, he ventures into the perilous country of the Song of Songs – 'Who is this that looks forth like the dawn, fair as the moon, bright as the sun, terrible as an army with banners?' He begs her to be a 'tower of strength' to the faithful. 'O Virgin Mother of God,' he exclaims, 'Gate of Heaven, and Ark, in thee I have a secure salvation. Save me, O Lady, out of thy pure mercy.' For him she is a symbolic Eden in whom the Fall is undone: 'Mary is the garden upon which descended from the Father the rain of benedictions. From that rain she herself sprinkled the face of Adam. Whereupon he returned to life, and arose from the sepulchre – he who had been buried by his foes in hell.' Addressing her directly, he says: 'My most holy Lady, Mother of God, and full of grace; glory of our common nature; dispenser of all good things; after the Trinity, mistress of all; after the Paraclete, another consoler; and after the Mediator, the whole world's mediatress . . .' Again: 'Hail, our Lady who by thy prayers obtainest for thy faithful ones a covenant, peace, and a sceptre wherewith to rule all.'[2]

Such phrases are not frequent or habitual. They have to be searched for. They are scattered through a luxuriant mass of verse, in a language, Syriac, which consigned it for the moment to a backwater of Christianity. Ephraem, alone among Syrian Fathers, came to be counted as a 'Doctor of the Universal Church', but not until 1920. In the context of his own time his salutations place him in a niche by himself, without precursors or companions, the single Christian to use such language so early; and he is not instantly famous for this, nor is it reflected in Christian practice even in Syria. Soon after his death, when Epiphanius writes 'Let no one worship Mary', it is still true that no one is perceptibly doing so except the Collyridians.

Who then influenced whom? The dates leave a margin for a theoretical doubt. Could it be that Ephraem's poetic flights were original with him and inspired Collyridianism, so that it was Christian-derived after all? Hardly. We would need to suppose that a manuscript of his poems got to Thrace almost as soon as they were written; that it came into the hands of a Thracian woman who could read Syriac (did such a person exist?) or had access to a translator; that she picked out the relevant verses; that a cult was founded which flowed back over the Middle East as far as Arabia, not to mention southern Russia; and that in a world without printing or mass-media, the entire process was completed inside ten years, ready for Epiphanius to pounce upon. Nothing short of explicit proof would excuse such a far-fetched set of notions. The better course is to accept the implied probabilities. We may regard Ephraem as one more in the succession from Justin and Irenaeus, a Christian who is Marianist-influenced, but does not mention the source. When he was at Edessa, Marianist ideas, in Collyridian form and otherwise, were already current over a wide area. Up to a point, some of them appealed to him . . . as, up to a point, others appealed to Epiphanius. His poems to Mary show it. They may be meant to offer a purified Christian version, in the spirit of his counter-heretical hymns.

Some of Ephraem's voluminous writings were translated into Greek during his lifetime, but there is no evidence that these were. To the Greek-speaking and Latin-speaking Christians who made up most of the Church, the Syrian poet's novel attitude to the Virgin remained unknown. Or nearly so. Early in 371 a momentous event took place. Ephraem went to Caesarea in Cappadocia (now the Turkish city of Kayseri) to visit its lately-appointed bishop, Basil. And Basil was very far from being a backwater figure. Native to Cappadocia, he was a Greek-speaker, one of the greatest among the Greek Fathers, chief organizer of monastic communities throughout the east. He had a brother named Gregory, known to history as Gregory of Nyssa from a town which he became bishop of himself. One of Basil's closest friends was another Gregory, also a Cappadocian, called Gregory of Nazianzus.

These three composed a group. They were all aged about forty, with years of Church leadership still ahead of them. All were well educated and unimpeachably orthodox. To judge from remarks by the younger brother, Gregory of Nyssa, Ephraem impressed them deeply. The tiny, venerable man was a strange being from a strange country, speaking an unfamiliar tongue, giving the mysteries of faith an exotic colour and freshness. Until his advent there had been almost no Christian poetry. Now, in this surprising quarter, it had suddenly dawned. Shortly after his death all three Cappadocians begin speaking of the Virgin in a new tone. This may be coincidence, but a Marian impulse transmitted from the Syrian is a great deal more likely.[3]

Basil's venturing beyond the earlier Christian norm is confined to a phrase or two. The phrases, however, are portentous. When re-asserting Mary's perpetual virginity he calls her the Mother of God, Theotokos, thereby planting the title in sober prose outside Egypt. Also, in a text which is probably his if not quite certainly, the *Magnificat* is cited to make her a 'prophetess'. This is her first emergence in a role going clearly beyond her maternity.

His brother Gregory of Nyssa prepares the ground further for a cult by extending to Mary a treatment hitherto restricted to Christ – the seeking out of Old Testament texts supposed to be prophetic of her. In the few prior attempts of this kind, such as Matthew's allusion to Isaiah 7:14, she is incidental to her Son. Gregory detects her in her own right, variously foreshadowed and symbolized. For instance, he expands an idea of which the germ is in Ephraem – that Mary is prefigured in the bush seen by Moses (Exodus 3:2–4), which was the place of divine manifestation, and burned before his eyes without being consumed. Similarly Mary contained God in her womb, yet was intact: 'the flower of her virginity was not made to wither.' Again, Gregory hits on Ezekiel 44:1–2, a visionary description of a new Jewish Temple. The east gate of the sanctuary is shut, and the prophet is told: 'This gate shall remain shut; it shall not be opened, and no one shall enter by it; for the Lord, the God of Israel, has entered by it; therefore it shall remain shut.' The application to Mary Ever-Virgin, Mother of God, is obvious.

Also – first among Christians to do so – Gregory considers the original Mary, Moses's sister Miriam, and claims her as a 'type' of the Virgin. By this concept he can connect the two without risking a commitment to reincarnation. God, creating the first Mary with foreknowledge of the second and greater one, built anticipatory hints into her life. Gregory extracts meaning from the timbrel she played after the Israelites' crossing of the sea-bed: 'As the tympanum, from which all moisture has been removed so that it is exceedingly dry, gives out a loud noise, so also is virginity, which receives no life-giving moisture, illustrious and renowned.' With such conceits as these a scriptural Mariology is launched. Later theologians adopt the 'bush' and 'gate' symbols, and add many others. Mary is said to be pre-figured by the untilled soil of Eden, the Ark of the Covenant, Gideon's fleece (Judges 6:36–40), the garden and sealed fountain in the Song of Songs. Several more women become 'types' of her under various aspects – Rachel, Deborah, Ruth, Esther.[4]

The same Gregory contributes two further items, both paving the way, like his scriptural ingenuities, for much that is to gather round Mary afterwards. Discussing the Resurrection, he breaks with the Fathers' discreet silence about her exclusion from it. He denies that she was excluded. He maintains that the 'other Mary' of Matthew 28:1, who sees Christ risen in the company of the Magdalene, is actually the Virgin: 'for it was fitting that she, who was not absent from the Passion, but, as John tells us, stood beside the cross, should also proclaim the good news of joy, as she herself is the root of joy.' The idea raises difficulties over the 'other Mary' being described else-where as the mother of James and Joses. Gregory invokes the *Protevangelium* notion of their being sons of Joseph the carpenter by a previous marriage, so that 'mother' means 'stepmother'. The reason for such misleading language is said to be that the secret of Mary's virginity had to be concealed from the Jews for her own protection.

This is an awkward theory, and few Christians have ever agreed with it (though one who did tried to father it on Ephraem, a further hint at a Marian link between the Syrian and the Cappadocians). The point to notice, however, is the way Gregory opens up a general line of Marian reasoning: what may be called the 'must have' logic. Christ *must have* appeared to his mother, therefore he did, and we can legitimately torture the Gospels' words till they say so. In due course theologians are to claim that he *must have* willed her absolute purity – hence the Immaculate Conception; and that he *must have* willed to preserve her body from corruption, and take her to himself in heaven – hence the Assumption.[5]

Gregory also tells the first known story of Mary appearing in a vision. This is alleged to have happened to an earlier Gregory, called the Wonder-Worker, towards the middle of the third century. When he was made a bishop, unusually young, he was diffident about preaching. One night he was lying awake wondering what to say in his sermon. Suddenly he saw an old man, who, it transpired, was the apostle John, sent by divine command to instruct him. John pointed across the room to where a woman stood, seeming more than life-size, and surrounded by a blaze of light. Gregory dared not look any longer, but he heard her telling John to speak. John answered that he would do as the mother of the Lord wished, and gave a discourse on Christian doctrine. Then the visitants vanished. The bishop wrote John's message down and found that it gave him all he required for his preaching.

There is no contemporary evidence to confirm this tale. Gregory of Nyssa really knew very little about the Wonder-Worker. What little he did know seems to have consisted mainly in gossip handed down by his grandmother, who lived in the same town as the asserted visionary, but not early enough to have talked with him herself. The story is a legend of the kind that becomes current when a new doctrine seeks a history and a pedigree. Gregory feels that Mary's reality as a living friend of the saints will be more credible if it is less of a novelty, if she can be shown as active in that capacity far back towards the beginning. Perhaps the story is based on a genuine tradition; perhaps the Wonder-Worker did have a dream. But it is only in the Marian burgeoning of the late fourth century that anybody thinks it worthy of notice, puts it on record, or offers it as more than a dream.[6]

With the third member of the Cappadocian trio, Gregory of Nazianzus, we glimpse the cult just beginning to take root in the Church. This Gregory was a poet of some talent, if less fluent than Ephraem, and studious by temperament. His written references to Mary are few, but sweeping in their implications. He not only calls her Mother of God as his friend Basil does, he makes this title a part of the Christian system, even a test of orthodoxy: 'if anyone does not accept the holy Mary as Theotokos, he is without the Godhead.' He also provides the first Christian case-history of the Virgin as a hearer of prayer, thereby giving substance to Ephraem's rhetoric.

The sermon in which he does so was delivered at Constantinople in October 379. He had come there less than a year before under peculiar circumstances. As bishop of Nazianzus, a small town in Asia Minor, he seemed to have found his level in the hierarchy. But a crisis happened to have developed in Constantinople. It was the eastern capital of the Roman Empire, and it was also the last stronghold within the Empire of the Arian heresy. Two pro-Arian emperors of the east, Constantius and Valens, had severely restricted orthodox worship in the city. In 378 Valens died fighting the Goths at Adrianople. The repressed Catholic party recovered slightly and invited Gregory to the city as their shadow-bishop. A relative who thought highly of him, and had probably suggested his name, put a hall at his disposal. It was christened the 'Anastasia' or Resurrection, to express hope of a Catholic revival. This chapel became the chief meeting-place of the surviving orthodox congregation, and it was here that Gregory preached.

In his sermon mentioning the Virgin's response to a prayer, he dates the event much earlier, like his namesake of Nyssa in a similar case. The sermon commemorates a martyr, St Cyprian of Carthage. Gregory says that when Cyprian was still a pagan, a Christian maiden named Justina was seized by an 'unholy love' for him and 'implored the Virgin Mary to help her, a virgin in danger'. Her battle against her soul's peril included fasting, sleeping on the bare ground, and disfiguring her looks to make herself unattractive. Mary sustained her and enabled her to survive intact. Cyprian was converted by her example, and both were martyred in the year 304.

The trouble with all this is that Gregory has confused Cyprian of Carthage with Cyprian of Antioch, who was almost certainly fictitious. His legend, as told in later and fuller versions, makes him out to have been a sorcerer who desired Justina and tried to win her over by black arts. It is the theme of a well-known Spanish drama, Calderon's *El Magico Prodigioso*; some scenes translated into English by Shelley are included in the poet's works. Justina does not belong to the biography of the real Cyprian, but to that of the fictitious one, and there is no reason to suppose that she ever existed. Hence, her prayer to the Virgin is not history. The only historical fact about it is that it is part of a story told by Gregory to his flock in 379. We cannot reliably trace it farther back. What is significant is that he should have begun *now*, in his fifties, to produce such stories.

Among his disciples at this time was the formidable St Jerome, fresh from ordination at Antioch. That city being the locale of the Cyprian-Justina fable, it is tempting to guess that he was Gregory's source for it. Certainly his later work supports the belief that Mary was an important person at the Anastasia. The building was endangered when an Arian mob tried to wreck it, but deliverance was near. In 380 the new eastern emperor, Theodosius, was baptized a Catholic and deposed the Arian patriarch of Constantinople. Gregory was enthroned instead. The office exposed him to political malice and he soon gave it up, retiring to Cappadocia. But his courageous tenure left a legend behind.

One aspect of it is deeply interesting. A church was built on the site, and we are told by the historian Sozomen, writing in the 440s (well within the lifetime of contemporaries), that it enjoyed a singular favour.

A divine power was there manifested, and was helpful both in waking visions and in dreams, often for the relief of many diseases and for those afflicted by some sudden transmutation in their affairs. The power was attributed to Mary, the Mother of God, the holy Virgin, for she does manifest herself in this way.

She conferred a blessing, in other words, on the headquarters of Gregory's triumph over heresy. Furthermore she revealed her presence very much as she was to do fifteen centuries later at Lourdes.[7]

2

Surprisingly then, the dawn of Mary's cult in the Church can be fixed with some accuracy. It did not exist – at least in any organized or recognized form – when Epiphanius completed his marathon tract. Ephraem had foreshadowed it poetically during the 360s, but in 377, four years after the Syrian hymnographer's death, there was still nothing in Christian worship to correspond. Two years later again, there was. The words of Gregory of Nazianzus about Justina imply that his hearers were already acquainted with the practice of praying to the Virgin. All clues suggest that the three Cappadocians learned of it from Ephraem as a private devotion, with odd but not damnable antecedents, and Gregory made it a collective one at the Anastasia, in 378 or '79. Mary's presence on the site as a 'divine power' was an acknowledgment of the homage paid to her there, and probably, for a while, in no other Christian building.

Such a thing could happen because of the unique plight of Catholics in Constantinople. In other major centres throughout the Empire, their faith had won its battle and was predominant. In the eastern capital they had been driven back to the catacombs, or so at least the contrast made it appear. Two results followed. First, they desperately needed a miracle of rescue. Forty years of fidelity to the true Godhead seemed to have led nowhere. They were ripe for a new deliverer; and to judge from the papyrus quoted on p. 171, the Mother of God was so regarded by those who invoked her. The other result of Constantinople's pressure on its Catholics was that they met in relative privacy. The innovation of praying to Mary could scarcely have been made in a Roman or Alexandrian church. It could be made in the Anastasia, by an underground poet-priest, behind doors that were barred against Arian intruders.

And deliverance came, soon and marvellously, with the conversion of Theodosius. It was not yet politic to speak out about the Virgin's deed. But rumours spread, and the religious climate altered. The Constantinople miracle was not the sole reason for this or even the main one, but it was a potent contributory cause.

There was another – the advance of the monastic movement with both sexes. At first, as we saw, this had tended to cut Mary down by making her simply an unreal and unlovely model for celibates. Now her perfect chastity began to be viewed in a more expansive spirit. She became a patroness. This perhaps was a legacy of Basil, the other Cappadocian, who had himself been a major monastic founder. His work in that field was done before his meeting with Ephraem, and he did not live to share in his friend Gregory's triumph at Constantinople. But a practice which he taught or favoured was likely to commend itself to religious communities, and this one was peculiarly apt to their mode of life. The Virgin would be a heavenly helper to the vowed celibate, male or female, as she had once been to Justina. St Ambrose, writing 'on the instruction of a virgin' about 392, quotes Isaiah 19:1 – 'Behold, the Lord comes seated on a light cloud' – and claims that the light cloud is a symbol of Mary, free from any burden of vice. 'Receive,' he continues, 'receive, O consecrated virgins, the spiritual rain that falls from this cloud, which will temper the burning desires of the body.'[8]

Egypt, which had been the first home of Christian monks and was still the chief, took the living Virgin to its ecclesiastical heart. The Coptic Christianity of the Nile valley, and presently Ethiopia, was soon to surpass most other forms in its adoration and in its output of strange fancies about her, some of them adopted (if the reconstruction in the previous chapter is right) from Marianists outside the Church. It was not, however, an eastern monk but a pioneer western one who had the first Marian visions for which there is any real evidence. This was St Martin of Tours, the founder of monasticism among the Gauls. His disciple Sulpicius Severus tells how he could be heard in his cell talking with people whom no one else ever saw. Martin explained that he had visits from angels, and also from several of the blessed including Mary. He described their appearance; unhappily the descriptions were not preserved. These meetings probably took place not very long before his death in 397. It is clear that the milieu was now receptive to such reports, even as far west as Gaul.[9]

Apart from the vows of monks and nuns, the special value of sexual continence had for some years been a theme of earnest discussion in the Church at large. Priestly celibacy was not yet a binding rule anywhere, but it was growing to be a widespread custom, on the ground that virginity was superior to marriage. A certain Helvidius ventured to protest that it was not. In support, he inverted the argument from the mother of Jesus and defied Christian tradition. Mary, he declared, was a pattern of both states. She was a chaste virgin when she bore Jesus, but she was a model wife afterwards in the fullest sense. The Lord's 'brothers' and 'sisters' were quite simply that, her subsequent children by her husband Joseph.

St Jerome – who had travelled west soon after his fruitful contact with Gregory – replied to Helvidius. His crushing weight of biblical learning established the view of the Holy Family which became standard in the western Church: a virginal Mary with a virginal Joseph, and the 'other Mary' as mother of a brood of cousins headed by James. Though, as a matter of history, Jerome seems to have got close to the truth, his motive in the attack on Helvidius was frankly to make a case for the ruling opinion.

The negative side of it was of course anti-sexual prejudice. Mary 'must have' been Ever-Virgin. Ambrose, in the tract just quoted, expresses it thus: 'Would the Lord Jesus have chosen for his mother a woman who would defile the heavenly chamber with the seed of a man, that is to say one incapable of preserving her virginal chastity intact?' This view of the matter is endorsed by the contemporary pope, Siricius, in much the same language. However, it is fair to stress that the doctrine had a positive side. Rightly or wrongly, the perfect purity of the Mother of God was seen in the closing years of the fourth century less as a sterile abstinence than as a kind of glory, which overflowed on to others around her – not only her husband, but John the Baptist and the beloved disciple to whose care Jesus entrusted her, both of whom also rose above their physical nature. [10]

Ambrose and Jerome both have more to say about Mary. For instance, they both pursue Gregory of Nyssa's quest for allusions in the Old Testament. A certain interchange occurs, marking the dawn of a consensus. Thus the Isaiah image of the 'light cloud', used by Ambrose, seems to be borrowed from Jerome. The former, as Bishop of Milan, is careful in his approach. Aware that the pagan cult of Cybele, Great Mother of the Gods, is still alive in Italy, he seldom employs the title 'Mother of God' (in Latin, *Mater Dei*): it might be misconstrued. His search for Old Testament prophecies and types reflects a wish for a plainly orthodox Mariology. Besides the cloud, which he is fond of, he detects Mary in the rod of Jesse (Isaiah 11:1) from which the flowering branch of Christ grows. Also he dares to detect her in the Song of Songs, in such verses as 2:10 – 'my fair one' – and 3:11, where the King is crowned by his mother.

As Ambrose evolves his scrupulously Catholic thoughts, several of the Church's Marian teachings can be seen taking shape. Thus the Virgin's consent to Gabriel's message is said to mean that she has an active part in the salvation of mankind. She is a type of the Church, and mother of Christians – Ambrose brings this idea to a sharper focus, though still without reference to Revelation 12. He takes the first step towards making her a flawless pattern of virtue in general, an all-round saint. Also, like Gregory of Nyssa, he maintains that she did see the risen Christ and indeed that she was the first to do so . . . the inexorable logic which is not afraid to add to the Gospels, centuries after the event.[11]

Jerome is more erudite, and his handling of scripture is the most interesting aspect of what he says about Mary. He too plunges boldly into the Song of Songs, emerging with such images as the 'garden enclosed' and 'fountain sealed' (4:12). He recognizes – at last – some of the Old Testament passages that really do have a bearing on the idea of the Virgin-Mother: the Wisdom texts, and the texts personifying Israel as the Daughter of Zion. He singles out Jeremiah 31:22, 'a woman shall compass a man' (p. 100), though he interprets the 'new thing' as simply a woman 'compassing' a man-child in her womb unaided. His following-up of his insights is disappointing, but he brings the Christians of his time into closer contact with the true imaginative sources.[12]

St Augustine, the greatest of Roman theologians, was a disciple of Ambrose. Besides expanding some of his mentor's ideas, he makes two contributions of his own to the growing edifice. One of these is the unhappy notion that Mary took a vow of virginity in her early youth, and that this is the reason for her bewilderment at the Annunciation. The ultimate basis is the *Protevangelium*, and Gregory of Nyssa gives a more precise hint, but the suggestion has no tradition of any value behind it. The motive for it is simply to make Christ's mother more like the vowed celibates who, at the time of its invention, were exalting her as their patroness. Though its tenacity has been amazing, it is no longer seriously held. Augustine's other contribution is his firm pronouncement that Mary was sinless. Whether his words imply the Immaculate Conception – that is, her freedom from original sin as well as sins of her own – is a vexed question. But after Augustine, hardly anyone dares to find a fault in her. Finally, whether or not in reflection of his own teaching, a disciple of his named Quodvultdeus makes a belated discovery. Like Jerome rediscovering Wisdom and the Daughter of Zion, Quodvultdeus – at last – discerns Mary in the woman of the Apocalypse, not in Epiphanius's peculiar sense, but as 'herself showing forth the figure of the holy Church'.[13]

Reading these authors, we still find few allusions to her as an intercessor, a hearer of prayer, or a recipient of anything remotely like worship. They give little reason to think that anything has happened to her officially. Yet the atmosphere has altered. The post-Nicene shrinkage has been reversed. She has become a richer, more complex figure, and, while it might be difficult to explain how, a more present figure. Ambrose, for instance, discusses her in the Gospel setting like earlier Fathers, but does not give the same impression of something that was complete and done with long ago. The story seems to unfold in a timeless eternity, where Mary is still with us because her Son is.[14]

An annual Marian festival day may have been observed by a small number of churches in the east, and a smaller number in the west, even before the close of the fourth century. Such a day was undoubtedly being kept in the early years of the fifth. Mary's liturgy was as yet only an offshoot of her Son's. Its appointed date was, in most places, the Sunday before Christmas, and the feast was a general commemoration of her as mother of Christ. The first church dedicated to her seems to have been in the valley of Josaphat near Jerusalem. But the first city where the cult of the living Theotokos became a mass enthusiasm was Ephesus.

Here stood the famous temple of Artemis, 'Diana of the Ephesians', whose adherents caused Paul such trouble. (About 400 a Christian smashed her image, but the temple, though derelict, continued to stand as a mighty reminder of female numinosity.) Here John had come, and according to local legend – disputed elsewhere – had brought the aged Mary with him. Here his Apocalypse had been published, and the Johannine school had produced Justin and Irenaeus, who extolled Mary as the Second Eve. An Ephesian document speaks of 'John the Theologian and the holy Virgin Theotokos' as being present in the city. It is not clear what the writer means. If he had tombs in mind, or bodily relics, he would surely have said so. More probably the city possessed two shrines where they were believed to be present spiritually, as Mary was at the Anastasia in Constantinople. At all events Ephesus had a basilica called the Church of Mary by 431, and she was then the subject of passionate public honour.[15]

3

As the Marian tide slowly rose, the unspoken question was whether this new thing invading Christianity would transform its character. If the Mother of God became in effect the Goddess restored, the Collyridian sect could be said to have converted the Church. The alternative was that the Church would confine Mary-worship within bounds, and adapt the resurgent Eternal-Womanly to its own system . . . well enough, at any rate, to avert the former contingency.

Where was the pressure coming from? Not from the top. A factor that did carry weight was the influence of monks over the Church at large, especially in the east. Another was the decline of urban life, the ruralization of a bankrupt social order, the return of the peasant. Agricultural peoples had been the Goddess's mainstay and always tended to favour a divine motherhood. But the main reason is almost too huge and too obvious to see.

Catholicism, as it stood, seemed a bringer of ill-fortune. Its progress had gone hand in hand with public calamity. In 363 the last anti-Christian emperor died and the faithful rejoiced; then, in 367, Britain was lost to the Empire through a barbarian onslaught. Britain was reconquered, but in 378 the Goths won their first major victory at Adrianople. Soon after that, Theodosius began issuing edicts to make Catholicism the sole recognized religion; over the next two decades heresy withered and the pagan temples were closed, sometimes wrecked by clerically led mobs; again the faithful rejoiced . . . and then, in 406, barbarian hordes crossed the Rhine and overran Gaul. In 410 Britain was lost for ever and Rome itself was sacked by the Goths. Furthermore the triumphant invaders were heretics, converts to Arianism.

Throughout these disasters, the Church not only failed to avert collapse but was palpably uninterested in even trying. As Bertrand Russell remarks of St Jerome:

> Jerome's letters express the feelings produced by the fall of the Roman Empire more vividly than any others known to me. . . . [Yet] with all Jerome's deep feeling about the fall of the ancient world, he thinks the preservation of virginity more important than victory over the Huns and Vandals and Goths. Never once do his thoughts turn to any possible measure of practical statesmanship. . . . It is no wonder that the Empire fell into ruin when all the best and most vigorous minds of the age were so completely remote from secular concerns. [16]

Few of the Empire's citizens could have worked it out so rationally. But the sequence of events made the ordeal look like a judgment, indeed a series of judgments, and that was easy to understand. Even for convinced Christians there was at least the suspicion of a shortcoming, an abuse of success perhaps. Among the indifferent and the pagans, a feeling grew that all these catastrophes were a consequence of deserting the old gods. The Rome of Jupiter had been powerful and prosperous, the Rome of Christ was pitiable. Augustine wrote his principal work, *The City of God*, in reply to such reproaches.

Though the old gods lacked the vitality to fight back against the Galilean, events were spreading a nostalgic unrest. Society remained religious in spirit. There could be no escape into what would now be called a secular attitude. So the case of Constantinople in 379 was repeated on a larger scale. Christians sought a new protective celestial power, the intermediate power spoken of by Newman, closer than the seemingly indifferent Trinity. Non-Christians, meanwhile, were in a mood to welcome a restoration of something like pagan deity and religious practice. Mary, Mother of God, could satisfy both kinds of aspiration. She was already within the Catholic scheme of things, and she could now be promoted. Her title recalled the still-not-quite-dead Cybele (as the western Fathers were well aware), and Cybele had been brought to Rome, long ago, to repulse Hannibal . . . a task she punctually performed.

The process which had begun at Constantinople also came to a head there. Ironically, the dispute which had that result was not in theory over Mary at all, but over Christ. In 428 Constantinople acquired a new patriarch, Nestorius. He was a product of the scriptural school of Antioch, which had been waging a rearguard action against what its leaders held to be novelties. One of these, in their opinion, was the Church's exaltation of Christ to a point where he was no longer genuinely human. The Antiochenes were so anxious to preserve his humanity that they came close to treating him as a split personality – a complete divine person (the Logos) and a complete human person, incomprehensibly partnered in the same body. It was inferred that since the divine partner had existed from all eternity, the Virgin could not be said to have given birth to him. Mother of Christ, yes; Mother of God, no.

This was the view of Nestorius's principal teacher, Theodore, and the new patriarch approved of it. He was still fresh in office when a certain Proclus preached a sermon at his cathedral that reads like an attempt to provoke him. Proclus may have resented Nestorius's appointment and thought that he himself had been unfairly passed over (he did in fact become patriarch himself later). The sermon, at any rate, was delivered from Nestorius's pulpit in Nestorius's presence, and was a soaring flight of Marian rhetoric, drawing in most of the symbolism of Ambrose, Jerome and others.

We have the text. It begins 'Today, on the feast of the Virgin' –

that is, the commemoration already noted, which in 428 fell on 23 December. Proclus goes on:

> We have been assembled by the holy Mary, the stainless jewel of virginity, the rational paradise of the second Adam, the workshop of the unity of the natures [of Christ], the scene of the saving contract, the bridal chamber, in which the Word espoused the flesh, the living bush, which was not burnt by the fire of the divine birth, the truly light cloud that bore him who is above the cherubim together with his body, the fleece cleansed by the dew from heaven . . . servant and mother, virgin and heaven, the only bridge between God and men, the awesome loom . . . on which the garment of union was woven. . . .

The sentence does eventually end. Later, he dwells on the mystery of the Incarnation:

> I see the miracles and proclaim the Godhead; I see the sufferings and do not deny the manhood. Emmanuel has, indeed, opened the gates of nature, because he was man, but he did not break the seals of virginity, because he was God. As he had entered through the hearing, so he went out from the womb [without violating it]; he was born as he was conceived; he had entered without passion, he went forth without corruption, according to the prophet Ezekiel.

This last phrase recalls the passage about the east gate of the Temple. Proclus quotes it, and then exclaims: 'Behold, an exact description of the holy Theotokos Mary!'[17]

Nestorius could not very well remain silent. When Proclus had finished, he rose from his episcopal chair and went up into the pulpit himself. He acknowledged that Mary was worthy of every praise, but to say that she gave birth to God was to bring Christianity close to pagan myth. The Christ whom she bore had a beginning and was carried in her womb for nine months. The Second Person of the Trinity did not have a beginning and was never gestated. Mary's Son was mysteriously 'joined' to God. He was a temple wherein the Logos dwelt. But the man died and only the God rose.

However these utterances were meant to be taken, one thing was clear. Nestorius denied Mary the title Mother of God. His comments on the fatal sermon were reported to Cyril, Patriarch of Alexandria. Two factors combined to precipitate a crisis. Alexandria and Constantinople, which disputed second place in the Church after Rome, were bitter rivals. Also, Cyril himself was an ardent Marian.

Cyril of Alexandria was an ex-monk, handsome, loud-voiced, and, it must be confessed, a fanatic. He had an unattractive flair for stage-management. He could raise hundreds of monks to demonstrate against an opponent, and he stationed friends in the cathedral to lead the applause which was then customary when a sermon was well received. In view of the sequel, it is psychologically interesting that his name is linked with the murder of a notable virgin. Hypatia was a mathematician's daughter and a skilful mathematician herself. She was also a woman of unusual beauty and charm. Choosing to remain unmarried, she taught philosophy and astronomy to a circle of disciples, some of whom came hundreds of miles to hear her. Unfortunately for herself she was a pagan, one of a small party of intellectuals still opposing the Church. In 415 Cyril denounced her as a trouble-maker. During Lent, a holy season, one of his mobs of monks halted her chariot in the street. A group led by a member of the cathedral clergy pulled her down, tore off her clothes, dragged her to a church, scraped the flesh off her bones with oyster-shells, and burned what was left. An early historian says that Hypatia was martyred 'for her exceeding wisdom'.

One may speculate whether the Virgin whom Cyril came to adore so lavishly was, in part, Hypatia's ghost projected into the heavens by his own guilt. Certainly the adoration was lavish. He dared (as Proclus dared too, but no one else had till then) to apply to Mary the luscious 'sister and spouse' verses of the Song of Songs (5:1-2). He also hit on the argument from Cana which was to enjoy so much favour – that as Christ performed his first miracle at his mother's insistence, she has the power not only to intercede with him but, virtually, to put pressure on him. Now Cyril flung himself on the startled Nestorius.[18]

At Easter 429, and again soon afterwards in an encyclical to his trusty monks, Cyril published his case for the title Theotokos.

If Christ was God, Mary was the Mother of God; it was as simple as that. He wrote to the Pope, Celestine, as Nestorius did too in self-defence. Also he wrote directly to Nestorius urging him to abjure, and received a politely negative answer; tried again, and received an answer that was still negative but not so polite. Meanwhile he was erupting further letters in other directions – to the Emperor Theodosius II, to the Emperor's consort, to the Emperor's sisters. In April 430 he compiled a dossier on the case and sent it off to Celestine.

The Pope accepted that he had to take action. He convened a synod in Rome, which declared against Nestorius. On 10 August Celestine wrote letters to the Patriarch, clergy and people of Constantinople. His ruling was firm, even severe: the complicated notion of the double Christ could only harm Christianity. However, he took the bizarre course of sending his messages, not to Constantinople, but to Alexandria. Cyril was to pass them on and see that the verdict was enforced. Nestorius's enemy was thus not merely upheld but appointed as Rome's agent to discipline him. When Cyril forwarded the documents he enclosed an additional broadside of his own. But his triumph was spoilt. By the time the package got to Constantinople, Theodosius and his colleague Valentinian had intervened, summoning a general council of the Church to meet in Ephesus at Pentecost 431. Nestorius was free to claim that the papal ruling was superseded, and to retort to Cyril's diatribes. When the Council assembled, a strong Nestorian party had formed.

Cyril, however, had lost none of his political talent, and he held more cards. The Bishop of Ephesus was a friend of his. When Nestorius arrived he found obstacles placed in his way and hostility among the people. Many of his supporters from the more distant east were held up on the journey, and so were the envoys of the Pope. On 22 June, without waiting for them, Cyril opened the proceedings and appointed himself chairman. The Emperor's representative tried to protest and was thrown out. Nestorius had already refused to attend on such terms.

The agenda consisted of readings from the documents in the case, chosen by Cyril, with almost no discussion. Nestorius was declared deposed, and excommunicated. When his backers reached Ephesus four days later they held a rival Council and excommunicated Cyril. Celestine's envoys arrived later still and reinstated him. A new imperial commissioner arrested both the contending patriarchs and put them in prison. The wrangle was resolved when the eastern bishops who had supported Nestorius worked out a formula enabling them to confess Mary to be Mother of God. In September the Emperor let the patriarchs go, but confirmed Nestorius's deposition and sent him back to Antioch. Cyril returned to Alexandria. A breakaway Nestorian Christianity spread through Asia and flourished disjointedly for a long time, but the verdict of the main Church at Ephesus remained unshaken.[19]

The most revealing event in the whole affair did not take place among the bishops at all. During 22 June, while Cyril was presiding over his rigged Council, crowds gathered and demonstrated outside. The pronouncement against Nestorius was the signal for an explosion of joy, not because of the conclusion about Christ but because of the by-product: Mary was the Mother of God and could safely be worshipped. Cyril and his henchmen were escorted to their lodgings through a delirious city, with torchlight processions and shouts of 'Praised be the Theotokos!' Great indeed, after her brief eclipse, was Diana of the Ephesians.[20]

It was in the public acclaim, not in the sordid squabbles at high levels, that the truth of these happenings was displayed. Cyril was not imposing a dogma but recognizing and ratifying a trend. Though counted as a saint, he owes that honour chiefly to his role as an unworthy agent of Providence . . . or the Zeitgeist. Because of him the hierarchy surrendered to what the masses demanded.

While in Ephesus he inaugurated the new era with a speech which has been called the most famous Marian sermon of antiquity. It was delivered in the church already dedicated to her. A long verbal salute opens with the significant phrase 'Hail Mary'. 'Hail Mary Theotokos [says Cyril], venerable jewel of the whole earth, never-extinguished lamp, crown of virginity, sceptre of orthodoxy. . . .' And so forth. 'Sceptre of orthodoxy' takes up Gregory of Nazianzus's idea that belief about Mary is a test and safeguard of Catholic faith. Her liturgy will in due course be praising her for having 'destroyed all heresies'. Cyril goes on to a startling list of things Mary has done. Through her, the Holy Trinity is adored on earth; the angels are gladdened; the tempter-devil has been expelled from heaven; fallen man is restored; all creatures have attained knowledge of the truth; holy baptism has come to believers; churches have been built all over the world; nations have been led to repentance for their idolatry. Cyril says that these things have been done by her 'through whom the only-begotten Son of God has shone forth', thus allowing the orthodox interpretation that it is all due to her bringing Christ into the world, and Christ alone is the real doer. But a Mariolatrous audience, listening to the sermon with no text in front of them, would have been unlikely to work this out; and a veteran public speaker like Cyril could hardly have been unconscious of the way his words would in practice be taken.[21]

The citadel had fallen. Proclus, who had launched the attack, became Patriarch of Constantinople. Rome itself took the lead in a proliferation of Marian churches, new or rededicated. Its own Santa Maria Maggiore quickly acquired a vast mosaic on a triumphal arch, depicting the Virgin enthroned and glorified. Almost every large city throughout the Empire followed suit in architectural homage. Predictably perhaps, several of Mary's churches stood on ground once sacred to female divinity. Santa Maria Maggiore replaced Cybele's temple on the Esquiline hill. In due course Santa Maria in Aracoeli, on the Capitoline, succeeded to a temple of the Phoenician goddess Tanit. Another Roman church adjoined Isis's sanctuary near the Pantheon, another was on a site which had long been consecrated to Minerva, the Roman form of Athene. This last goddess, virgin daughter of Zeus, handed over to the new Virgin in a number of places, notably the Greek city of Syracuse, and Athens itself.

The lingering popular cults made the same transition. Rustic shrines of Aphrodite in Cyprus turned painlessly into shrines of Mary, where she is hailed to this day as *Panaghia Aphroditessa*. Goddesses surrendered their functions to her. Like Cybele she guarded Rome. Like Athene she protected various other cities. Like Isis she watched over seafarers, becoming, and remaining, the 'Star of the Sea'. Like Juno she cared for pregnant women. Christian art reflected her new attributes. She wore a crown recalling Cybele's. Enthroned with her Child she resembled Isis with Horus. She even had touches of Neith about her. The title and office of Queen of Heaven passed to her naturally from Isis, Anath and Astarte, and preserved her own Collyridian character.[22]

A battered, disillusioned society had looked for a new protector and found one. In psychological terms, the nature of the protection is obvious. It is defined not only by the Theotokos crisis but by a shift of emphasis which begins about the same time. In the fourth century, Christians had thought of Mary as primarily the Virgin. In the fifth, they thought of her as primarily the Mother. She represented a refuge of unique value in an age of peril and insecurity: the womb. In her, the Mother of *God*, the entire Christian nature-of-things was safely enclosed. To quote the words of a much-loved devotional paradox, 'he whom the heavens could not contain was contained in her womb'. Christ himself, the divine humanity, became foetal, and so – vicariously – did the mystical body of the faithful.

This withdrawal was the Catholic world's spiritual response to the barbarians. However irrationally, it went far towards restoring nerve. If it implied birth as well as protection – well, at least it would be a new birth, a fresh start. Hence the surprising phrases of St Peter Chrysologus already quoted on page 147: 'Mary is called Mother. . . . Was it not she who conceived in her single womb the people going out of Egypt, that it might come forth a heavenly progeny reborn to a new creation?' In the non-Christian perspective, Mary was She through whom, in association with her Saviour Son, the ancient power of the Eternal-Womanly could revive.

It might appear that since the Roman world did in fact continue to crumble, her protection was manifestly useless. Why, therefore, was she not discredited in her turn? But the worst shocks were already past. The western Empire had suffered its death-wounds long before 431, and the remainder of its career, though doomed, was not so utterly traumatic as the phase through which St Augustine lived. There could now be resignation and readjustment. Rome even summoned the strength to win a victory. Attila, the worst of all the barbarians, was defeated, and Europe never succumbed to the total savagery of the Huns. A few decades later Italy, Spain and Gaul settled down as Teutonic kingdoms, which at least gave their subjects a degree of calm, and relief from the oppressions of the imperial decadence. It was a long time before westerners learned to worship Mary with fervour, but they had no reason to turn away from her as an outright failure.

In the Greek-speaking east, meanwhile, her protection showed every sign of working, and her status was correspondingly high. The Byzantine Empire survived, recovered, even counter-attacked, and it did so under the banner of resurgent Marian Christianity. In the rich mosaics of its churches, in the exquisite metal-work of its craftsmen, the Virgin sat or stood: an august blue-clad figure, hooded and haloed, receiving the Magi with the Child on her lap, or lifting her hands to heaven as Christ ascended. She was portrayed in the style deemed suitable for sovereigns and consuls, not for humble citizens. Even at the Annunciation she was a princess rather than a girl. She belonged among the rulers, and with their subjects' glad acquiescence they made her their patroness, in war as well as peace. The ships of the Byzantine navy carried her image. Byzantine generals such as Narses entrusted their armies to her care. So also, it is said, did Arthur, fighting for the remnants of Imperial and Christian order in Britain. Though his repulse of the Saxons was only temporary, his later legend sustained the honour of his protectress.[23]

Chapter 9

NOTES FOR AN UNWRITTEN HISTORY

I

A conclusion therefore emerges. After four centuries of growth, Christianity was completed, in its essentials, when the cult of Mary was made a part of it. That happened at Ephesus in 431. Much more was yet to come, including a protracted debate over the Marian doctrines themselves. But the Catholic Church of the fifth century can be recognized as the same that flourishes today; and while countless groups have diverged from it, claiming to purify or reform the religion it taught, that religion remains a common inheritance and is the fountainhead of nearly everything known as Christianity.

Only – as now appears – the word 'religion', in the singular, disguises a more complex fact. The Christianity shaped in the Ephesian mould was not strictly one religion but a combination of two. The Church of Christ was of course the paramount partner. It had existed since the early Empire, survived many ordeals, and won through to toleration and then to power. Having a male Godhead, a male Saviour, a male priesthood, it received attention in a society ruled by men, and is well known to us because of what they said and wrote. Alongside it, however, there was . . . something else. It was a dissident body which also traced its inspiration to the Gospel events, but paid its chief homage to the Virgin, as Queen of Heaven and (in effect) a form of the Goddess; and it was composed mainly of women.

No one even knows what its adherents called it. We have a glimpse of it under its 'Collyridian' nickname, and probably another in the papyrus prayer to the Mother of God. It is likely to be older than either: first, because there are hints that it grew from a mystery over Mary's passing, and a rumour that she was immortal, a female Elijah; second, because several Marian themes in the Fathers, as far back as Justin Martyr, make better sense if we assume borrowing from a school of thought outside the Church.

In the 360s Ephraem borrowed more boldly, at least for poetic purposes. From him the idea of looking to Mary as a living intercessor in heaven reached the Cappadocian group. Basil and his brother began giving substance to it in Christian terms, and about 379, at Constantinople, Basil's friend Gregory of Nazianzus introduced the custom of praying to Mary. For various reasons it proved acceptable, and the new cult developed and spread. The process moved into a higher and higher tempo, till, in 431, the Church swallowed its shadow-religion up. After that there was no sufficient basis for the separate sect and we hear no more of it. Yet arguably the shadow was no less than the substance. Arguably it was the women, and the Eternal-Womanly as Mother of God, that saved Christianity as an effective religion. Certainly the rival Nestorian Church, despite missionary zeal and early success, failed to maintain its non-Marian Christianity and dwindled away.*

But did the Church succeed in assimilating what it had taken over?

Its theologians never surrendered their main position. They could not admit Mary as divine. To do so would mean that the Collyridians had taken over the Church. She had to be adjusted to the Catholic framework, and kept subordinate to Jesus. To this end the more orthodox forced her into the unreal harmony with him surveyed on pp. 112–15. The Church's view was, in the words of Newman, that 'the glories of Mary are for the sake of her Son'. All Christian spokesmen including Cyril insisted that

---

* It was only after arriving at these conclusions that I discovered Elizabeth Gould Davis's book *The First Sex*. Published in 1971, it makes the same point in a radical-feminist spirit. The argument, however, is chiefly sociological. Having approached the topic from a different angle, I would simply remark that the history of the Church supports Elizabeth Gould Davis a great deal more powerfully than she seems to realize herself.

the Virgin was strictly human, no goddess but a created being. To this day the most ardent Catholic Mariolaters have never said otherwise (though, as will be seen, they long since devised a formula for having it both ways). Since she was a creature, she could not be worshipped as the Triune Godhead was worshipped. Yet on the other hand, she was higher than all the saints, and therefore not to be treated like them. The official position – implied from the outset, though not defined till later – was that the worship proper to God was *latria*; the sub-worship due to saints was *dulia*; and Mary should be given a special kind of devotion called *hyperdulia*, which was hers alone.

The word, being based on *dulia*, seemed to anchor her on the human level. In practice, however, *hyperdulia* tended to float upwards into *latria*, 'Mariolatry' strictly so-called. It could do this all the more easily because there were no other instances of it to determine its limits. When the Virgin became 'Our Lady', a title echoing Christ's title 'Our Lord', she sounded like his equal. Some zealots seriously urged, on a courtly analogy, that the honour due to the King was due also to the King's mother. So if the King was God, what, in practice, was she?[1]

The set prayers which the Church presently began to use (and still does) appeared at first to be linking Mary firmly to Christ and the approved pattern of redemption. Chief of them in favour has always been the *Ave Maria*, Hail Mary. This was composed in the fifth or sixth century as a salutation, combining Luke 1:28 and 42.

> Hail Mary, full of grace, the Lord is with thee: blessed art thou among women, and blessed is the fruit of thy womb, because thou didst conceive the Redeemer of our souls.

In later usage the last part was shortened to 'blessed is the fruit of thy womb, Jesus', and a petition was added:

> Holy Mary, Mother of God, pray for us sinners now and at the hour of our death.

Her role and relationship to her Son are no less clear in a similar brief petition:

Pray for us, O holy Mother of God, that we may be made worthy of the promises of Christ.

But in other prayers the link became tenuous. One that found a place in the Roman liturgy as well as the Greek was the *Sub tuum praesidium*. This was based on the prayer in the papyrus fragment already quoted, and thus looked to the Virgin rather than Christ.

Under thy protection we seek refuge, O holy Mother of God; despise not our petitions in our necessities, but deliver us continually from all dangers, O glorious and blessed Virgin.

First used in Byzantine circles, this reached the west by way of an eighth-century monk, Ambrose Autpert, who was abbot of a southern Italian monastery and in touch with Greek communities. Probably through the same Ambrose Autpert the western liturgy acquired a further prayer in the same spirit, the *Sancta Maria*:

Holy Mary, succour the wretched, help the faint-hearted, comfort the sorrowing, pray for the people, mediate for the clergy, intercede for all women vowed to God: so that all may experience thy help who devoutly praise thy name.

Here too, though auxiliary to God and his Church, Mary sounds like an independent agent. It is her own choice whether she does mediate for priests, or intercede for nuns; she might not.

The doctrinal scheme is still holding together in the most moving of these prayers, the *Salve Regina*, which was composed towards 1100 and sponsored by the religious orders. This can hardly be separated from the Latin, and the music which the Latin is sung to. Its august accents are only dimly heard in the standard English, which reduces *mater misericordiae* to 'mother of mercy' and *dulcedo* to 'sweetness', and sinks towards the maudlin.

Hail, holy Queen, mother of mercy; hail, our life, our sweetness, and our hope! To thee do we cry, poor banished children of Eve; to thee do we send up our sighs, mourning and weeping from this valley of tears. Turn then, O most gracious advocate, thine eyes of mercy towards us, and after this our exile show unto us the blessed fruit of thy womb, Jesus: O clement, O loving, O sweet Virgin Mary.

The doctrinal scheme, it must be repeated, is holding. Yet the emphasis has altered. Mary is indeed to unite us with Christ, but Mary is active and Christ is passive. It is almost as if she were Isis summoning us to approach the child Horus whom she cradles in her arms.

Much the same bias is apparent in the Rosary, which dates from about this time. In its fully developed form it guides the bead-teller through a series of meditations on scenes from the Gospels, during which the Hail Mary is to be recited. True, the Lord's Prayer as well is said at intervals. But the Hail Marys vastly outnumber the Our Fathers; and the last of the fifteen themes, taking leave of the Bible altogether, is Mary's coronation as Queen of Heaven.[2]

When we turn from the Church's language to its calendar, the impression is no different. The feasts of the Virgin always conserved doctrine, but they gradually shifted emphasis. Her pre-Ephesian commemoration, taking place on the Sunday before Christmas, made her strictly and solely 'the Christ-child's mother'. Even here, however, there was an awkwardness, because the usual practice in commemorating a holy person (at that time normally a martyr) was to do so on the anniversary of the person's death. Whatever traditions may have existed about Mary's death, or at any rate her departure from common life, they did not assign it to December. By about 500, the churches in Antioch and Gaul had moved her commemoration to 18 January, and those in Jerusalem had opted for 15 August. Detached from Christmas, it was well on the way to being a holy day for the Virgin in her own right.

A little later, she virtually annexed two of her Son's feasts. One was the 'Encounter', Candlemas, marking the day when Joseph and Mary took Jesus to the Temple, and Simeon acknowledged the awaited Messiah. By the Ephesian period this was already being named from the 'Purification' instead – that is, Mary's purification after childbirth, which was part of the Temple ceremony – and as such it became a general feast of the Byzantine Church in the sixth century, under the Emperor Justinian. The same happened with 25 March, marking Christ's conception. Justinian turned it into the 'Annunciation', Lady Day, with the stress on the dialogue between Gabriel and Mary. In the second half of the sixth century the Byzantines reached the point of decreeing holy days for Mary alone, which recalled events fifteen years before Christ was born. Her conception by her own legendary mother St Anne was observed on 9 December, and her birth on 8 September. Rome adopted three of these feasts for the western Church during the following century. There, the Purification began to be observed as such somewhere about 600, and was fixed on 2 February. The Annunciation and Mary's birth or 'Nativity' were added to the calendar between 650 and 700.

Two of the Marian holy days became involved with special teachings about her. The early commemoration, transferred to the reputed date of her passing or 'falling asleep' (the Dormition), ended up as the feast of her Assumption or bodily ascent to heaven, which might be supposed to have followed quickly afterwards. The Jerusalem date, 15 August, was made obligatory by the Emperor Maurice about 600, and it became general in the west towards 650. For obvious reasons the Assumption reinforced belief in Mary's intercessory powers. Many of the warmest assertions of them are to be found in sermons preached on that day – by Greeks from an early period, and first in the west, so far as any record reveals, by the Marian enthusiast Ambrose Autpert. The December feast of Mary's Conception, shifted to the more logical 8th, carried less weight and was slow to reach the west at all; but it gained ground with the doctrine that the Conception was Immaculate.[3]

By the early Middle Ages, then, Mary had five holy days of her own, covering the whole course of her earthly life – the Conception, the Nativity, the Annunciation, the Purification and the Assumption. The Church added one more for general observance, the feast of Our Lady Queen of Heaven, kept on 31 May. (As far back as the sixth century Venantius Fortunatus had written a grandiose Latin poem on her coronation; saints from all countries, including Britain, take part in the ceremony.) A further feast which became important was the Visitation, commemorating her stay with Elizabeth. This was kept on 2 July.

But devotion did not halt there. Over the centuries she acquired a whole series of optional minor feasts, such as Our Lady of Victories, a thanksgiving for Christian successes against the Turks. The Carmelite Order, which held her in special reverence and hymned her as Flower of Carmel, allotted her no fewer than twenty-three days of its calendar. In the mid-twentieth century, besides the five ancient feasts, Carmelites were observing the Betrothal of Our Lady; the Patronage of Our Lady; the Apparition of the Blessed Virgin Mary at Lourdes; the Seven Sorrows of the Blessed Virgin Mary (on two different days); Our Lady, Help of Christians; Our Lady, Mediatrix of all Graces (an alternative to the 'Queen of Heaven' feast); the Visitation; Our Lady of Mount Carmel; Our Lady of the Snow; the Most Pure Heart of Mary; the Most Holy Name of Mary; Our Lady of Ransom; the Most Holy Rosary of the Blessed Virgin Mary; the Maternity of the Blessed Virgin Mary; the Purity of the Blessed Virgin Mary; the Presentation of the Blessed Virgin Mary; and Our Lady's Expectation. Though Catholics at large were not imitating the Carmelites in detail, they were treating the whole of May as, in a general sense, Mary's month.

2

This accumulation of separate honours speaks for itself. Yet it is not the whole story, or even the essential story. Despite all dogmatic constraints, the person honoured had been changing and growing in the eyes of the faithful. To trace that deeper trend we must revert to the century after Ephesus.

Among much else it witnessed a second flowering of poetry in Syria, where Ephraem wrote. First came Jacob of Sarug, author of a long and fervent *Ode on the Blessed Virgin Mary*. His chief successor was Romanos, whose language was Greek. In Romanos's poems, as in some of the prayers, we catch hints of the Virgin's being pictured as independent from Christ, or at least of her having a distinct will and a distinct function. Thus Romanos imagines her speaking to her Son, making common cause with a humankind which he almost seems to stand aloof from:

I am not simply *your* mother . . . but for all men I beseech you. You have made me the mouth and the glory of my whole race; in me your world has a mighty protectress, a wall and a support. The exiles from the paradise of delights look to me.

Purely as a poet Romanos would not be conspicuous. But he had a special and enduring impact as the author of the first major Marian hymn to be sung in churches, the *Akathistos*. He composed this during the first half of the sixth century. The Greek title means 'not sitting', and is a reminder that those who sing it must rise in respect. Its twenty-four stanzas, one for each letter of the Greek alphabet, recall various Gospel events and praise Christ and Mary. The odd-numbered ones are followed by salutations to the Virgin alone, ending with a refrain *Chairé, nymphé anympheuté*, 'hail, unespoused spouse'. She is extolled as the source of all Christian truth; as the ladder whereby God descended; as the bridge leading from earth to heaven; as the vanquisher of demons; as the strength of martyrs; as the opener of paradise; as the vessel of the wisdom of God; as the fortress of all who have recourse to her; as the citadel of the Church; as the healer of bodies and the rescuer of imperilled souls.

Romanos's writing of this hymn, and its adoption in the Church (by the Greeks at once, by the Latins in the ninth century at latest), had two sequels. In 626 Constantinople was threatened by barbarians. When the danger receded, the *Akathistos* was enlarged into a song of thanksgiving for deliverance. In 717 the city was threatened again, this time by the army of Leo the Isaurian, who proposed to suppress the use of holy images and was therefore anathema to the Church. Leo's siege failed — it was claimed, because of the Virgin's intercession. The Patriarch Germanus held a festival in her honour, at which the *Akathistos* was sung, and preached a sermon on the day of the Assumption, hailing her as virtual Co-Saviour. 'No one, Lady all-holy, is saved except through you. . . . No one, Lady most venerable, is given the merciful gift of grace except through you.'

Germanus injected two ideas into Marian thinking – two highly radical ideas. One was that God's earthly mother retains authority over him in heaven. This astounding inference from Luke 2:51, which says merely that Jesus as a boy was obedient to his parents, inspires Germanus to address Mary as follows: 'You, having maternal power with God, can obtain abundant forgiveness even for the greatest sinners. For he can never fail to hear you, because God obeys you through and in all things, as his true mother.' It might seem difficult to go any further, but Germanus manages it. Mary, he maintains, does not simply put requests to the Deity on matters they could agree about; she actively and successfully opposes him. 'You turn away the just threat and the sentence of damnation, because you love the Christians . . . therefore the Christian people trustfully turn to you, refuge of sinners.' The universe is split at the summit. God stands for Justice, and since we are all sinners more or less, most of us have little to hope for at his hands. Mary stands for Mercy, and it is only because of her influence at court, not because of love or goodwill on God's part, that heaven is within reach for more than a handful of human beings.

All this is easier to understand if imagined against the visual background. Byzantine ecclesiastical art turned Christ into a world-ruler so tremendous that he was dehumanized, alarming, remote. It underlined the effect of the theologians' decisions about his nature, making the Virgin, even the majestic Byzantine Virgin, seem the only friend close to the throne and the only rescuer from utter awestruck despair. Even so, the Patriarch went further than logic or doctrine warranted.

Though his special teachings remained for the moment in reserve, quietly ripening, the Greek Church agreed that Mary was indispensable to salvation. An edict issued from Constantinople in 754 condemns anyone whatsoever who withholds worship from her: anyone, in its own words, who 'does not confess the holy Ever-Virgin Mary, truly and properly the Mother of God, to be higher than every creature whether visible or invisible, and does not with sincere faith seek her intercessions, as one having confidence in her access to our God.'

She is no longer the gentle Lady to whom Christians *may* turn
for help. She is the unique being, above the archangels, to
whom they *must* turn or be in peril of losing their souls for
ever.[4]

3

In this exaltation of Mary in heaven, we have the key to her
expanding glories on earth: to the heaping up of praises and the
evolution of prayers and rites, first among Byzantine Christians
and then among Roman ones. It would be futile, here, to go
further in detail, tracing the structures of Mary-worship through
the Middle Ages and into modern times. The story is too vast,
and its fundamentals are now sufficiently clear. However, there
is some point in asking how it looks as a whole in the light of the
facts which have emerged. If these seem to shed fresh light and
give an improved perspective, the summing-up may serve as a
preface to the adequate history which is yet to be written.

As anyone might guess from the effusions quoted, Mary's
devotees have a habit of running to extremes. Germanus is not a
mouthpiece of dying superstition, he is the herald of a trend
which is to persist and strengthen, right into the twentieth
century. In this a curious contrast appears. One of the Virgin's
attributes, according to the liturgy, is that she 'overcomes all
heresies'; and it is true, simply as historical fact, that her
worship does tend to conserve Catholic loyalty. Protestant
seceders have always felt compelled to oppose it. Yet it hardly
seems reliably orthodox itself. Again and again enthusiasts make
claims on Mary's behalf which defy scripture, distort tradition,
and would, on any impartial reading, be branded as heresy.

Catholics palliate these as 'devotional excesses'. But in a
system as powerful and well-defined as Catholicism, one would
expect aberrations to be swiftly corrected. The norm should
return, the interrupted stream should flow as before. It does not.
The history of Marian doctrine is largely a history of extreme
positions gradually becoming official ones. Debate may meander
on for hundreds of years, but in the end the extremists triumph.

If the Virgin has kept her worshippers securely wedded to orthodoxy, it is partly because orthodoxy has proved unable to break with Virgin-worship, has always adjusted itself so as to remain at one with it – not of course by changing the basic creed, but by restating and enlarging, and tolerating those who restate and enlarge more boldly. This at least was the rule till the death of the late Pope Pius XII. While the Marian tide has ebbed sharply since the Second Vatican Council, it is too soon to be sure that the Church's bias has altered. Over most of its history the nature of the bias is evident. Even where a Mariolatrous author or preacher is admitted to have gone too far, and has been disowned by more prudent Catholics, we are still apt to find that he has been canonized and that his works have been re-issued without ecclesiastical protest.[5]

Whatever compulsion is at work here, it is more than the odd ripple of 'devotional excess'. The sexual sublimations of a celibate priesthood may well be a factor, but they cannot account for the Mariolatry of the masses, which has often ranged far ahead of the clergy. Moreover the whole process seems against the grain. As Henry Adams put it (*Mont-Saint-Michel and Chartres*, pp. 261–2):

> A heretic must insist on thinking that the Mater Dolorosa was the logical Virgin of the Church, and that the Trinity would never have raised her from the foot of the cross, had not the Virgin of Majesty been imposed, by necessity and public unanimity, on a creed which was meant to be complete without her.

The 'necessity and public unanimity' appeared first at Ephesus and have surged up in repeated waves ever since. But why? Where has this compulsion come from?

If the cult began as a separate religion, we have the answer. The separate religion, though absorbed by the Church, was never fully digested. It stirred restlessly in the system and sometimes, directly or indirectly, shaped it. There is no call for romantic theories of an underground movement or a conspiracy of Collyridian diehards. Enough that the Church tried to assimilate a pattern of thinking which proved, in the upshot, to be unassimilable.

An early hint that this was so is to be found in a surprising place, the Koran. While Mohammed revered Jesus and Mary, he condemned Christian teaching about them as he understood it to be from his contacts with Arabian Christians. The form of his condemnation is very odd. Allah, he insists, did *not* make these two divine; the Virgin was simply a holy woman in whom he worked a miracle, and her Son was simply a great prophet; there is no Trinity of God, Jesus and Mary. The protest would make more sense if we knew of any Christians who did preach a Trinity of God, Jesus and Mary. No record of such a group survives. Yet some in Arabia were apparently doing so when Mohammed wrote, during the first quarter of the seventh century. What Marian pressure was at work distorting their Christianity? It is little use trying to guess, but pressure there evidently was. Furthermore, Arabia had been Collyridian country. [6]

Back in the mainstream, we have seen how several Christian motifs, hard to account for in themselves, can be construed as inferences from the lost separate religion. Mary's status as Second Eve, her symbolism of the Church, her motherhood of Christians, all follow from her manifestation in the woman of Revelation 12 . . . which, however, is not admitted in Christian writings till too late to be relevant. Plausibly this was a Marianist theme which Christians at first did not like to adopt, yet which had consequences they approved of and did adopt. As we push on further into the history of doctrine, that plausibility grows, and earlier events illuminate later ones.

The same chapter of Revelation points to the belief in Mary as a female Elijah; and the same Christian process of thought, working on that belief, can account for both the Marian dogmas, the Immaculate Conception and the Assumption. As with Elijah (we may infer), Mary's deathlessness was taken by her worshippers to imply that she was free from sin. As with Elijah, her only fitting destiny in their eyes was a triumphal ascent, body and soul complete, to a post near God's throne. Christians' behaviour is in keeping with the view that they did the same with these two ideas as with the earlier ones. When the Church affirms them, it censors out the original basis and destroys the logic. They are left hanging in a void, two dogmas coming from nowhere.

The Church refused to admit Mary as an immortal like Elijah, partly because of male prejudice, partly because the legend, despite Epiphanius's willingness to entertain it, was suspect as giving no place to Christ. She must be held to have died like anyone else, or at any rate 'fallen asleep', and if that event had a special sequel it was only because her Son raised her. Denying the Virgin Immortal, many Christians still asserted the two corollaries, the Virgin Sinless – but now for no reason – and the Virgin Assumed into Heaven – again for no reason. Neither dogma is intelligible in terms of scripture or Christian tradition. Both are intelligible as branches from a Marianist trunk. The Church's scheme had no place for that trunk. Yet it made its ghostly presence felt, because, in trying to subsist without it, the branches grew ever more contorted. A new logic was demanded which Catholicism could not supply from its primary resources, and therefore had to improvise.

The Immaculate Conception, cut off by itself, was hard to justify or even explain. To accept – as most Christians did by the fifth century – that Mary never did wrong, was one thing; to pin this down to a doctrinal statement was another. The reason alleged now was that when God became man, the act required total purity in the human vessel, a mother without blemish. Christian stress on 'original' sin as well as 'actual' made the notion more complex, especially in the west where Augustine's influence was strong. To be totally pure, Mary had to be not only innocent through her entire life but free from the original stain, even at the first instant of existence in her own mother's womb.

Furthermore, Christians tended to connect original sin with sex, and assume that a child received its taint from the sexual act involved in creating it. Therefore, if Mary was truly spotless, the only way this could have happened was through a special exemption by divine grace at the moment of conception. Some theologians were willing to argue thus, others were not. The prudish atmosphere of the whole debate produced a misunderstanding which is still not extinct: that in order to make Mary perfect the Catholic Church teaches that she too was virgin-born like Jesus, or even (as Bernard Shaw apparently thought) that she was descended from a line of virgins stretching back to Creation.

Not so. But however stated, the Immaculate Conception was odd, and so devoid of clear logic that the growth of delusion was understandable. It could even be faulted as inconsistent with the Assumption, because, if Mary was unaffected by Adam's sin, why did she suffer the Adamite penalty of dying before her translation to the celestial world?

In the effort to cope with the Assumption, invention was more colourful. If Christians knew any Collyridian tradition of Mary's passing, they blotted it out as valueless. Having resolved that she did die or 'fall asleep' before being taken up to heaven, they needed a legend of their own. Late in the fifth century that need was met by a Greek narrative ascribed, absurdly, to John. As time passed its story was repeated with improvements and variations in Latin, Syriac, Arabic, Coptic and Ethiopic. Essentially it tells how Mary spent her last years in Jerusalem, often praying at her Son's tomb that she might be re-united with him. One day an angel appeared to her and announced that her prayer was granted. She asked Jesus to let her see his apostles again before she died. They were scattered through the world – John in Ephesus, Peter in Rome, Thomas in India – but the Holy Spirit lifted them up in clouds, and brought them, including Paul, to Jerusalem. Mary, now on her death-bed, roused herself and spoke with them. Angels appeared around the house. Sick people recovered. Presently Christ himself came to summon his mother; her soul passed visibly into his hands. The apostles took up her lifeless body for burial. Jews menaced the funeral procession, but their assaults were miraculously repelled and conversions resulted. Though the body was laid in a tomb in the usual way, the apostles soon afterwards discovered it to be gone.

Details of the story vary from text to text. Sometimes Mary receives the apostles in Bethlehem. The tomb is in Gethsemane or in the valley of Josaphat (pilgrims were shown it in the latter location), and there is also a version which transfers it to Ephesus. Some accounts are more explicit than others. The chief Latin text goes so far as to describe Jesus coming to the sepulchre, re-infusing Mary's soul into her body, and returning to heaven accompanied by his living mother. But no account has authentic tradition behind it. The Christian legend of the Assumption is fiction, and so plainly fiction that the Church has seldom appealed to it and never required assent to it. All that is insisted upon is the belief around which it grew. It was composed to lend substance to that belief, to plant Mary firmly in heaven as an intercessor . . . and, it seems, to fill the gap left by suppression of the earlier legend.[7]

Neither Marian dogma established itself quickly. Eastern Christians, while seldom contesting Mary's flawlessness, never adopted the Immaculate Conception as a rigid tenet. (The Greek and Russian Orthodox Churches still do not.) They accepted the Assumption early, and continued to do so in their eventual schism from Rome. But they rarely argued with any heat over either. Among westerners, with their greater thirst for exactitude, both the doctrines aroused disagreement. The Immaculate Conception caused more outright disputes. In 1854 Pius IX silenced them at last by defining it as an article of faith. The Assumption tended for a long time to remain a pious opinion, not so widely debated and seldom challenged. Since it was less audibly controversial there was less pressure for a decision, and it had to wait till Pius XII's action in 1950.

Both papal definitions showed that Rome had succeeded in evolving its special method of Marian reasoning. The documentation of the two edicts refers to scripture only in passing, and cites its handful of texts in very fanciful ways. The Immaculate Conception is supposed to be implied by Mary's absolute opposition to evil, as witnessed by the crushing of the serpent's head (Genesis 3:15); also, by her fullness of grace (the mistranslated Luke 1:28 again). The Song of Songs reappears. Its verse (4:7) about the Beloved being all-beautiful without flaw may be read to this day, with Mary's name interpolated, over the entrance to the Lady Chapel in Westminster Cathedral. The Assumption is alleged to be hinted at by a verse in the same book (3:6), 'Who is that coming up from the wilderness like a column of smoke?' Other Assumption texts are Psalm 45:10–16, describing a king receiving a princess into his palace, and Psalm 132:8, 'Arise, O Lord, and go to thy resting place, thou and the ark of thy might' – the argument being that the ark symbolizes the Virgin.

It is not seriously pretended that the texts matter. The appeal is to 'tradition'. But even this does not seem to work, because, over the centuries, it is easy to find both beliefs ignored or opposed by theologians and even saints; they are both present in the Church, but scarcely traditional in the sense of a general acceptance. Nor, of course, can either be traced as far back as the apostolic age. What then does 'tradition' mean? The modern Catholic view, owed largely to Newman, is that doctrine can develop. Something may be implied in tradition, even in scripture, which it takes hundreds of years to realize.[8]

A sceptic may urge that this claim is bogus. What it amounts to is that a doctrine is 'implied' if the Pope says it is, and since he takes his decision after sounding out Catholic opinion, the determining factor is the consensus of the moment. Tradition, so-called, is retroactive. If the faithful *now* choose to think of the Virgin as immaculate, and the Pope bestows his approval, then she *has always been* immaculate, and no further reasons are required.[9] To which a more severe sceptic might add an economic footnote. Mary-worship is lucrative – at Lourdes, for example. But such criticisms are less than fair, and the truth is more interesting. Both definitions have a genuine process of thought behind them. The way in which the doctrines are 'implied' by Christian belief can be put into words. To be specific, their advocates' answer to the demand for reasons is the 'must have' argument . . . which goes far to reveal what Mariology is really about.

Launched by Gregory of Nyssa, this argument was used to prove the Assumption as early as the sixth century by a bishop named Theoteknos, preaching near Jericho. It was fitting, he maintained, that Mary should be assumed into heaven body and soul. Christ, after all, took his own flesh from her, and he would not have allowed hers to suffer corruption any more than his own did. Since he prepared places in heaven for his apostles, he must have prepared a more honourable place for his mother. Since Elijah ascended in the body, so much the more must Mary have ascended, and to a more exalted level. The bishop's main line of proof is in fact to cite other cases and then infer that whatever happened to the Mother of God must have been superior.

Theoteknos might seem to be of purely antiquarian interest. Yet, in essence, this is the argument that prevails. It was redeployed in the west five centuries later on behalf of the same doctrine. Opinion had been swayed against the Assumption by a forged letter of St Jerome, declaring that nothing was known of Mary's passing except that her tomb in the valley of Josaphat was empty. Pseudo-Jerome was probably Paschasius Radbert, a French abbot. The author who swung opinion the other way is known as Pseudo-Augustine, because his treatise was ascribed to that saint. He may in reality have been English. 'There are truths on which scripture is silent,' he observes, 'but not reason. Of these is the Assumption of the Blessed Mary.' He repeats Theoteknos's point about the physical unity between Mary and Christ. It would not have been fitting for the body from which the Saviour himself proceeded to be eaten by worms. Obviously Christ was able to save his mother from corruption. Therefore, since he honoured her, he must have done so, translating her to heaven as a complete and glorified human being.[10]

Whatever Pseudo-Augustine's nationality, it was an Englishman who first used this formula in defence of the Immaculate Conception. He was a monk named Eadmer, and he took a hint from the more famous Anselm, William Rufus's Archbishop of Canterbury, inventor of what is known as the ontological argument for the existence of God. Anselm did not endorse the Immaculate Conception, but Eadmer noticed a sentence in his works which, if thought out to the end, seemed to prove it. 'It was fitting,' Anselm had written, 'that this Virgin should shine with a degree of purity than which no greater can be imagined apart from God.' Quite so, Eadmer contended. Fittingness is a valid test. It was in God's power to make his mother supremely pure, and it was fitting that he should. Any other choice would have made her inferior to what she should be. God must have willed it, he was able to do it, therefore he did it. And it was this maxim of Eadmer, taken up and polished by the Franciscan philosopher Duns Scotus, that steered the doctrine into relatively calm waters. Some dissent rumbled on at intervals, and Rome's long-delayed verdict was not superfluous. The proof, however, was decisive. It showed how Christianity could be made out to 'imply' Marian dogma, and it underlay the papal rulings.[11]

What is the inwardness of this argument? Taken at face value it is merely presumptuous. The pretence to know what God 'ought' to do or 'must' do is vetoed in the Bible. It is the error of Job's friends, whom God rebukes, while commending Job for abandoning all claim to understand (Job 42:7). The truth, however, is not on the surface. Anselm betrays it by what might almost be described as a Freudian slip. His phrase about Mary's purity, 'than which no greater can be imagined apart from God', echoes his own description of God as 'that than which nothing greater can be conceived', which is the basis of the ontological argument. Elsewhere he says, in effect, that Mary is 'that than which nothing is greater except God'. The psychological ground for the 'must have' formula is not the dubious reasoning about God and his options, it is a prior notion of Mary as – on her own level – divine herself. On that level she can be discussed theologically in her own right. Just as every glory that is appropriate to God can be attributed to him, so every glory that is appropriate to the Virgin can be attributed to her. In Christianity, however, this Marianist mode of thinking can no more be allowed than the related myths. Therefore the logic of her nature has to be twisted into rationalization about what God 'must have' done for her, which preserves a touch of the original spirit but snaps under pressure.[12]

That her devotees actually have thought of her thus, quite apart from the two dogmas, is confirmed by some of their marginal fantasies. These include, for instance, a recurring daydream of her as incredibly beautiful. An ancient Ethiopic text is entitled *Salutations to the Members of the Body of the Blessed Virgin Mary*. It praises her in forty-two sensuous paragraphs, feature by feature, right down to her toenails. The implied portrait is a frontal and standing nude, and very little that would be seen is left unpraised, though here and there the language is circumspect. About 1245, at the height of medieval culture, a certain Richard of St Laurent treads the same path as the naive Ethiopian. In a long book *On the Praises of Holy Mary* he devotes forty pages to her physical loveliness, which is made the starting-point for various allegories. Further on he recommends honouring her by saying the Hail Mary while meditating on parts of her body. A modern Mariologist, Gabriele Roschini, still feels able to assert that she 'must have been' beautiful.[13]

Richard of St Laurent was not a major author, but he was not a negligible crank either. His book won a fair-sized public, largely because it was supposed to be the work of a far greater man, the Dominican Albertus Magnus. Another book wrongly ascribed to Albert, the anonymous *Mariale*, extends the same principle. 'The Virgin does not cede place to any of the famous in any matter whatsoever.' In fact she usually excels them. Even on earth, the writer maintains, she had a perfect knowledge of the Trinity; she could see angels and demons; she understood scripture in every detail; she foresaw the future; she was expert in mathematics, geography, astronomy and canon law . . . though the Church which enacted canon law did not yet exist. A second *Mariale*, written in 1478 by the Franciscan Bernardine of Busti, reaffirms her proficiency in all sciences and lengthens the list with the 'must have' argument ('if anyone else had this knowledge, God must have given it to his Spouse in a much higher degree'). Bernardine adds that she was as wise at three as a woman of thirty.

Both the *Mariales* became popular handbooks. In the end theologians recoiled from the cruder marvels. But they went on using the same logic to raise the Virgin above all beings in the moral and spiritual realms. The aforesaid Roschini considers that whatever is true of any saint must be true of her. She is a compendium of all human perfections, and more so. Though below God, she is above everything else, the entire cosmos and even the supernatural order. 'Her greatness borders on the infinite.' Roschini, like the unnamed Pseudo-Albert, seeks a Christian basis for all this in the phrase 'full of grace'. As with so much else, the text is only a bad reason for things believed from a deeper motive: the ineradicable presence of female divinity.[14]

4

Far back, I have suggested, Mary's priestesses deified her as an avatar of Wisdom. That is conjecture, yet now it falls into place. By way of doctrine, where her numinosity lingered and its effects on the Church's mind were felt, Wisdom did actually re-enter the system and blend with her.

As Bouyer remarks in a passage already quoted (p. 147),

there was no reason in Christianity for this to happen. Despite Jerome, few of the Fathers had ever mentioned the two together. Yet it happened. Under a compulsion that was never discussed, the two Marian dogmas drew Wisdom into the liturgy of their feast-days. Proverbs 8:22ff became the Lesson for the Immaculate Conception. Parts of Ecclesiasticus 24 were read at the Assumption. Thus, almost casually, Mary was conceded the Jewish demigoddess's attributes. Proverbs 8 was also read at the feast of her Nativity, and Ecclesiasticus 24 at her feast as Queen of Heaven, when she was once again the Lady hailed by the Collyridians. In the Ecclesiasticus readings Rome excluded one verse – 'From eternity, in the beginning, he created me, and for eternity I shall not cease to exist.' But the thought was not to be suppressed, and even that extreme-sounding verse found its way into Vespers according to the Carmelite Rite.[15]

Censorship in detail could not remove the sting. Mary's Wisdom aspect was subversive in any case. The siting of several of her churches on ground sacred to Athene was a perilous continuity. It evoked not only the pagan wisdom-goddess but others connected with her. The Greek Church dallied with the Mary-Wisdom equation but, on the whole, drew back. In the dedication of the cathedral of Constantinople, the phrase 'Sancta Sophia', Holy Wisdom, was explained as meaning the wisdom of Christ. But Russian churches of the same name, at Kiev and Novgorod for instance, applied it to Mary and expressed that idea in their icons. They held their 'feasts of title' on Marian days. Orthodox Russia instituted a special Mass combining the Holy Wisdom with the Assumption.

That union carried some of the country's religious minds to hazardous extremes. It was still active in the attempts of a Russian theologian, Sergius Bulgakov, to re-think Orthodoxy after the Revolution. Bulgakov saw Mary as 'the creature glorified and deified'. 'In her,' he wrote, 'is realized the idea of Divine Wisdom in the creation of the world; she is Divine Wisdom in the created world.' The Russians were influenced by the Protestant mystic Jacob Boehme, who also speculated about Mary and Wisdom. The Catholic Church, having inserted the Wisdom texts in its liturgy, sensed the danger and left them unexpounded. Recent forays by a few of its theologians have all tended towards a near-deification in Russian style, and been tacitly discouraged.[16]

The concept of Mary as Wisdom-taking-visible-form seems to underlie the bizarre sermons of an isolated fourteenth-century Greek, Isidore Glabas. It is uncanny to see something very like the conjectured Marianist religion re-assembling itself, as though by a latent logic, after a thousand years of silence, and then lapsing into silence again. The Virgin, Isidore declares, existed in heaven ages before her birth below. In her eternal nature she is not a human being or even an angel, but above both orders. Her title Mother of God implies far more than the birth of Jesus. She is the cause and condition of God's manifestation in general. All things came into being because of her, and even for her. Isidore pictures her as an active co-creatress with God, 'drawing creatures into being together with him', aeons ago. Though the relevant Wisdom passage in Proverbs 8 is not cited, the reminiscence of it seems obvious. God was so captivated by her beauty in her celestial form that he united himself as closely to her as possible. He did not place her in his world at its dawn, because her unearthly loveliness would have been too much for it. Yet his creating humanity 'in his own image' refers to her and not Adam; she alone was the true mirror of his perfection. That sounds like another echo, of the Wisdom of Solomon 7:26. A statement that she was enlightening human beings long before her own earthly life sounds like another, of the tenth chapter of the same book.

According to Isidore there was no reason for her to leave heaven at all. She did not belong on earth. However, she descended when its inhabitants grew corrupt, so that God could become incarnate through her and save them. Her advent was a renewal of creation, which is not only holier but literally more beautiful because she was once in it. Isidore re-words biblical texts to suit his purpose. Thus John 1:14, 'We have beheld his glory, glory as of the only-begotten of the Father', becomes 'We have beheld her glory, glory as of the only-begotten Mother of God.' When Mary took the burden of human flesh there was no sin in her conceiving, and she was faultless herself. As a child of Adam she inherited mortality like the rest of us, but she 'threw it off'. Now she is with God and a light for all generations. The comment of the Catholic scholar Jugie, 'Isidore's eyes are so unswervingly fixed on the Mother that he seems to forget the Son', is putting it mildly.[17]

<h2 align="center">5</h2>

More might be guessed about Marianist loose ends in the Church – for example, Peter Chrysologus's hint at reincarnation. There is also the bond between Mary and Elijah in Carmelite and Islamic contexts. The Virgin was at least juxtaposed with the prophet, if no more, at an early stage of Russian Christianity: in Kiev, the Marian 'Holy Wisdom' church was not far from the first church in Russia with its 'Saint Elias' dedication. Guesswork aside, however, it should now be clear that the once-divine Virgin was never trimmed into conformity even by Rome. The effort to do it twisted Catholics' thinking. Parts of the liturgy they devised for her turned out to be so redolent of a dangerous past that the only course was to avoid commenting on them.

Her modern Catholic cult is rooted in the Christendom of the high Middle Ages. Once again, all that can be attempted here is a preface to a vast story which has yet to be completely unravelled. But tracing its continuity with the origins may help to bring its unravelling nearer.

The Marian tide did not flow strongly in western Europe till the Crusades. When it came, the causes were mixed. New art, new poetry, a new romanticization of women, all had their share. But contact with the Byzantine Church, in a briefly united struggle against the infidel, gave substance to what might otherwise have remained no more than a sentiment. At least one of the factors, the troubadour convention of courtly love, possibly owed more to the cult than the cult did to it. Mary was a major irruption of the Eternal-Womanly. Catholics in the west, who had revered her and prayed to her without (as a rule) waxing extravagant, now picked up the thread from the Patriarch Germanus and his successors.[18]

At first the atmosphere of the cult was happy and gracious. Byzantine awe was toned down, and cathedral art had few images of pain or sorrow. In that early, exploratory phase the chief spokesman of Marian piety was St Bernard of Clairvaux, who lived from 1090 to 1153. He still kept matters in proportion, writing on the topic with glowing eloquence and very much to the point, but not copiously. Bernard disapproved of the feast of the Immaculate Conception, then a novelty in France, while the bodily Assumption had no special interest for him. In his teaching the Virgin was a friend to the humble, and to those abashed by the majesty of her Son. She could act as a mediatrix, an 'advocate with the Advocate'. The focus, however, was still on Christ, and a Christ of love, not wrath. Transposed into literature by such poets as Dante and Petrarch, the Virgin according to St Bernard became a figure of rare beauty and vividness. The prayer to her which opens the final canto of the *Divine Comedy* ranks among the supreme utterances of western religion. Mary was queenly yet human and attractive. Without the absurd fancies which made her a prodigy of learning, she was the patroness of humanity's highest gifts. In Chartres Cathedral the Seven Liberal Arts attended her.[19]

But the growth of Chartres itself, and other cathedrals, soon showed that Byzantine extremism was not to be kept out. It was simply taking a western form which ignored St Bernard's caution. The cathedrals have been aptly described as 'palaces of the Queen of Heaven'. Those dedicated to her in France – not only Chartres, but Paris, Reims, Amiens, Rouen, Bayeux, Coutances, Noyon, Laon – were far more splendid than the palaces of earthly queens. The Virgin liked to dwell in colour and light and ample space, and some cathedrals had an air of being designed for her rather than the public. It was against a background of Marian architecture, Marian art, Marian craftsmanship, and Marian financial investment, that theologians disputed over doctrine. Within a few decades the vested interest in the cult was enormous, and it was not the interest of a static and docile institution but of a strongly developing one. The same tendencies were at work here as among the schoolmen, giving Mary an autonomous life in the public realm as well as in the arena of debate; and each process reinforced the other.

She was soon being hailed with complete litanies of her own – long lists of titles, such as 'Spiritual Vessel', 'Cause of our Joy', 'Tower of Ivory', 'House of Gold', 'Ark of the Covenant', and (significantly perhaps) 'Seat of Wisdom', which were recited in church with the words 'pray for us' after each. When such litanies had been first composed, they were addressed to lists of saints, but the Virgin under her various titles had always come to fill so much of the list that she was taken out and addressed separately. Some of the new Marian litanies had their ancestry in the *Akathistos* hymn. The oldest known text of the most important, that of Loreto, was written about 1200 and contains seventy-three invocations.[20]

In cathedral imagery the Mother-with-her-Son crowded the Holy Trinity into the background. Her sovereignty at first had imperial rather than royal trappings, but preachers spoke of her in contemporary courtly terms, and presently dynastic chance brought her closer in spirit to feudal monarchy. The twelfth century happened to produce a famous Queen-Mother, Eleanor of Aquitaine, and the thirteenth produced another one, Blanche of Castile, whose loving son was the good and sainted King Louis. Pictorially the Virgin became Queen-Mother of Heaven, with a retinue of ladies-in-waiting disguised as allegorical Virtues and Beatitudes. In her dealings with her own Son she was not unlike Blanche with Louis, even, in one legend, literally going to see him to ask a favour for a dependant.

To imagine her (in effect) giving him orders – the first of Germanus's more daring ideas – was not too huge a step beyond. The Crusades had promoted the great ladies of Europe to a new ascendancy. They were in charge while their husbands were away fighting, and they retained influence even when their husbands were back, partly through friendship with the clergy. The casting of Mary in a dominant role was easy and natural. Also, it led on to Germanus's other idea: that she could oppose her Son on behalf of human petitioners, or, at any rate, suspend his decrees.

Some such escape from the trap of official doctrine was needed more and more as time passed. In the thirteenth century, despite tremendous achievements, the sky was already starting to cloud. The Crusades had failed, and that and other disasters looked like divine judgments on unworthy Christians. Westerners were learning to follow the same path as Byzantines and regard Christ with dread rather than love. The Godhead stood for unshakable cosmic law; it could not grant favours, or make allowances for the frailty of mortals. Since nearly all were sinners, nearly all must be doomed, and the increasingly legalistic tone of theology made the doom all the more certain. The only real hope for most lay in a celestial power that was closer, that could understand and sympathize, could accept excuses and make exceptions . . . and could enforce them, even against the rules. So Mary's regal independence became an independence of Mercy as against Justice. The supernal kingdom was divided. She, in her sphere of action, was virtually equal to Christ in his. She could stand up to him in defence of those who loved her.[21]

Her reputed miracles were many. In the most characteristic, she befriended erring humans who turned to her in devotion or despair. All such legends descend from a single ancestor, the tale of Theophilus of Adana. This is pre-medieval. A Greek form of it is known to have existed before 600. It has a second, more famous family of descendants, the assorted versions of the Faust story. Theophilus, excluded by his bishop from a post he greatly desires, approaches the Devil through the agency of a Jewish sorcerer and sells his soul. After this he prospers, but the thought of the damnation ahead fills him with horror. His remorseful prayers attract the Virgin's attention. She obtains God's forgiveness for him and induces Satan to hand the contract back. Translated into Latin in the eighth century, widely popularized, and included in the *Golden Legend*, Theophilus's rescue was taken up in the west as it had never been in the east. It was cited in all seriousness as proof of Mary's power, and it spawned hundreds of fables on the same lines.

Even in a collection compiled before 1233, the norm of Marian miracles is hardening. As a rule, here and later, the people concerned are not spectacular sinners like Theophilus. Their misdeeds are apt to be commonplace and sometimes repellent. The sole redeeming feature they have in common, 'redeeming' quite literally, is their love for the Virgin. This protects them against the consequences of wrongdoing. Her devotees seem able to get away with anything. A thief prays to her before going out to rob, and when he is hanged, she sustains him in the air till the hangman acknowledges the miracle and lets him live. A nun who leaves her convent to plunge into vice, but keeps praying to Mary, returns at last to find that Mary has taken her place and no one has missed her. And so on. It is unfair to treat this mythology as a licence to sin; by saving misguided mortals the Virgin enables them to repent. But the moral is not always conspicuous. Sometimes she refers to a person as 'my sinner', with a hint that she is a feudal protectress. The dependant can rely on her to fulfil her obligation.

She herself, with all her greatness, is far from being an Olympian sovereign above the battle. Not only does she perform tricks like impersonating the nun, she has jealousies and caprices, and can descend towards our own level. A young man prays to her to soften his beloved's heart. Mary appears and asks which of the two is more beautiful, the beloved or herself? If he insists, she will grant his prayer, but he must choose between them and take the consequences. She forbids another man to marry: she herself, she says, is the better mistress, with a 'rich bed' prepared for him in heaven (which is a metaphor, but a startling one). She can even, in appearance, be blackmailed. A widow whose son is a prisoner of war begs Mary to release him. When nothing happens, she goes to a Madonna and takes away the Child as a hostage. Mary, amused, sets free the widow's son and the Child is put back.

All such legends convey the same message. The medieval popular Virgin represented the all-too-human, the irregular, the exceptional. She was superior to the system and she could break through every rule. Humanity had her on its side in its perpetual protest against divine law and human ordinance. For her, every case was a special case. A suppliant's love for her was what mattered, and it was this that extracted mercy where mercy was needed. She could draw 'her' sinner up out of hell itself, giving him another chance.[22]

Faced with these pyrotechnics of wayward majesty, we ask where God was supposed to stand. After all, the power was still his, not Mary's. In the teaching of St Bernard she had been simply an intercessor, who laid the prayers of the humble before her Son. Technically no one ever said otherwise. Even her miracles were not, strictly speaking, worked by her but by the Triune Godhead at her request. However, one legend gives blackly comic expression to the view of their relationship which was more and more widely taken. A group of devils complain about her. With God they have a fair working arrangement: he is just, and hands over the souls that should be theirs. But Mary interferes, constantly putting in a word on some sinner's behalf . . . and God 'loves and trusts her so much that he will never refuse or contradict her, whatever she does, whatever she says.' Germanus's opinion comes through here with a slight shift of emphasis but no real weakening. Though voiced by agents of Satan, it echoes the belief of countless good medieval Catholics. God never refuses what Mary asks – therefore, in effect, he obeys her, and she has a mother's authority.

In a sense this can still be squared with orthodoxy. If the Virgin is supremely holy she is at one with God, and knows better than to ask anything he is unwilling to grant. He never does refuse her, because she never makes a request which he would refuse. But the autonomous Virgin of medieval Christendom was regarded quite differently. She had a will of her own. She could oppose Mercy to Justice and get her way. Nor was this purely a popular or decadent aberration. A few teachers in the monastic orders had been laying a basis for it even before St Bernard; the thirteenth century simply increased the need and brought it out into the open. Thenceforward, in defiance of many distinguished men who taught otherwise, it came nearer and nearer to being the standard doctrine. Mary was equal with her Son in a heavenly division of labour, and when she wanted a favour, he always did what she asked.

One perfectly logical conclusion was that she was omnipotent. Few spokesmen of the Church said so outright. Some, however, did – Richard of St Laurent, for instance, the same who anatomized her beauty – and many more acquiesced. It was not a direct omnipotence but an 'intercessory' one, working through God who obeyed her will, but it amounted to the same thing. Thus Christians could have it both ways. Mary remained human and accessible, even suffering like ourselves as Mother of Sorrows, when they chose to remember her at the foot of the cross. But she was also a kind of informal goddess, not of course truly divine (a blasphemous thought) but able to arrange whatever one would pray to a goddess for. Chaucer dignifies the concept in a magnificent line: 'Almighty and all-merciable Queen.'[23]

She was planted at the summit, in a class by herself above the angels, Co-Saviour with a dutiful Son whom most men and women could hardly reach except through her. It might seem that this was the limit and no one with a vestige of Christian orthodoxy could go any further. Mary might be virtually equal with God, she surely could not be above him? Yet even that sanctified impiety hovered in the air of the Middle Ages.

Psychologically, it has been claimed, the Trinity was absorbed into the Mother through the Second Person. In poetry 'the Temple of the Trinity' was a title actually given her, and a Madonna in the Cluny Museum has all three Persons inside it. Less recondite, and more surprising, was the influence of the Franciscans. From about 1300 onwards, the tendency of their preaching was to humanize Mary further. Art reflects this in a new realism and warmth of treatment. She becomes a recognizable mother, often fondling a recognizable child. Yet it was precisely this enhanced humanity which led to the most vertiginous notions about her. Flesh and blood and natural feeling seemed to give her a positive advantage over the abstract Deity.

In a sermon on the Assumption mistakenly ascribed to the Franciscan St Bonaventure, the preacher reverts to the theme of Mercy and Justice with a fresh evaluation. He maintains not only that the Virgin was made Queen of Mercy while her Son remained King of Justice, but that she 'chose the best part' (an allusion to Luke 10:42, in the Assumption Gospel reading), because mercy is better than justice. On this ground and others, she has an actual moral superiority.

In the fifteenth century another Franciscan, Bernardine of Siena, outdoes Pseudo-Bonaventure. The Virgin, for Bernardine, may almost be described as doing favours to God rather than receiving them from him. By bringing him into the world of space and time, she added to his nature in ways that surpassed his unaided power. The Father's generation of the Son in eternity was less remarkable than Mary's giving birth to him in a human shape. 'God could only generate someone infinite, immortal, eternal . . . in the form of God; but the Virgin made him finite, mortal, poor . . . in the form of a servant, in a created nature.' Furthermore she did what she did through her own transcendent gifts. She was wiser, holier, richer in grace than all other creatures put together. 'Even if she had not been the

Mother of God, she would nevertheless have been the mistress of the world.' In the relationship with God the Father which produced Jesus, Bernardine credits her with what amounts to a sexual ascendancy, and an active role. 'O the unthinkable power of the Virgin Mother! . . . One Hebrew woman invaded the house of the eternal King; one girl, I do not know by what caresses, pledges or violence, seduced, deceived and, if I may say so, wounded and enraptured the divine heart.'

These are not the words of a lonely heretic or fanatic. They were spoken in public by a leading member of a major religious order, a man of intelligence and integrity, a promoter of Christian reunion, one of the most popular preachers of the age; and they were not forgotten. Even Bernardine's weirdest fancy, the seduction of God, persists after the Reformation in yet another Franciscan, Lawrence of Brindisi. Despite Mary's total innocence and chastity, Lawrence compares her intercession with God to Esther's wheedling of the King of Persia on behalf of the Jews, and likens God himself to an infatuated husband, tamed by the bride who has been 'united' with him (the word is *copulata*, and Lawrence takes the language of Luke 1:35 in a sexual sense).[24]

This, at last, was too much. But by Lawrence's time such fancies had taken root in Catholic Europe, Reformation or no Reformation. Little was done to weed them out. Bernardine of Siena, canonized within six years of his death, continued to be venerated: a policy which was bound to be seen, however wrongly, as bestowing Roman approval on his teachings. In the reign of Louis XIV Henri Boudon, archdeacon of Evreux, found that the layfolk of his diocese considered the Virgin to be 'as much as, or more than God himself'. Another subject of Louis XIV, the ebulliently successful preacher Louis-Marie Grignion de Montfort, composed a *Treatise on the True Devotion to the Blessed Virgin* reaffirming bluntly (among much else) that she has power over God.[25]

It might be suspected that the Virgin of these imaginings was largely a projection of male fantasy. Surely men like St Bernardine were essentially poets and romancers whose poetry and romance took a clerical form? The query is fair enough. Indeed, if some of the more reckless notions are put together,

Mary acquires a curious likeness – in her own sphere – to Shakespeare's Cleopatra. For Bernardine and Lawrence, she is even a lass unparallel'd. We may still ask, however, whether women imagined her with any more restraint.

The Church being what it was, comparatively few left any record of their thoughts on the subject. One who did was the seventeenth-century Spanish nun Maria d'Agreda, a Franciscan, like Bernardine and Lawrence. Maria was no woolly-minded dreamer, but a woman of vivid character and active intellect. She corresponded with King Philip IV, giving him sound advice which he seldom followed. Her immense book *The Mystical City of God* is a life of the Virgin based on alleged private revelations. While it borrows from earlier authors, and from apocryphal legend, a great deal of it is genuinely original; and it is just as flamboyant as the work of male Mariolaters. It differs chiefly in being more systematic, and, though distended by pious verbiage, more interesting.

Sister Maria detects the Virgin in the logic of Creation itself. She does not share the usual Christian belief that Christ came because man had strayed and needed a Saviour. On the contrary, Christ would have come in any case. The Incarnation was the first thing to be willed by God, before the world was made; and since it involved a birth, it involved a mother. Jesus and Mary existed together in God's mind from the beginning. He made the world as their destined dwelling-place and kingdom. Adam was formed in Jesus's image, Eve in Mary's. The Fall did not cause the Incarnation, but changed its nature, when it happened in historical time, from glory to suffering.

Several of the obvious texts (such as the Wisdom passage in Proverbs, and Revelation 12) are skilfully applied to the Virgin. Maria d'Agreda notes – and pushes to extremes – Mary's mystical identification with Zion. Even the New Jerusalem, in Revelation 12, is construed as a symbol of her. Here, in the guise of the celestial city, she comes so close to being man's sole refuge and destination that her Son fades into the background. Elsewhere she is called the Godhead's 'unique image', and the 'redemptress' eternally united to it. She often sounds in fact like a goddess herself, and on that point, intriguingly, Maria inverts the Catholic norm: she remarks that she has to take it on faith that the Virgin is *not* divine. The natural supposition would be that she was.

And in practice, loopholes appear. Maria depicts the Mother of God as a special, unclassifiable creature, not indeed divine (since the Church says she is not), but hovering in single glory above all other natures. Even in her own mother's womb, it transpires, she was a sentient being with more than mortal wisdom. Throughout her life a thousand angels were at her command, though the reason for this, and for other privileges, was withheld from her in her mortal nature till the Annunciation. On the eve of that event God gave her complete knowledge of the universe, and complete power over it, with *carte blanche* to work miracles. She assisted her Son's labours on earth and guided the Church afterwards, making frequent visits to heaven for consultations. Today, says Maria, she is the omnipotent Queen to whom all should turn for mercy and deliverance. At the end of the world she will sit as Co-Judge with Christ.

The Mystical City is never credible for an instant as a human being's life-story. All the same it is the product of a vigorous mind, with many adroit touches. Maria strives, of course, to be strictly orthodox, yet a reader sometimes feels that Christian theology does not suit her. Despite punctilious homage to the Trinity, her thoughts seem to be straining towards a rival one composed of God, Jesus and Mary. This, it will be recalled, is the same mysterious triad which Mohammed denounced, and which may just possibly have been a relic or after-effect of Arabian Collyridianism. Islamic conquest brought the Koran to Spain, and with it the idea of the God-Jesus-Mary Trinity, even if only as a delusion. Did some speculative mystic pick up a hint from it which trickled through to Maria d'Agreda? Certainly her book was regarded as suspect. Two popes tried to ban it, and the mighty Bossuet opposed its circulation in France. Nevertheless, it was translated into a number of languages, and remained popular reading far into the Age of Reason. One of its readers was Casanova; it gave him nightmares.[26]

6

The Virgin's modern cult is largely a re-editing of the medieval, after a phase of decline. From the definition of the Immaculate Conception in 1854 till the death of Pius XII in 1958, the main trend was towards the revival and triumph of extreme views. Symptomatically, Lawrence of Brindisi was canonized in 1881, Grignion de Montfort in 1947. Besides the two pronouncements on dogma, and increased papal encouragement in general, Marian progress was furthered by apparitions.

Mary of course had manifested herself before: through visions, as at Guadalupe in Mexico, and through miraculous images and pictures, as at Czestochowa in Poland. Now, however, a whole series of such events took place. The Lourdes manifestations in 1858 remain the best known and the best recorded. Bernadette's meetings with the Lady in the grotto created a centre of pilgrimage which became a Marian capital. But a few years previously Mary had appeared to a nun, Catherine Labouré, at a Paris convent, and to two children at La Salette. In 1871 she appeared at Pontmain; in 1917 at Fatima, in Portugal; in 1932 at Beauraing, in Belgium; and in 1933 at Banneux, likewise in Belgium. Between 1930 and 1950 twenty-eight other such incidents were reported and investigated.

All the visionaries except Catherine Labouré were children, a fact suggesting 'eidetic' imagery, though events at Lourdes and Fatima cannot be fully explained by this alone. Whatever the nature of the visions, they reflected and reinforced the belief in Mary's autonomy. She appeared by herself. Once or twice she had forerunners or attendants (Catherine Labouré was guided to her by a small boy in white), but always she was the sole figure of importance. Her actual messages to the children are often difficult to sort out. Accounts of Fatima, in particular, are overlaid with alleged warnings against Communism which were not published till long afterwards. The most credible sayings usually take the form of simple advice, and convey a sense of goodness and courtesy. The crucial point is that the voice of heaven speaks through the Virgin, not Christ.[27]

During the first half of the twentieth century enthusiasts were talking of a 'Marian Age' in the Church. They hinted at what would be, in effect, a fresh revelation. A French priest named Doncoeur spoke for many in 1927 when he said: 'There yet remains the achievement of the discovery of the Madonna.'

Rumours spread about a secret entrusted to the young seer of Fatima, which was to be given out (it was not) in 1960. Meanwhile Gabriele Roschini proposed his theologized Virgin who was by definition unique, perfect, an epitome of all sainthood, and so close to Christ in her nature that it was hard to draw any distinction. New associations arose and flourished, among them the Legion of Mary, inspired by Grignion de Montfort, the same who asserted that the Virgin has power over God himself. New books, pamphlets and articles poured out, on an average a thousand a year by the mid-century.[28]

Theologians of the post-Lourdes era discarded the opposition of Mercy to Justice. Their Christ was again a Christ of love. Mary, however, retained her place as his indispensable partner in the work of salvation. In the Mariology of Matthias Scheeben of Cologne it was put forward as a serious principle, not simply a flourish of rhetoric, that Mary was Christ's spiritual bride as well as his mother and that this was the key to her whole position. Scheeben came to the brink of restoring the Goddess-and-Son duality. The formula of the *gottesbräutliche Mutterschaft* (it does not go readily into English) never had much influence in itself, but related teachings of the same German seminary professor were welcomed and in due course exaggerated.

Mary was made out to be the Co-Redeemer, or rather Co-Redemptress, in concert with Christ. At the foot of the cross she shared consciously in his mystical sacrifice, with a kind of priesthood. Through his words to her about John she was appointed mother of the faithful. In heaven, it was further maintained, she is the Mediatrix, and all divine grace is channelled through her. She is therefore essential to salvation, though, of course, many are saved without ever knowing what she does for them. This latter doctrine is chiefly due to St Alphonsus Liguori, whose credulous work *The Glories of Mary*, published in 1786, is the main bridge between the medieval and modern forms of the cult.

In Catholic treatment of the Co-Redemption idea, a familiar scene was re-enacted. Attempts were made to rationalize it in terms of official doctrine. But it was not amenable. Scripture gave it no warrant at all. Rather than squeeze the text of the Fathers for a few doubtful drops, some authors tried to support it philosophically. Co-Redemption was alleged to have perfected the divine act by involving both sexes in it, in other words the entirety of human nature. This was a Gnostic way of thinking, and it became involved with new speculations about Wisdom and claims that Mary somehow 'completed' the Trinity and hence added to it, making it more than it would have been without her. Understandably these notions were viewed askance in Rome. Still, despite the lack of basis, it seemed for a time as if the definition of the Assumption in 1950 might be followed by yet another, declaring the Virgin to be Co-Redemptress and dispenser of all graces. Pope John XXIII, however, tactfully applied the brakes. 'The Madonna is not pleased,' he said, 'when she is put above her Son' . . . striking testimony that in the judgment of a wise pontiff, the obsessions of many Catholics were tending that way. Since then the impetus has slackened. Other interests, for the moment at least, have supervened.[29]

Morally, the Marian devotion of recent times has shown an advance. Our Lady no longer favours detestable characters whose sole virtue is their attachment to her. Lourdes, miraculous or not, is a place of spiritual therapy and physical healing. Yet the dominant factor is still the medieval desire to have it both ways, to square the theological circle. Mary has divine powers without actually being divine. She is human, tenderly and comprehensibly human. She has been made more so by a non-medieval interest in her husband as well: Catholic homage to St Joseph is quite a recent growth. Being still, after a fashion, one of us, she can sympathize. Her eyes of mercy are eyes of pity. But one result is that from the ordinary worshipper's viewpoint she can seem to condone *self*-pity, culpable weakness, ethical irresponsibility.

Meanwhile her more thoughtful devotees have sometimes drifted towards an un-Christian humanism. In the Virgin of their belief, human nature rises above its fallen state. It is instructive that the Romantic Movement gave Mary a new attraction for poets, even Protestants such as Wordsworth, who called her 'our tainted nature's solitary boast'. Through her as its exalted representative, that tainted nature gropes its way upward and saves itself. The goal of its pilgrimage is still Christ, but a Christ who is no longer the all-in-all, only the bestower of a sort of royal assent. The current pause has shelved such problems rather than solved them.[30]

As in earlier ages, the cult has produced great art, great literature, great music. It has comforted and strengthened. It has aided the suffering and spread the works of mercy and charity. Yet it remains an anomaly, a discord Catholicism has failed to resolve, repeatedly distorting itself in the effort to do so. The cult has an intense, mysterious life of its own – the life of the Goddess, mediated through a living daughter of Zion – which the Church has not only been powerless to control but has often submitted to, obeying its dictates and then evolving reasons.

Sooner or later that life will surely uncoil itself again, and become newly operative. If not, some will greet its quiescence as a sign that Catholicism is coming to its senses. It is more likely to be a sign that Catholicism is moribund.

EPILOGUE

What issues has this inquiry raised?

Several. One of them is mainly for the theorists of Catholicism. They take their stand on a body of teaching, handed down (they affirm) from Jesus and his apostles, and divinely preserved from error. Their two Marian dogmas are clearly not easy to defend as belonging to this, but the plea has been that they are 'implied' in the apostolic tradition. However fragile the proofs, that plea could carry a certain weight so long as no one proposed a better basis, a better way of explaining where the dogmas came from. Now, however, we have such a basis. It is partly documented, and by a Father of the Church, Epiphanius. We can explain the dogmas as originating from an Elijah-type legend of Mary's immortality.

To the Catholic Church, this legend poses a dilemma. On the one hand, it was certainly no part of any teaching received from the apostles. On the other, the infallible Church cannot repeal its own definitions. The Marian dogmas proclaimed in 1854 and 1950 have to be true. But the only way of conserving them is to allow some validity to the legend. A portion of the faith, it appears, was transmitted outside the apostolic succession, from sources that may not have been in harmony with Christ. The Church drew this portion into itself during the fifth century, rejecting the legend as a whole but extracting truths it was deemed to contain. Until then the line of transmission was external.

I do not know whether Catholic logic could stretch so far without snapping. The implied picture, however, agrees very well with the impression given by the New Testament when it is read impartially with Mary in mind. Christianity emerged from a group which comprised more than Jesus's chosen circle, and existed before it. This began in his mother's family, and she herself was the central figure till her Son's launching. He was a resultant – though of course far more than a resultant – of conflicting hopes and aims in a long preparation for his Messiahship. More than one tradition was set in motion. That which came down from Jesus via his apostles (plus the latecomer Paul), and formed the early Church, was not the entirety. Something else ran alongside, something associated with Mary, its divergence hinted at in her absence from the Resurrection stories. We can fairly connect this with the immortality legend and the traces of a Marianist religion. Christianity in its eventual fullness tried to graft it back on to the apostolic stem.

Protestants reject the Marianist doctrines in any form. But they cannot shake off the Marianist inheritance. It descends through the Middle Ages, inspiring art and literature and a less barbaric Christian attitude towards women; and because of all these things, it remains embedded in Christianity and its culture. The Puritans did try to get rid of it, and they failed. In any case the Protestant objection to Mary's cult, as distinct from Marian excesses, now looks much more doubtful. Granted, the cult is no part of the apostles' teaching as recorded in scripture. But that does not make it a late perversion or innovation. It flows down from the beginnings by a different route, influencing Christian thought on the way, and joins the apostolic stream at the Council of Ephesus. To excise it with a view to restoring 'pure' Christianity would be as misguided as trying to put a chicken back in the egg.

Another argument collapses as well, for Catholics as for Protestants who use it: the case against the ordination of women. True, the apostles were men, and so were the priests who succeeded to them. But the early cult of Mary was served by priestesses. Epiphanius says so, and is annoyed about it. The historical argument for a male priesthood of Christ lets in a similar argument for a female priesthood of Mary. Or better, for a priesthood of both sexes, in a Church that venerates both Mother and Son.

Such topics may be thought to concern Christians only. I believe, however, that the Mary cult with its implications has a far broader interest. It is the most impressive of all psychological case-histories. That has little to do with the Freudian cliché about sexual sublimation by priests (which, it is worth recalling, was completely annihilated in another religious connection by Marghanita Laski, whose study, *Ecstasy*, can scarcely be charged with partiality towards Christians). The cliché diverts attention from the profounder mystery, which is simply this – that the cult is valid. It works. It is proof against analytic destruction. Therefore its true nature is a vital and continuing question.

I am not speaking merely of mystical experience, or of religious emotion, or of apparent answers to prayer, or of art and poetry and music before which criticism falters. Facts are facts. The Church's adoption of the cult in the fifth century was wildly irrational, a flouting of its own rules. Yet this *was* what was needed; it *did* retrieve the situation; it *did* create a richer, revivified Christianity able to face the barbaric era. It was an act of supreme unconscious wisdom. Theologians afterwards could only rationalize it, and not very well.

Much the same could be said of the second upsurge during the Middle Ages, with its extraordinary unfolding of a new Christendom. It could even be said of the third which started in 1854. The papal edict on the Immaculate Conception was seen by the enlightened as ecclesiastical hara-kiri. Rome had gone insane and was finished. All the trends of the age were sweeping Catholicism away as an outworn superstition. And, indeed, they were. Yet Pius IX's act of Marian suicide turned out to be the beginning of a recovery. The popular devotion at Lourdes and other shrines, plus the second definition in 1950, fortified the Church to an amazing extent against forces which were expected to dash it to pieces, and, by every rule of reason, ought to have done so. The Church is still there, whereas most of the nineteenth-century movements against it have petered out or changed course. There are signs also that the converse holds. In England during the 1950s, when restored Marian centres at Walsingham and Aylesford were flourishing, conversions rose to a peak of fifteen thousand a year. Then came the toning down; and by the 1970s the figure had dropped to three thousand.

A believer might interject that the answer is simple. However inflated, however badly put, Catholic teaching has been in substance true. The Virgin is a living being, does actually exist in some other sphere, has actually accepted a role in the affairs of mankind. When Christians have turned to her she has intervened, protectively or creatively or both. When they take less notice of her she is less active. Here I will argue neither in favour nor against. Her literal existence could not be allowed to affect the present requirement: to ask how the human approach to her, and the human response to her, can be assessed in human terms.

In the Prologue I mentioned two names, Robert Graves and C. G. Jung. Despite the vagaries which have exposed these authors to attack, some of their ideas have come through triumphantly. One such idea is common to both. It lies in a zone of overlap where, if in very different ways, they are talking about the same subject. Between them they provide the most promising clue to the enigma.

Graves's book, *The White Goddess*, is a study of poetic myth. It becomes, to a large extent, a study of the imaginative role of the Eternal-Womanly. Graves portrays the history of religion as governed by a male-female conflict, with male gods ousting the Goddess. This is a process which we are now well aware of, having traced it, notably, in the oscillation between Wisdom and the Logos. What emerges is that the myth of the Muse is accurate. The Female is the authentic source of inspiration and life. The Male in his would-be dominance is a usurper, and his attempts to drag her divinity down have been self-stultifying.

By acquiring the attributes of Wisdom and older deities, Mary became a renascent form of the Goddess. It would follow on Graves's showing that she was invested with the Goddess's magic – not merely the left-overs of paganism, but the power of spiritual awakening, endlessly renewed. As an activity extending through the whole Church this might be hard to define, but strictly on Graves's poetic level it makes curiously good sense. The singer of the *Magnificat* does indeed have an air of being a Muse towards others. The first Christians to apply the language of worship to her were two poets, Ephraem of Syria and Gregory of Nazianzus; this at a time when the number of Christian poets was microscopic. The odds against its being coincidence are immense. For many reasons it is plausible to go on in a Gravesian spirit, and see Mary as the source of a vital imaginative energy which the male Godhead could not supply.

Are we toppling into a new theology, with the Goddess literally existing, and a literally-existing Virgin assuming her nature? Perhaps not. Perhaps the same thought can be stated otherwise. It is here that Jung has his point of entry. His theory of the Collective Unconscious is largely an attempt to avoid such hazards. It admits the intense reality of the gods and myths, the absurdity of reducing them to subjective fantasy; but it professes to find them deep in the human psyche, far below the level of individual consciousness. They are shaped by 'archetypes' or patterns which are constant from one human being to another. Once shaped, they are projected outwards.

When Jung is read alongside Graves, it is easy to see where they overlap, however different their explanations may be. Jung has his psychologized version of the Eternal-Womanly, and the echoes are multiple. In the male minds which have so long ruled society, there is, he claims, an unconscious feminine element which has been lodged there for thousands of years. It produces dreams and fantasies. It also produces imaginative creations which become society's common property. At an infantile stage it merely reflects the mother, but with maturity it develops (or should) into what Jung calls the anima, with the mother element still present but less to the fore. The anima draws together a man's experiences of women, and his ideals and wishes about them. In any individual it is the basis of falling in love. He projects the anima on to a real woman, usually with poor results. But the anima is also projected in other ways, transcending private misfortune: as the Not-Impossible She, and Helen of Troy, and Beatrice; as all priestesses and enchantresses; sometimes as a mythified harlot too, like Swinburne's Dolores. She has endless guises in legend, poetry and fiction.

Obviously the anima – with the maternal element in the background – is at least closely related to ideas of the Goddess. Furthermore, Jung's clinical work with his patients led him to the same view Graves was led to by his reflections on myth. The feminine factor in men is the source of the deepest insights and inspirations, and a key to self-knowledge and wholeness. The anima's arousal, according to Jung, is a giant step towards the total good of the psyche.

If Graves evokes the Female as Muse, Jung evokes her as a figure who has been haunting us throughout – Wisdom. This is so, at least, if we take Wisdom as intuitive rather than purely intellectual, a divine light rather than a rule-book. Mary herself expresses the anima at more human levels, and she blends into Wisdom in the liturgy. Therefore devotion to her should, on Jung's showing, activate the archetype and help to unlock the treasury of the psychical depths, with results which no rational or dogmatic system can keep under control. To say so is more than amateur speculation. In *Man and his Symbols*, a book edited by Jung and written by followers of his, Marie-Louise von Franz (who collaborated with Emma Jung in a study of the Grail legend) has the following:

> The first stage [in the full development of the anima] is best symbolized by the figure of Eve, which represents purely instinctual and biological relations. The second can be seen in Faust's Helen. . . . The third is represented, for instance, by the Virgin Mary – a figure who raises love to the heights of spiritual devotion. The fourth type is symbolized by Sapientia, wisdom transcending even the most holy and the most pure. . . . In the psychic development of modern man this stage is rarely reached.

It will be recalled that Mary was associated not only with Wisdom but with Eve, and that both motifs show signs of having begun in the Marianist context outside the Church: a fact which would suggest a high degree of perceptiveness in that quarter. As for the other image, Helen, Marie-Louise von Franz is thinking of Goethe's *Faust*, Part Two. It is in the closing lines of that drama that the phrase Ewig-Weibliche, Eternal-Womanly, is coined; and in the same lines the poet salutes Mary as a goddess. We have come, at last, into contact with a set of ideas from which a further progress in understanding may in time be possible.

But the Virgin is not a symbol, she is a person. Whatever she may now have become, she appears first at the earthly beginning of a great religion, and it would be wrong to think our last thoughts of her in any setting but that. Graves himself does not forget it. He argues in *The White Goddess* that the only religion with a credible future in the west would be a Christianity restoring the ancient Goddess-and-Son relationship. Here he touches the crowning paradox. Christian scripture and doctrine totally preclude placing Mary above Christ. Yet the vitality of Christ's own Church has often seemed to depend on her rather than him. Humanly speaking, one would say that without her he would probably have lost his kingdom. I do not know whether the paradox can be resolved in Christian terms. In any case there is reason to concur with Graves in spirit if not in detail, and conclude that a revived Christianity would need to be based, not on progressive or ecumenical programmes, but on a fresh approach to origins.

Such an approach might be dismissed with contempt as antiquarianism, a diversion from the real issues of suffering and injustice. I am not so sure. The Marian issue has turned out to be more 'real', even in a contemporary sense, than most. It calls in question the nature and credentials of a worldwide religion in which nearly all direct power is held by men, a fact with vast social ramifications. To point this out is not to disparage the churches' work for the betterment of the human condition. Yet arguably much of that work is itself a diversion, to the extent that it blunts awareness of the sexual wrong in their own structure: a wrong sustained by an appeal to origins which this inquiry has undermined. If a revised Christianity is to take shape, it cannot escape its ancestry. The first need is that the numinous figures at the source should be re-thought, re-interpreted, and differently related to one another.

Notes

Short headings only are given here. The full title of a work may be found by looking up its short heading in the Bibliography. 'Adams', for instance, refers to Henry Adams's *Mont-Saint-Michel and Chartres*.

Chapter 1: *Ewig-Weibliche*

1 Mascall and Box, pp. 77, 90, 104-7.
2 Campbell, vol. 1, pp. 139-40, 313-31, 374-5, 396; James, E. O. (1), pp. 11 ff., 21-2, 24, 41-2, 47, 141, and (2), pp. 59-60, 145-171; *Man, Myth and Magic*, art. 'Mother Goddess'; Neumann (1), pp. 94-6 and Plates 1 and 2, and (2), pp. 13-15.
3 Boslooper, pp. 150-1; Cassuto, pp. 58, 65; James, E. O. (1), pp. 69, 76-8; *Man, Myth and Magic*, arts 'Astarte', 'Ishtar', 'Mother Goddess'.
4 Cles-Reden, *passim*; Guthrie, p. 99; James, E. O. (1), pp. 42-6, 60-2, 147, 150-1, and (2), pp. 161-71, 241; Neumann (2), p. 71.
5 Campbell, vol. 1, pp. 315-25; Neumann (1), p. 91.
6 Boslooper, pp. 167-8; Campbell, vol. 3, p. 86; Graves (1), Section 3, 'The Olympian Creation Myth'; James, E. O. (1), pp. 22, 60-1, 230, and (2), pp. 152-3; *Man, Myth and Magic*, art. 'Cybele'; Neumann (1), pp. 63, 220-1, 269-70, and (2), pp. 13-14, 46-51, 102-7, 135.

I will not here debate the vexed question whether the male High God of Heaven is actually older still, but was eclipsed in remote prehistory and then rediscovered. Even if he was, his eclipse is a fact, and the Goddess-era is a fact, and the rediscovery of male godhead – if it was a rediscovery – frequently happened through Goddess-centred myths as described. See James, E. O. (2), pp. 206-8, and Neumann (2), pp. 147-8.

Related to the High God theory is an obvious query: 'If goddesses in general are aspects or fragments of one Goddess, surely we should regard gods in general as aspects or fragments of one God?' Anthropologically, however, there is not the same case for such a being, and he cannot be reconstructed as the Goddess can. The

Zeus of classical myth, for instance, is a fusion of a northern sky-deity and a Cretan Attis-type figure. Both may perhaps be derived from the primordial Goddess, but it is very hard to see them as aspects or fragments of a prior male divinity. They are simply unlike.

If analytical psychology is admitted as evidence, we have the further fact that Jung's researches revealed a single feminine 'archetype' in the Unconscious, the anima, but no equivalent masculine animus; the latter archetype is not single but multiple, and could not project a similarly cohesive God. Cp. also Campbell, vol. 3, p. 70.

7 Cassuto, pp. 64–5, 89, 91; Guthrie, p. 103; Neumann (2), p. 52.

8 Campbell, vol. 3, pp. 9–14; James, E. O. (1), pp. 47–8, 73–4, 129–131, 138–9, 235, 238, and (2), pp. 164, 189, 195, 198; *Man, Myth and Magic*, arts 'Baal', 'Syria and Palestine'; Neumann (2), pp. 48–51.

9 Cp. Miegge, p. 80.

10 Campbell, vol. 3, pp. 17–21, 50–3; James, E. O. (1), pp. 16–17, and (2), pp. 248–9; Neumann (1), pp. 162–3.

11 Campbell, vol. 3, pp. 148–9; Guthrie, pp. 37, 52, 55, 63; James, E. O. (1), pp. 140–60, and (2), pp. 221–4; Neumann (1), pp. 55–6; Seltman, pp. 33–4.

12 Campbell, vol. 3, pp. 76–85, 92; Cassuto, pp. 18–20; James, E. O. (1), pp. 78–81; *Man, Myth and Magic*, art. 'Baal'; Neumann (1), pp. 213–15. For the Israelite shrines, see e.g. Judges 6:25–32. For the religious compromise underlying them, see Ashe (3), pp. 121–9, and Kaufmann, *passim*. Cp. Hosea 2:16.

13 James, E. O. (2), p. 50.

14 James, E. O. (1), pp. 61–3, 161–2, 168–70, 174–82; Knox, p. 85; *Man, Myth and Magic*, art. 'Isis'.

15 Campbell, vol. 3, p. 171; *Man, Myth and Magic*, art. 'Demeter'; Neumann (1), p. 307.

16 Robert Graves's translation, pp. 268–71.

17 Thurian, pp. 13–14.

18 For some of the issues raised by Wisdom, see Dodd (1), p. 109 fn 2, and (2), p. 85; Knox, pp. 55–89. Also Albright, pp. 367 ff, and Bulgakov, pp. 47–9.

19 Knox, pp. 60, 70; and cp. p. 112 for the attempt to maintain Wisdom's identity with the Torah by representing the Torah itself as existent from all eternity.

20 Bouyer, especially Chapter 2, and p. 276 and notes on p. 294; also Bulgakov, *passim*.

21 Albright, pp. 367–70; Knox, pp. 57, 60–1; Williamson, pp. 67–9.

22 Albright, pp. 373–4; Cassuto, pp. 64–5; Ions, p. 74; James, E. O.
(1), pp. 77–8; Knox, p. 56; *Man, Myth and Magic*, art. 'Phoenicians and Carthaginians'. Cp. E. M. Parr cited in Graves (2), p. 369.

23 Cp. Miegge, p. 70.

24 Knox, p. 23.

Chapter 2: *From the Son to the Mother*

1 The main early non-Christian sources are Tacitus, Josephus, Pliny the Younger and Suetonius. See Ashe (1).

2 Cp. Dodd (2), p. 285.

3 Brandon, pp. 76–7; North, *passim*.

4 Brandon, *passim*; Dodd (2), pp. 273–7. The divine Christ of John, with a unique relation to God the Father, is not as sharply different from the Synoptic Jesus as is often asserted. Thus Matthew 11:27 and Luke 10:22 are entirely in the style of the Fourth Gospel.

5 See e.g. Matthew 2:16–18, 4:12–16, 8:16–17, 12:15–21, 21:1–5, 27:3–10. Likewise John 12:14–15, 19:23–4, 32–7.

6 Behind the Gospels we may of course assume written notes, letters, oral traditions. In particular, a document known as 'Q' has been inferred as a common source for the three Synoptic writers. There is no reason to think, however, that even 'Q' was an earlier full-scale Gospel telling an earlier tale. Cp. Brandon, p. 185.

7 The oldest of all Christian evidences may be an inscription at Nazareth in which the Emperor Claudius decrees the death penalty for tomb-violation. Complaints may have reached him about the subversive rumours started by the disappearance of the body of the Nazarene prophet. See Brandon, pp. 119, 123.

8 The apparent irrefutability of the Gospels is seldom given enough weight by scholars. Many theories of the growth of Christian 'legend' really presuppose a kind of imbecility or bewitchment preventing anyone else from contradicting it. The point is touched on by Brandon (pp. 193–4) with regard to a point of detail only. There he takes the view that the Gospel concerned, Mark, was written for a public a long way from Palestine where no one could check. But this is to ignore the hostile authorities' very strong motive for checking, in order to discredit the Christians, and their resources for doing so.

9 Despite all divergence, there may still be a 'rational' majority view. Many people still favour the Jesus of Victorian liberal churchmen, the Great Moral Teacher overlaid by theology. But he is no longer a consensus figure or anything like it, and he was a product, not of

impartial study, but of preconceived ideas working against the evidence. The Sermon on the Mount was made out to be virtually the whole of the real story. But Mark, the earliest Gospel and presumably the one nearest the facts, gives no Sermon on the Mount and almost no moral teaching at all. Jesus exhorts his hearers to repent in general terms, and advises a man to obey the Ten Commandments, but he spends most of his time in healing, exorcism and apocalyptic warning.

Chapter 3: The Strength of the Absurd

1 See the *Jewish Encyclopaedia*, art. 'Miriam', and Patsch, pp. 25-7. Cp. Polano, pp. 122-3.
2 The Egyptians had no cavalry then, but 'rider' can mean 'chariot-rider': Vaux, p. 224.
3 Graves (2), pp. 393-4. Cp. Fortune, pp. 46, 156, 160.
4 Mascall and Box, p. 32.
5 Boslooper, p. 230; Mascall and Box, p. 45.
6 Brandon, *passim*, and especially p. 181; James, M. R., pp. 1-2, 8-10; *Man, Myth and Magic*, art. 'Ebionites'. For a point against the 'primitive Jewish Christian' theory, see Dodd (1), pp. 39-40.
7 Boslooper, pp. 214-16; Miegge, p. 30.
8 Boslooper, pp. 39-40; *Man, Myth and Magic*, art. 'Mary'.
9 Graef, vol. 1, p. 12.
10 Boslooper, p. 135, and discussion following.
11 Boslooper, p. 203; Graef, vol. 1, p. 4. The possible bearing of the 'daughter of Zion' texts quoted on pages 24-6 is best deferred.
12 Boslooper, pp. 159-60; Cottrell, pp. 99, 175; Ions, pp. 103-4, 106-9; James, E. O. (1), pp. 60-1; Neumann (1), pp. 220-1. The lore of the priests of Saïs included the story of Atlantis.
13 For Neith-Athene see Herodotus, II.59, 175; IV.180, 188-9. E. M. Parr, cited in Graves (2), p. 369, seems to suggest that Anath and Neith can be directly equated. On the idea of a fresh beginning, cp. Miegge, p. 29.
14 It has been claimed that Mark attaches no importance to the Davidic descent, because of the incident in 12:35-7. But Matthew and Luke, both committed to the Davidic descent, record the same incident. They cannot have thought it to be in conflict.
15 Graef, vol. 1, p. 42; Palmer, pp. 24-7.
16 *Antiquities*, XX.ix.1.
17 Patsch, pp. 69-71.

18 This is the view laid down in the fourth century by the greatest biblical scholar among the Church Fathers, St Jerome. Western Christians moved slowly towards agreement with him and achieved virtual unanimity in the Middle Ages. Eastern Christians dissented, but still regarded Mary as Ever-Virgin and Joseph as a widower with children by his first marriage. Graef, vol. 1, pp. 90–1.

19 I have drawn largely on Patsch, pp. 71–5, but think his reconstruction can be improved on. For a medieval version see Adams, p. 164. Cp. Thurian, pp. 38, 146.

20 There are several possibilities, depending chiefly on how we relate the two Marys, but, as stated, the result is always substantially the same. I have chosen the arrangement which seems to me to explain most.

21 Brownrigg, p. 142; Patsch, p. 73. 'Chalpai' occurs in the Old Testament Apocrypha, 1 Maccabees 11:70. The name Alphaeus is also borne by the father of Matthew, but the lists do not suggest kinship with James or Jesus, and this Alphaeus appears to be a different person. See Herbert G. May and Bruce M. Metzger, *The Oxford Annotated Bible*, note on Mark 3:18.

22 The mystery is not artificial. It is the main basis of a well-known modern theory of the Church, Brandon's, noted here on page 52. He argues (p. 5) that the sudden emergence of the Lord's brother in Acts, despite the Gospels' not recognizing him as a disciple, proves that there was a Jewish Christianity in Jerusalem which he headed. After the Gentile takeover, Christian origins were re-written to tone this down, but James was too eminent to suppress, so he was left hanging without explanation. Brandon is driven (p. 50) to say that James 'must have' followed Christ during his lifetime, and that the Gospels ignore him out of hostility to his family and to the kind of Christianity he afterwards preached. The whole difficulty vanishes (and perhaps a good deal of the theory vanishes with it) on the simple supposition that James the Lord's brother is also James son of Alphaeus, the apostle. This, I reiterate, is and has always been the mainstream Christian opinion. Brandon's book never even mentions it, let alone offering a refutation.

23 I doubt if the process of rationalizing the data can go any further. We could however ask, as some have, whether Jesus might have been virgin-born as a natural event.

This is not science-fiction. In the third century AD Origen tried to relate the miracle to parthenogenesis in nature. It does happen, though not in mammals without artificial means. Apart from parthenogenesis proper, freak pregnancies occur even in humans.

For instance, a woman can pick up a man's spermatozoa by having a bath just after him in the same water. Such a pregnancy is extremely rare, and as it would not have been understood in Galilee, any child resulting might have been viewed with awe and given a flying start on a Messianic career.

However, I do not think the theory deserves much notice. Like some other would-be eliminations of the marvellous, it fails to do even that. We would have to suppose, not only that the multi-million-to-one chance occurred, but that the result was another multi-million-to-one chance – the birth of a child who actually was extraordinary, and could measure up to the Messianic hope. The odds are beyond reckoning. A 'rational' account as far-fetched as this would excuse belief in divine intervention after all; it would virtually let in the same miracle by another door.

There are some references in Boslooper, pp. 40, 159 fn, and Bouyer, p. 220 fn.

Chapter 4: *Magnificat*

1 Boslooper, p. 64; James, M. R., pp. 38–49.
2 Patsch, pp. 7–11.
3 See Ronald Knox's note, and Keller, pp. 329–30.
4 Keller, pp. 333–6; Patsch, pp. 23–4, 97.
5 Graef, vol. 1, pp. 8–9.
6 Budge (2), pp. xxii–xxiii; Cronin, p. 1; Graef, vol. 1, p. 182. The description is sometimes mistakenly attributed to an earlier Epiphanius, on whom see Chapter 7.
7 Patsch, p. 37. There is a large literature of the Shroud, pro and con. The restored image is very good on artistic, anatomical and medical grounds, and hard to explain as a medieval fake, but the utmost which can be said at present is that the Shroud's genuineness is seriously arguable – not proved.
8 Patsch, pp. 3–4; Thurian, pp. 11, 193–4.
9 Patsch, pp. 48–9, 97.
10 Dodd (2), p. 253.
11 Josephus, XI.v.2. Jewish ideas and hopes on this subject in the first century AD are set forth in the apocryphal *II Esdras* 13, especially verses 39–47.
12 Budge (2), p. 82.
13 Graef, vol. 1, pp. 10–12; Miegge, p. 33.
14 John 7:27. See Dodd (2), pp. 87–9. It has been urged that the Messianic exegesis of Micah 5:2 depends on Isaiah 7:14 – the

prophecy taken to mean that a virgin shall bear a son – because 'she who is in travail' in the next verse is the virgin in question. If the two texts are so closely linked, the idea of Bethlehem as the right birthplace may have originated in circles where Isaiah 7:14 had already been singled out, and Mary's child was already looked upon as the One promised. In that case Micah 5:2 was itself an afterthought and only became seriously 'Messianic' as confirmation, when the birth at Bethlehem had actually happened. Cp. Graef, vol. 1, p. 5.

15 James, M. R., p. 46.

16 Cp. n. 14 above. If the Micah interpretation was an afterthought occasioned by the Bethlehem birth, this would suggest that the priests' reply to Herod was indeed prompted by someone – let us say, Zechariah – who already regarded Mary's child as the Messiah. On the other hand the alleged link with Isaiah 7:14 might seem to imply that the Virgin Birth was a fact already known to Zechariah, or, at any rate, a belief held by him . . . which is getting very close to a fundamentalist view. Perhaps. We might suppose, however, that he merely drew attention to a prophecy with Bethlehem in it, regardless of any wider bearings; or that the priests simply referred Herod to Bethlehem as the source of the current rumour, and the actual Micah text was put into the story later.

17 Patsch, pp. 126–7.

18 James, M. R., pp. 49–90.

19 This view now commands wide acceptance. See Graef, vol. 1, pp. 7–8; New Catholic Encyclopedia, art. 'Mary, Blessed Virgin', I; Thurian, pp. 14–15, 20, 25, etc. Cp. Mascall and Box, p. 16.

20 See Ronald Knox's note, and cp. Graef, vol. 1, pp. 5–6, 54–5, 93. This verse, mistranslated, was applied to Mary by St Jerome and many others following him – an indication of some sort of awareness about it. In modern times the idea has been generally dropped, because the words, so far as they can be construed, do not fit the Mary of Christianity. But the way the text is embedded in others which reappear in the New Testament, suggesting a continuity with them, makes it hard prima facie to dismiss; and, as stated, it would have fitted Mary at a pre-Christian stage, suggesting her sponsorship of her still unknown Son.

21 Gaster, Introduction.

Chapter 5: The Heart of the Labyrinth

1 Cp. Dodd (2), p. 285.

2 Patsch, pp. 151–5; Thurian, p. 137.

3 Palmer, pp. 42–4. The passage is in Augustine's work *On the Gospel of John*, Treatise 8.

4 *New Catholic Encyclopedia*, art. 'Mary, Blessed Virgin', I; Thurian, pp. 124–6.

5 *Man, Myth and Magic*, art. 'Theosophy'.

6 Another brother, Jude, is an active Christian later, but I find it hard to accept the view that he is the apostle 'Judas, not Iscariot' who appears in Luke 6:16, John 14:22 and Acts 1:13, and is elsewhere called Thaddaeus.

7 Graef, vol. 1, pp. 67–8, 126; Livius, pp. 190–1; Patsch, pp. 199–200.

8 See for example O. R. Vassall-Phillips in Smith, George D. (ed.), vol. 1, chapter 15.

9 Mascall and Box, pp. 39, 48–9; Thurian, p. 20. Austin Farrer, author of the relevant essay in Mascall and Box, suggests reproducing the internal echo by 'Good day to you, since God's so good to you'.

Chapter 6: *A Bridge without a Span*

1 'Virgin motherhood' in this sense is found in Philo. Boslooper, p. 193.

2 I concur with the Protestant Mariologist Max Thurian, as far as he goes (Thurian, p. 25).

3 Swete, pp. cxxv–cxxix.

4 Boslooper, p. 103.

5 Bouyer, pp. 65, 235–6; Mascall and Box, pp. 50–1, 100–2; Swete, pp. 147–9; Thurian, pp. 9, 179–81. The plausibility of a double symbolism, both corporate and personal, is confirmed by the next chapter, where the Beast is both the persecuting Roman Empire and Nero as its embodiment: Swete, pp. 161–75 passim.

6 Graef, vol. 1, p. 28; Miegge, pp. 101–2; Swete, pp. ccvii–ccix.

7 Boslooper, pp. 28 ff.

8 Graef, vol. 1, pp. 42, 44–5. Tertullian denied the perpetual virginity, but he had seceded from the Church.

9 Boslooper, pp. 42, 49–51.

10 Graef, vol. 1, pp. 37–45; Miegge, pp. 37–8, 135; Palmer, pp. 12–14. Irenaeus's word 'advocate' might suggest intercession, but it could be rendered 'comforter' and the intention is doubtful. In any case the application is to Eve only.

11 Vawter, pp. 68–9. See also Graef, vol. 1, pp. 1–3, 46, 61. The Latin of the Vulgate rendered it '*she* shall bruise your head', a

reading which made it easier to bring in Mary. However, this was a mistranslation, and irrelevant to those who did not read the Bible in Latin.

12 Graef, vol. 1, pp. 28–30, 37 fn 3; Mascall and Box, pp. 22, 100–2; Swete, pp. cvii–cviii; Thurian, pp. 177–8. C. C. Martindale, in his *Catholic Commentary on Holy Scripture*, argues that the early emergence of the Second Eve theme implies an earlier emergence of Mary as the apocalyptic woman. Vassall-Phillips, that very traditional Mariologist, states flatly (Smith, George D., vol. 1, p. 524) that the Second Eve theme is not in the Bible. Even in the 'primeval prophecy in Genesis' it is only 'implied'. Ignoring the Apocalypse, he falls back on undocumented apostolic tradition. This confirms Martindale: without the Apocalypse, the notion has no discernible basis at all.

13 Graef, vol. 1, pp. 40, 41; Mascall and Box, pp. 5–6, 20–1; Origen, I.6; Thurian, pp. 146–9.

14 Here the traditionalist Vassall-Phillips is again relevant. On the topic of Mary's spiritual motherhood he does cite the Apocalypse, and admits that this is the only direct evidence. 'But once in the Sacred Scriptures our Lady is pointed out to us in her own person as the Mother of Christians.' He means Revelation 12 and goes on to discuss it. 'In her own person' is a shade misleading; he makes it clear that he recognizes the woman as a combined symbol, 'the Church under the figure of the Blessed Mother of God'. Smith, George D., vol. 1, p. 540.

15 Graef, vol. 1, pp. 40–6, 75–6, and vol. 2, p. 112; Livius, p. 43; Mascall and Box, pp. 7–8; Miegge, p. 180; Palmer, pp. 12, 15, 33–4, 41 and fn.

16 Boslooper, pp. 66 ff. James, M. R., pp. 70–9.

17 Budge (2), pp. 68–80; James, M. R., p. 81 and cp. 117; Patsch, pp. 112–13.

18 Boslooper, p. 55; James, M. R., pp. 81–2.

19 Cronin, pp. 8–13 and Plates 2, 3, 4; Grabar, p. 9; Charles Holmes in Marchant, p. xxi; Rice, Figure 219.

20 Ashe (3), pp. 314–15; Boslooper, pp. 56–9, 62.

21 Boslooper, pp. 60–2, 69–70; Graef, vol. 1, pp. 34–5.

22 Budge (3), pp. lxxvi, 628–30, 636–9; James, M. R., pp. 8, 87–8. Cp. Graves (2), pp. 141–2.

23 Budge (2), pp. xxxvii–xxxix; James, M. R., pp. 151, 181–6.

24 James, M. R., pp. 166–81.

25 Dodd (2), p. 107 and fn; Doresse, pp. 30–1; Grant, pp. 17, 24–7; *Man, Myth and Magic*, art. 'Gnosticism'; Miegge, pp. 71–4.

26 Ashe (3), p. 309; Bouyer, p. 71; Dodd (1), p. 109 fn 2, and (2), pp. 85, 273–7; Knox, pp. 70, 81–9; Williamson, pp. 38–9, 70.
The anti-feminist change of sex reappears in medieval Jewish mysticism. In the system of the Kabbalah, Chokmah – Wisdom – has mysteriously become male. See Fortune, chapter 16, and Scholem, pp. 37–8, 213, 219, 270.

27 Newman, pp. 104–5.

28 Graves (2), pp. 156, 159; James, M. R., p. 2.

29 Livius, pp. 287, 289–92; Miegge, pp. 135–6; *New Catholic Encyclopedia*, art. 'Saints, Devotion to the'.

30 Boslooper, p. 45; Graef, vol. 1, pp. 50–3; Miegge, pp. 40, 70–1, 135–6.

31 The remark about Christians' belief in the old gods was made by G. K. Chesterton as an aside in, I think, *William Blake*.

32 Budge (1), vol. 2, p. 220.

33 Bouyer, p. 76 (translation mine); Ronald Knox Bible, Appendix II, pp. 287–8; Williamson, p. 69.

34 Sermon 146 of St Peter Chrysologus, 'On the Generation of Christ', quoted in Palmer, p. 39. Early Irish verses relating to St Brigit are given in Butler, vol. 1, pp. 225–9 (1 February).

Chapter 7: The Seventy-Ninth Heresy

1 Epiphanius, 78. 23, 79.1 and 7; Graef, vol. 1, pp. 72–3; Livius, p. 302; Miegge, pp. 74–5; Palmer, p. 49.

2 Epiphanius, 78.11 and 24; Graef, vol. 1, p. 72; Livius, pp. 300–1, 343; Miegge, p. 85; Patsch, p. 217.

3 Graef, vol. 1, p. 72; Miegge, pp. 101–2.

4 Brandon, pp. 88–90, casts doubt on the early persecutions. But whatever the truth, they were accepted as Church history by the time the Apocalypse was written. In the persecution ascribed to Saul, afterwards Paul, Christians are stated to have scattered from Jerusalem, and women are stated to have been among his victims (Acts 8:1–3).

5 Livius, p. 346.

6 Jugie, pp. 77–81; Livius, pp. 349–54; Miegge, pp. 59(fn 2), 103.

7 Swete, pp. 136 and 151–2 (notes on Revelation 11:6 and 12:6).

8 Epiphanius, 79.5; Livius, pp. 301–2. In the first great age of monasticism Elijah's virginity made him a model for celibates, but this was not the original form of the idea. Epiphanius does not say that Elijah took a vow, but that he was 'virgin from the womb', with some special and unexplained significance attached to the fact.

It is not taken from Jewish tradition, which merely notes that scripture is silent about Elijah's family, and infers without fuss that he was unmarried.

9 Ashe (2), pp. 14–15, 22–4; Ginzberg, vol. 4, pp. 195–235, and notes in vol. 6; *Jewish Encyclopaedia*, art. 'Elijah'.

Two important movements of Jewish renewal, Kabbalism and Hasidism, both claimed that Elijah came in person to bless their founders.

10 Graef, vol. 1, pp. 48, 221; Miegge, p. 136.
11 Boslooper, p. 45; Graef, vol. 1, pp. 46–7, 49, 51–2; Miegge, p. 53; Newman, p. 106; Vassall-Phillips in Smith, George D. (ed.), vol. 1, p. 514.

Chapter 8: *The Road to Ephesus*

1 Miegge, p. 18.
2 Butler, art. 'Ephraem', 18 June; Graef, vol. 1, pp. 57–62; Livius, pp. 92–102, 288, 294–9, 397 ff; Marchant, pp. 6, 99–100; Palmer, pp. 16, 20–3; Sozomen, *Ecclesiastical History*, III.16.
3 For the Cappadocian group in general, see Graef, vol. 1, pp. 62–8. Ephraem's visit is discussed in Wace and Schaff, vol. 13, Introduction to his works, pp. 127–8, 143.
4 Graef, vol. 1, pp. 60, 63–6; Smith, George D. (ed.), vol. 1, pp. 541–2.
5 Graef, vol. 1, pp. 67–8, and cp. 189–90, 261.
6 Butler, art. 'Gregory the Wonder-Worker', 17 November; Graef, vol. 1, p. 47; Livius, pp. 316–18.
7 Butler, arts 'Gregory Nazianzen', 9 May, and 'Cyprian and Justina', 26 September; Gibbon, chapter 27; Graef, vol. 1, p. 64; Livius, pp. 318–19; Sozomen, *Ecclesiastical History*, VII.5. I have corrected one or two inaccuracies in the translation of Sozomen given by Wace and Schaff.
8 Boslooper, p. 45; Graef, vol. 1, p. 82; Palmer, pp. 27–8.
9 Sulpicius Severus, *Dialogues*, II.13.
10 Graef, vol. 1, pp. 79–81, 89–91; Palmer, pp. 24–8.
11 Graef, vol. 1, pp. 77–8, 83–8, and cp. 100; Livius, pp. 92–102, 191; Miegge, p. 109.
12 Graef, vol. 1, pp. 92–4.
13 Graef, vol. 1, pp. 8–9, 95–6, 98–9, 131–2.
14 Cp. Newman, pp. 106–8.
15 Graef, vol. 1, pp. 112, 133; *Man, Myth and Magic*, art. 'Diana'; Miegge, pp. 59–60, 84; Palmer, pp. 50–1, 57.

16 Russell, pp. 362–3.

17 Graef, vol. 1, pp. 74, 101–4, 133 fn 3; Miegge, pp. 54–5.

18 Gibbon, chapter 47; Graef, vol. 1, pp. 104 ff, and cp. 226; Livius, pp. 92–102; Palmer, p. 44 fn; Russell, pp. 387–8.

19 Gibbon, chapter 47; Graef, vol. 1, pp. 105–11, and cp. 124–5.

20 Graef, vol. 1, p. 109; Miegge, p. 67; Seltman, p. 137.

21 Graef, vol. 1, pp. 111–12; Palmer, pp. 50–1.

22 Boslooper, pp. 161–2; Grabar, p. 47; Graef, vol. 1, p. 112; Guthrie, p. 30; James, E. O. (1), pp. 212–13; Miegge, pp. 75–7, 81–2; Rice, pp. 138–40; Seltman, p. 91; Wilkins, pp. 133–4, 145.

23 Adams, pp. 91 ff; Ashe (4), p. 56; Cronin, pp. 14–16; Grabar, pp. 75–81, 97–8, 128–30; James, E. O. (1), pp. 211–12; Livius, p. 288; Miegge, p. 133.

Chapter 9: Notes for an Unwritten History

1 Miegge, pp. 83–4, 180.

2 Graef, vol. 1, pp. 48, 168, 221, 229–31; Miegge, p. 136; Palmer, pp. 53–4; Wilkins, *passim*. Much Marian liturgical matter can be conveniently read in the *Little Office of the Blessed Virgin according to the Carmelite Rite*, published in 1955. The *Sancta Maria* is in Vespers and the *Sub tuum praesidium* is in Compline.

3 Graef, vol. 1, pp. 48, 112, 133–6, 139, 142–3, 166; James, E. O. (1), p. 223; Miegge, pp. 84–5; Palmer, pp. 57–8, 61–2; Patsch, pp. 222–3; Williamson, p. 69.

4 Boslooper, pp. 46–7; Graef, vol. 1, pp. 119–23, 125–9, 145–50; Miegge, pp. 141–4; Palmer, pp. 54–7.

5 Miegge, pp. 167, 177.

6 *Encyclopaedia of Islam*, art. 'Maryam'.

7 Graef, vol. 1, pp. 134–8; James, M. R., pp. 194–227; Miegge, pp. 85–92, 103; Palmer, pp. 57–61, 64–7, 70 fn; Patsch, pp. 217–22.

The Assumption doctrine may have gone through a transitional stage. The earliest version of Mary's Passing ends obscurely: her body is translated to paradise, but nothing is said about its reanimation. Christians may, at first, have accepted that her deceased remains were nowhere on earth, but hesitated to go the rest of the way. Final capitulation came because of the need to establish her in the role of unique intercessor before God's throne, as complete a being as the rabbinic Elijah. Traces of a controversy appear in the sermon of Theoteknos cited on page 210, and elsewhere.

8 Graef, vol. 2, pp. 79–83, 130, 146–7; Miegge, p. 104; Palmer, pp. 81–9, 101–13; Patsch, pp. 223–5.

9 Cp. Miegge, pp. 104, 127–9.

10 Graef, vol. 1, pp. 134–6, 178–9, 222–4, and cp. 185–7; Miegge, pp. 95–7; Palmer, pp. 65–7.

11 Graef, vol. 1, pp. 211, 215–21, 298–302, and cp. vol. 2, p. 109; Miegge, pp. 105–6, 123–7; Patsch, pp. 226–8.

12 Graef, vol. 1, pp. 211, 213–14, 311–13; Mascall and Box, p. 49; Miegge, pp. 102–3; Russell, pp. 437–8.

13 Boslooper, p. 77; Budge (2), pp. xlviii–xlix, 236–44; Graef, vol. 1, pp. 249, 254–5, 260, 266–9; Miegge, pp. 130–2.

14 Graef, vol. 1, pp. 224–5, 270–3, 321; Miegge, pp. 21–2, 130–2.

15 Ronald Knox Bible, Appendix II, pp. 287–8. For the reappearance of the excluded verse, see the *Little Office of the Blessed Virgin according to the Carmelite Rite*, p. 94.

16 Bouyer, pp. 74–7, 276–83, 294; Bulgakov, pp. 16–17, 49, 173–96; Graef, vol. 2, pp. 62–3, 119, 132–3; Graves (2), p. 254; Miegge, pp. 12–13, 70, 76, 79–81, 179–80; Wilkins, pp. 111–12, 134, 145, 161.

17 Graef, vol. 1, pp. 342–6.

18 Adams, pp. 50, 91 ff, 198; Graef, vol. 1, p. 240 fn 2; Miegge, pp. 107–8.

19 Adams, pp. 71–3, 251, 257; Graef, vol. 1, pp. 235–41; Miegge, pp. 98, 112–16, 136–9; Palmer, pp. 68–71.

20 Adams, pp. 91, 94–6, 100, 103, 254–5; Graef, vol. 1, p. 232.

21 Adams, pp. 74, 83–4, 103, 199, 202, 252, 261–3, 272–3; Graef, vol. 1, pp. 146–7, 221, 240, 268–70, 289; Miegge, pp. 141–2, 152.

It is interesting to find Henry Adams, at this point, speaking of the Mary cult as a 'separate religion' – his own words (p. 261). He is thinking of the medieval and modern eras, not of antiquity. The impression of something autonomous is very persistent.

22 Adams, pp. 258–80; Cronin, pp. 37–8; Graef, vol. 1, pp. 170–1, 204–5, 269, 331; *Man, Myth and Magic*, art. 'Pact'; Miegge, pp. 150–1.

23 Adams, pp. 274–5; Graef, vol. 1, pp. 147, 225–6, 269, 297–8, and vol. 2, p. 69. The line from Chaucer is the opening of his address to the Virgin, *An ABC*, translated from the French of Guillaume Deguilleville.

24 Adams, pp. 97, 103; Cronin, pp. 38–42; Graef, vol. 1, pp. 288–90, 315–18, and cp. 253, and vol. 2, pp. 27–8; Jung, Emma, p. 339; Neumann (1), p. 331 and Plates 176 and 177.

The idea of a kind of sex-by-analogy in Mary's relation with God is very old, but it is not stated consistently. To which Person of the Trinity would it apply? Luke 1:35 would point to the Holy Spirit, and so do several commentators. Bernardine and Lawrence seem to prefer the Father. Some who expound the *Song of Songs* see Mary as mystically the bride of her Son. The impossibility of giving this notion coherence is perhaps a further proof that the Virgin Birth is non-sexual and therefore non-pagan.

25 Graef, vol. 2, pp. 40–1, 57–62, and cp. 32, 45–6, 76.

An English version of Grignion de Montfort's *Treatise* was reissued in 1962 with an Imprimatur – i.e. a bishop's official declaration that it was 'free of doctrinal or moral error' – and was on sale, under the auspices of the Catholic Truth Society, in 1975. It has a Foreword by Frank Duff, founder of the Legion of Mary. The Foreword is orthodox; yet the statement that the Virgin has power over God is still in the text, without comment, on page 3.

26 Graef, vol. 2, pp. 53–5; Kendrick, *passim*, especially pp. 80 ff.

27 Graef, vol. 2, pp. 83–106, 136–46; Laurentin, *passim*; Martindale, *passim*; Miegge, pp. 155, 167, 182–3.

28 Graef, vol. 2, pp. 105–6, 126–7, 151–2; Miegge, pp. 15, 16, 21–2, 130–2, 180–1.

29 Bouyer, *passim*; Graef, vol. 2, pp. 74, 118–26 (and preliminary page with the quotation from John XXIII); Miegge, pp. 133, 149, 155–67, 169–72, 179–80, 188–9.

It may be doubted whether any actual retreat has occurred. A programme issued in 1975 for an English pilgrimage contains ten processional hymns. Only one is unequivocally centred on Christ. One is addressed to both Christ and Mary. Four are devoted to her. In the remaining four, one refers to her in passing and never mentions her Son. The programme includes the very popular hymn 'O Mother blest', by St Alphonsus Liguori, with these thoroughly medieval lines:

> Most powerful Mother, all men know
> Thy Son denies thee naught;
> Thou askest, wishest it and lo!
> His power thy will hath wrought.

30 Cp. Miegge, pp. 173, 183. Wordsworth's line is in his *Ecclesiastical Sonnets*, Part II, No. 25.

Many more poems may be read in Marchant's anthology *The Madonna*. Francis Thompson's on the Assumption has an astonishing flash of insight: hailing the Virgin glorified, he expresses a doubt 'if thou art assumed to heaven, or is heaven assumed to thee'. The same doubt arises in the history of her relationship with the Church.

Select Bibliography

Adams, Henry, *Mont-Saint-Michel and Chartres*, Constable, 1913.

Albright, W. F., *From the Stone Age to Christianity*, Johns Hopkins Press, Oxford University Press, 1958.

Ashe, Geoffrey (1), 'The Church as Evidence of her Divine Foundation', in *Wiseman Review*, Winter 1964–5, pp. 351–60.

Ashe, Geoffrey (2), *Elias: Prophet and Saint*, Carmelite Press, 1965.

Ashe, Geoffrey (3), *The Land and the Book*, Collins, 1965.

Ashe, Geoffrey (ed.) (4), *The Quest for Arthur's Britain*, Pall Mall Press, 1968.

Bible, translation by Ronald Knox, 1955, and the Revised Standard Version 'Common Bible', 1973.

Boslooper, Thomas, *The Virgin Birth*, Preachers' Library, 1962.

Bouyer, Louis, *Le Trône de la Sagesse*, Éditions du Cerf, Paris, 1957.

Brandon, S. G. F., *The Fall of Jerusalem and the Christian Church*, SPCK, 1951.

Brownrigg, Ronald, *The Twelve Apostles*, Weidenfeld & Nicolson, 1974.

Budge, E. A. Wallis (1), *The Gods of the Egyptians*, 2 vols, Methuen, 1903.

Budge, E. A. Wallis (2), *Legends of Our Lady Mary the Perpetual Virgin and her mother Hanna*, Oxford University Press, 1933.

Budge, E. A. Wallis (3), *Miscellaneous Coptic Texts*, British Museum, 1915.

Bulgakov, Sergius, *The Wisdom of God*, Williams & Norgate, 1937.

Butler, Alban, *Lives of the Saints*, revised and edited by H. Thurston and D. Attwater, 4 vols, Burns Oates & Washbourne, 1956.

Campbell, Joseph, *The Masks of God*, 3 vols, Secker & Warburg, 1960–5.

Cassuto, U., *The Goddess Anath*, Magnes Press, 1972.

Cles-Reden, Sibylle von, *The Realm of the Great Goddess*, Thames & Hudson, 1961.

Cottrell, Leonard, *The Anvil of Civilization*, Mentor Books, 1957.

Cronin, Vincent, *Mary Portrayed*, Darton, 1968.

Dodd, C. H. (1), *The Bible and the Greeks*, Hodder & Stoughton, 1935.

Dodd, C. H. (2), *The Interpretation of the Fourth Gospel*, Cambridge University Press, 1953.

Doresse, Jean, *The Secret Books of the Egyptian Gnostics*, Hollis, 1960.

Encyclopaedia of Islam.

Ephraem of Syria, *see* Wace and Schaff.

Epiphanius, *Panarion*, in J. P. Migne, *Patrologia Graeca*, vol. 42. Excerpts in Graef, Livius and Miegge.

Fortune, Dion, *The Mystical Qabalah*, Benn, 1972.

Gaster, Theodor H., *The Dead Sea Scriptures*, Doubleday, 1956.

Gibbon, Edward, *The Decline and Fall of the Roman Empire*, Modern Library edition, 2 vols, n.d.

Ginzberg, Louis, *The Legends of the Jews*, 7 vols, Jewish Publication Society of America, Philadelphia, 1947.

Grabar, André, *Christian Iconography*, Routledge & Kegan Paul, 1969.

Graef, Hilda, *Mary: a History of Doctrine and Devotion*, 2 vols, Sheed & Ward, 1963, 1965.

Grant, Robert M., *Gnosticism: an Anthology*, Collins, 1961.

Graves, Robert (1), *The Greek Myths*, Penguin, 1960.

Graves, Robert (2), *The White Goddess*, Faber, 1952.

Guthrie, W. K. C., *The Greeks and their Gods*, Methuen, 1950.

Herodotus, *History*, trans. G. Rawlinson, 2 vols, Dent, 1910.

Ions, Veronica, *Egyptian Mythology*, Hamlyn, 1968.

James, E. O. (1), *The Cult of the Mother-Goddess*, Thames & Hudson, 1959.

James, E. O. (2), *Prehistoric Religion*, Thames & Hudson, 1957.

James, M. R., *The Apocryphal New Testament*, Milford, 1924.

Jewish Encyclopaedia.

Josephus, *Antiquities of the Jews*, trans. William Whiston, 1825.

Jugie, Martin, *La Mort et l'Assomption de la Sainte Vierge*, Biblioteca Apostolica Vaticana, Vatican City, 1944.

Jung, C. G., *The Archetypes and the Collective Unconscious*, Collected Works, vol. 9, part 1, Routledge & Kegan Paul, 1968.

Jung, Emma and von Franz, Marie-Louise, *The Grail Legend*, Hodder, 1970.

Kaufmann, Yehezkel, *The Religion of Israel*, trans. Moshe Greenberg, Allen & Unwin, 1961.

Keller, Werner, *The Bible as History*, Hodder, 1974.

Kendrick, T. D., *Mary of Agreda*, Routledge & Kegan Paul, 1967.

Knox, W. L., *St Paul and the Church of the Gentiles*, Cambridge University Press, 1939.

Laurentin, R., *Lourdes*, P. Lethielleux, Paris, 1958.

Livius, Thomas, *The Blessed Virgin in the Fathers of the First Six Centuries*, Burns Oates, 1893.

Man, Myth and Magic (ed. Richard Cavendish), 7 vols, 1970–2.

Marchant, Sir James (ed.), *The Madonna: an Anthology*, Longmans, 1928.

Martindale, C. C., *The Message of Fatima*, Burns Oates & Washbourne, 1950.

Mascall, E. L. and Box, H. S. (eds.), *The Blessed Virgin Mary*, Darton, 1963.

Miegge, Giovanni, *The Virgin Mary*, trans. Waldo Smith, Lutterworth Press, 1955.

Neumann, Erich (1), *The Great Mother*, Routledge & Kegan Paul, 1955.

Neumann, Erich (2), *The Origins and History of Consciousness*, Routledge & Kegan Paul, 1954.

New Catholic Encyclopedia.

Newman, John Henry, *The Development of Christian Doctrine*, New Ark Library edition, 1960.

North, Christopher R., *The Suffering Servant in Deutero-Isaiah*, Oxford University Press, 1948.

Origen, *Commentary on John*, trans. Allan Menzies, Ante-Nicene Christian Library, 1897.

Palmer, Paul S. J., *Mary in the Documents of the Church*, Burns Oates & Washbourne, 1953.

Patsch, Joseph, *Our Lady in the Gospels*, Burns Oates & Washbourne, 1958.

Polano, H., *The Talmud: Selections*, Frederick Warne, 1876.

Rice, David Talbot, *Byzantine Art*, Penguin Books, 1968.

Russell, Bertrand, *A History of Western Philosophy*, Allen & Unwin, 1946.

Scholem, Gershom G., *Major Trends in Jewish Mysticism*, Schocken, 1955.

Seltman, Charles, *The Twelve Olympians and their Guests*, Max Parriser, 1956.

Smith, George D. (ed.), *The Teaching of the Catholic Church*, 2 vols, Burns Oates & Washbourne, 1948.

Smith, William and Wace, Henry, *Dictionary of Christian Biography*, 4 vols, Murray, 1877–87.

Sozomen, *see* Wace and Schaff.

Sulpicius Severus, *see* Wace and Schaff.

Swete, H. B., *The Apocalypse of St John*, Macmillan, 1907.

Thurian, Max, *Mary: Mother of the Lord, Figure of the Church*, trans. Neville B. Cryer, Faith, 1963.

Vaux, Roland de, *Ancient Israel*, Darton, 1961.

Vawter, Bruce, *A Path through Genesis*, Sheed & Ward, 1957.

Wace, Henry and Schaff, Philip (eds.), *Select Library of Nicene and Post-Nicene Fathers*, second series, vol. 2 (Sozomen), 1891; vol. 11 (Sulpicius Severus), 1894; vol. 13 (Ephraem), 1898.

Wilkins, Eithne, *The Rose-Garden Game*, Gollancz, 1969.

Williamson, Hugh Ross, *The Arrow and the Sword*, Faber, 1947.

Index

Books of the Bible are indexed under short forms of their titles, e.g.
Isaiah, Acts